Business Ethics as Practice

In recent years, a succession of corporate scandals has rocked the international business community. As a result, many companies have invested considerable time, money, and effort on the development of ethics management programs. However, in many cases, such programs are nothing more than insurance policies against corporate liability, designed merely to limit the fallout of scandals should they occur. In *Business Ethics as Practice*, Mollie Painter-Morland urges us to take business ethics seriously by reconsidering the role of ethics management within organizations. She redefines the typical seven-step ethics management program from within – challenging the reader to reconsider what is possible within each aspect of this process. In doing so, she draws on the insights of Aristotle, Nietzsche, Heidegger, Foucault, and numerous contemporary organizational theorists and sociologists to create the space for the emergence of a morally responsive corporate ethos.

MOLLIE PAINTER-MORLAND is Associate Professor in the Department of Philosophy at DePaul University, Chicago. She is also Associate Professor in the Department of Philosophy at the University of Pretoria, South Africa, where she was, for many years, Director of the Centre for Business and Professional Ethics. In this capacity she acted as ethics management consultant to various business corporations and the South African government. In 2006, she was awarded an International Ethics Award by the Society of Corporate Compliance and Ethics (SCCE) for her contributions to the ethics profession internationally.

Business, Value Creation, and Society

Series editors
R. Edward Freeman, *University of Virginia*
Stuart L. Hart, *Cornell University* and *University of North Carolina*
David Wheeler, *Dalhousie University, Halifax*

The purpose of this innovative series is to examine, from an international standpoint, the interaction of business and capitalism come to be seen as social institutions that have a great impact on the welfare of human society around the world. Issues such as globalization, environmentalism, information technology, the triumph of liberalism, corporate governance, and business ethics all have the potential to have major effects on our current models of the corporation and the methods by which value is created, distributed, and sustained among all stakeholders – customers, suppliers, employees, communities, and financiers.

Published titles:
Fort *Business, Integrity and Peace*
Gomez & Korine, *Entrepreneurs and Democracy*

Forthcoming titles:
Crane, Matten & Moon, *Corporations and Citizenship*
Rivera, *Business and Public Policy*
Yajizi & Doh, *Corporate Governance, NGOs and Corporations*

Business Ethics as Practice

Ethics as the Everyday Business of Business

MOLLIE PAINTER-MORLAND

CAMBRIDGE
UNIVERSITY PRESS

CAMBRIDGE UNIVERSITY PRESS
Cambridge, New York, Melbourne, Madrid, Cape Town, Singapore, São Paulo, Delhi

Cambridge University Press
The Edinburgh Building, Cambridge CB2 8RU, UK

Published in the United States of America by Cambridge University Press, New York

www.cambridge.org
Information on this title: www.cambridge.org/9780521877459

First published 2008

Printed in the United Kingdom at the University Press, Cambridge

A catalogue record for this publication is available from the British Library

Library of Congress Cataloguing in Publication data

Painter-Morland, Mollie.
  Business ethics as practice: ethics as the everyday business of business / Mollie
Painter-Morland.
    p.   cm. – (Business, value creation and society)
  Includes bibliographical references and index.
  ISBN 978-0-521-87745-9 (hardback)   1. Business ethics.   2. Corporations–Moral
and ethical aspects.   I. Title.   II. Series.

HF5387.P352 2008
174'4–dc22
2008020514

ISBN 978-0-521-87745-9 hardback

Contents

Tables

Preface

Though all writing can be described as an attempt at conversation, writing this book confronted me with the considerable challenge of engaging in a conversation with a number of disparate audiences, each with its own set of expectations and priorities. Academic writing is always directed at one's academic peers and senior students, but the intended audience of this book also includes fellow consultants, and those in the corporate and public sectors who are charged with ethics and compliance programs. In fact, it is one of the primary objectives of this text to engage this practitioner audience. However, having emerged, as it has, not only from the experience of a consultant, but also from the reflections of a philosopher, the text is informed by a number of scholarly preoccupations and fascinations. To sustain this kind of conversation required a delicate balancing act in which detailed analysis had to be weighed against accessibility, philosophical interest against immediate relevance, and the exploitation of existing literature against the exploration of new ideas. As such, a certain degree of compromise was both inevitable and unavoidable. I am not entirely convinced that the right "balance" was always struck, but then, finding "balance" would mean accepting the compromise, whereas avoiding it means that the struggle continues.

The questions to which this text is a response originated in and through my engagement with ethics management projects. This exposure presented a much-needed reality-check to a young scholar, eager to put into practice what she had the privilege of studying and contemplating. I soon came to the sobering realization that many of the well-reasoned theoretical constructs with which I set out did not translate well to the messy realities of corporations and public service departments with which I began grappling as a consultant. This may not come as any great surprise to practitioners, nor, one suspects, to some scholars. However, I remain convinced that in its various iterations, all philosophical ethics is concerned, informed and precipitated by practice. As such, merely accepting that philosophical ethics does not have much to say to business practice would undermine my motivation for pursuing it in the first place. It is precisely the reintegration of theory with practice that this text seeks to accomplish. To do so, I judged it necessary to make use of both philosophical insights and multidisciplinary studies of organizational life. This hybrid approach is likely to test some people's endurance and I can only beg the reader's patience and indulgence in light of the objectives that I have outlined above. I can only hope that the reader will become convinced, as I am, of the necessity of the many "compromises," "translations" and "negotiations" that have shaped this text. For the sake of better understanding and by way of preparation, I would like to outline just a few of these.

Some practitioners may not be aware of this, but the philosophical landscape is divided into distinct traditions. For instance, in the US, there is a definite divide between so-called "analytic" and "continental" philosophical traditions. The differences between these traditions have become so marked that analytic and continental philosophers do not generally attend the same conferences, publish in the same journals, or read one another's work. The majority of business ethics scholars in the US subscribe, either explicitly or implicitly, to the basic epistemological suppositions of the analytic tradition. For me, this represents yet another challenge in sustaining the kind of inclusive conversation that I consider necessary in business ethics. I broadly describe myself as a continental philosopher, at least in research interests and style, and hence I often find myself having to "bridge the gap" between the two traditions. At conferences and during peer review processes, I have to "translate" my ideas into terms that are more familiar and palatable to my audience. To do so I am compelled to resist, as much as possible, dwelling on the continental philosophers' preoccupation with the ineffability of experience and the hermeneutic complexity of representation and to try to convey my ideas in the sober, unembellished prose and syllogistically precise logic that is valued in analytic scholarship. Though it is often challenging and uncomfortable, putting oneself through the analytic "paces" makes one "multilingual" in a way that fosters conversation. This book is another experiment in this "multilingualism," drawing equally strongly on continental thought, pragmatism, communitarianism and the work of some of my more analytically inclined colleagues in business ethics.

I suspect that many of my colleagues in continental philosophy will wade through the corporate jargon and the data drawn from empirical studies with great difficulty.[1] Many of them will feel that the text could have explored the philosophical traditions employed in far greater detail, and described them in a more nuanced way. They would, of course, be entirely correct. Others will wonder why I chose to accept the terms within which "ethics" is pursued in the corporate environment so uncritically and why I did not level macro-economical critiques against the broader capitalist regime. These would all have been legitimate agendas, but they bring me back to what this book is. It is an attempt at conversation, and as such, it requires accommodation and translation. A certain measure of accommodation is indispensable if the conversation through which the tensions between ethics as theory and ethics as practice may be resolved is to be productively sustained. It means that theory starts, and ends, in a situated practice, i.e. one that is not only shaped and informed, but also bound, by the particulars of a specific material, temporal, and epistemological context. Here I take the advice of those philosophers who would have us start right where we are, in the here and now, in our own skin, and within the parameters of whatever constraints we may presently be subject to. From this perspective, it is our task is to try to ascertain who we are, how we got to where we are, and how we may change where we are, should that prove necessary.

If the book therefore reflects the conversations brought about by my own particular philosophical identity, it is also significantly shaped and informed by the unavoidable practical constraints to which business ethicists working in South Africa and the US are subject. As a practical matter, business ethics is limited, in many respects, by a fairly rigidly delineated and regulated set of organizational practices. This is especially true in the US with its well-developed regulatory framework. One of the practical implications of such a developed regulatory environment is that legality often inadvertently becomes conflated with morality in organizational practice. When and where this is the case, it is something that may rightfully be bemoaned. However, it would simply be impractical, at this particular historical juncture, to advocate

---

[1] Not to mention the philosophical objections against such objectifying empirical work and the critique of the power dynamics that inform its hypotheses! Those philosophers who are driven up the wall by this kind of academic work should scan – with forebearance – the last part of Chapter 1.

the abolition of an extensively entrenched regulatory system, such as the one that exists in the US, on the basis of such an objection. The truth is that with so many people so deeply invested in the idea, it simply isn't going to happen any time soon. This being the case, it is perhaps more sensible to set our sights on, and invest our efforts in, more realistically attainable goals – in other words, to play with the cards that we have been dealt. I therefore chose to start the conversation right here, in the current reality of ethics officers and corporate counsel – a context that is fraught with legislative demands and in which liability threats abound. However problematic we may find this notion from a philosophical point of view, the legal and regulative context requires certain step-by-step ethics interventions, the "management" of ethics, if you will. One can argue that "ethics management" undermines the essence of what ethics is, and as this book will indicate, in some respects I agree. But we still have to start right here, and reconsider the practices that exist, in order to redefine ethics as such.

In the process of reconsidering established corporate ethics management practices, I also have to beg the patience of my practitioner audience, who may feel that I really did not need that much philosophical justification to make my point. Such objections are certainly understandable, but this book is also an attempt to involve my graduate students and my colleagues in a conversation (there are, of course, many others) that I truly believe makes what we do in philosophy exciting. It wants to restore us to our role as public intellectuals who care deeply about the realities navigated by those without the luxury of living primarily as readers, writers and teachers. The role of public intellectuals relies on the ability, and willingness, of both audiences to translate. Practitioners have to share their questions, and their answers, and scholars have to relate their insights into how the history of thought informs our options in the present and in the future. This is no simple task, as many of the thinkers whose ideas still inform our presuppositions and prejudices in the present lived in completely different times, and as such could not possibly have anticipated the contemporary relevance of their proposals. Yet there is so much to be gained from knowing where our understanding of ourselves and our beliefs comes from. It provides us with the kind of perspective that is necessary to effect change.

In this text, certain chapters are more deliberately focused on providing the philosophical background to why we do things in particular ways in ethics. They try to explain why and how certain assumptions prevent us from exploring rewarding new avenues of thought and practice. I leave it up to my practitioner readers to decide whether they want to accompany me on this part of the journey. For instance, Chapter 2 provides a detailed analysis and critique of some of the most prevalent approaches to ethical decision making, which may be of interest to some practitioners, especially those involved in designing ethics training programs, but certainly not to all. Chapter 3 makes a case for the need to rethink who we are as moral agents on the basis of a number of philosophical considerations. Managers and executives who are not interested in exploring these issues in such philosophical depth may simply scan Chapters 2 and 3 without fear of losing the thread of the overall argument.

In each conversation, some common ground has to be established, and in this text, I suspect that Chapter 4 is it. It contains a lot of philosophical analysis, but it employs these perspectives to redefine values in a very practical sense. I would therefore suggest that regardless of what the reader's specific reason for picking up this text is, he/she would need to read this chapter as conceptual framework for the propositions put forward in the last part of the book. It lays out the basis of a new epistemology, advocates a new understanding of what business is about, redefines what values are, and ultimately what business ethics could be.

The book ends with practice, as I think all books should. Chapters 5 and 6 explain why we may need to rethink leadership and "ethics management." In following the broad argument of the book up to this point, as well as the various observations offered along the way, it may be possible for some readers to conclude that all the elements of ethics management programs are best abandoned. However, I deliberately chose not to go that route. I believe that changes to practice occur incrementally. From the perspective of complex adaptive systems, small changes can have large effects. If you tinker with enough elements in the system, new patterns emerge. But you have to tinker often, and insistently. It is the initiation of such a process to which this book aspires.

The arguments and observations offered here potentially have many other applications, but the focus of this book is on rethinking ethics management. I have focused in this text on the practice of which I have had the most experience, and for the moment it ends there. But this ending opens many other avenues, which I hope to explore in future projects. However, for that research to happen, the places, people and problematic conversations that will shape and inform it are yet to announce themselves with sufficient immanent force. In a sense, I have no choice but to wait patiently until they do, because to me, it is this that makes ethics as practice possible.

Foreword

Mollie Painter-Morland has written an important book. It charts a new direction for business ethics as a discipline along a number of dimensions. First of all the book introduces more of the continental and post-modern traditions to the largely Anglo-American conversation about business ethics. Second, this is accomplished by paying attention to the practical problems of ethics in modern organizational life. Third, by merging theory and practice, Painter-Morland offers us real wisdom about how to think about ethics in corporate life.

Professor Painter-Morland begins by arguing that most of our thinking about ethics has become disconnected with the practical problems that we face in our lives. And nowhere is this clearer than in business, where the scandal of the day seems to drive the analysis of most philosophers, who simply conclude that people need to be more ethical. Typically they mean by this phrase, "become more in tune with the tenets of Anglo-American ethical theory." She rightly claims that "business ethics is supposed to be as much about business as ethics," but shows us how the kinds of narratives that are present in the current business ethics conversation can never really be about business. And she eschews the idea that ethics can be built into business practice through the traditional means of ethics officers and codes of principles and behaviors.

What Painter-Morland offers in the place of this tradition is a view of business ethics that does not make the theory–practice distinction, but rather is grounded in practice. It is a view that puts questions such as "how should we live" and "who am I and what kinds of relationships with others are possible" squarely in center stage. She makes it abundantly clear that in the traditions on which she draws, "there is a general acknowledgement and appreciation, . . . of the role that people's emotions, bodies, relationships, histories and contexts play in shaping one's sense of self, and any perceptions and beliefs that one may have."

After opening chapters which set the stage for her new approach, we find concrete discussions of the role of context and relationships in business, the nature of moral values and their place in an epistemology that is skeptical of the tradition of moral reasoning and the search for normative certainty and foundations.

Nietzsche, Heidegger, Lakoff and Johnson, Young, Nussbaum, Bourdieu, Polanyi, Marcuse, Butler, Merleau-Ponty and others join the conversation about the connection between business and ethics. We find topics like authenticity, sexuality, gender, power and domination, embodiment, and others alongside management theory, stakeholders, rights, leadership, and decision making. What holds the conversation together is its profound concern with the practical Socratic question of how should we live.

Business ethics as a discipline is in danger of becoming irrelevant. It has held onto its foundational roots for too long. As others discover the power of thinking about values and ethics in business, the role of philosophers, mired in traditional ethics, will become increasingly marginal. Painter-Morland offers hope to philosophers working in business ethics, and she offers a sound philosophical roadmap to those in business schools who find the current landscape problematic.

By integrating the work done in continental philosophy, traditional business ethics, and management theory, Painter-Morland gives us a multi-layered argument that should set a new direction for the conversation about business and its role in society. Indeed it is an honor to publish this book in the series on *Business, Value Creation, and Society*. The purpose of this series is to stimulate new thinking about value creation and trade, and its role in the world of the twenty-first century. Our old models and ideas simply are not appropriate in the "24/7 Flat World" of today. We need new scholarship that builds on these past understandings, yet offers the alternative of a world of hope, freedom, and human flourishing. Mollie Painter-Morland has given us just such a book. She has breathed new life into business ethics.

R. Edward Freeman
Olsson Professor of Business Administration
Academic Director, Business Roundtable
Institute for Corporate Ethics
The Darden School
University of Virginia
Charlottesville, Virginia, USA

Acknowledgements

So many people, places and experiences contributed to the conversation that takes shape in this book. Naming them is a daunting task and thanking everyone who has somehow helped me along the way is simply not possible. In some respects this book is the culmination of a journey that started a number of years ago, and as I retrace my steps over the past seven years, scores of faces drift into focus.

My journey in Business Ethics started during my time as a PhD research scholar on a Fulbright grant at the Center for Business Ethics at Bentley College in 2000–2001. I cannot give enough credit to Professor W. Michael Hoffman, and his wonderful team of people, for the support, resources, and companionship they offered me during my stay in Boston. The time I spent at the CBE provided me with the best possible exposure to best practice in ethics management. The Ethics Officer Association (now ECOA) under the leadership of Ed Petry was also instrumental in exposing me to the practical roll-out of ethics management programs. I learnt a great deal from practitioners within the ECOA and Society of Corporate Compliance and Ethics (SCCE) and I continue to do so.

Many decision-makers and mentors at the University of Pretoria deserve thanks for the trust they put in me by appointing me as Director of the Centre for Business and Professional Ethics upon my return to South Africa in 2001. This position gave me the opportunity to gain consulting experience in both the South African public and private sectors. Thrown in at the deep end, I was fortunate enough to have had wonderful clients, who learnt with me, debated the issues with me, and believed in me. I owe so much to their practical advice, experience and dedication. The dilemmas we confronted together informed the questions that led to this book. I hope that my new ideas and proposals will enhance their programs and will stimulate further conversation between us. I also want to thank some of the consultants who partnered with me on large projects, especially Deon Rossouw,

Kris Dobie, Stiaan van der Merwe, John Mafunisa, and Leon van Vuuren for their loyalty, conversation and perspective.

The University of Pretoria deserves thanks for appointing me to a challenging position early on and then being gracious in allowing me some focused research time when I needed it most. My research leave greatly contributed to bringing this book project to fruition. Their support since my move to DePaul University has remained unfaltering, and I continue to work with the Centre for Business and Professional Ethics (CBPE) and the Philosophy Department there on a part-time basis.

My current institutional home has been the perfect base from which to further my research. Not only did DePaul University support my research through a Summer grant, but it is also an institution that has become well-known for its wealth of Business Ethics expertise. I was fortunate to have two of the strongest women in the field, Patricia Werhane and Laura Hartman as colleagues and friends. This was not the full extent of my good fortune however. DePaul University's Department of Philosophy provided me with the collegial environment that any philosopher could only dream of. Not only did I have access to some of the best minds in continental thought, but I was offered the friendship and moral support of an amazing group of people. Nothing inspires writing more than that. I often found myself exploring new research ideas during happy hour-long conversations with Peg Birmingham, Tina Chanter, Jason Hill, Sean Kirkland, Rick Lee, Bill Martin, Will McNeil, Darrell Moore, Michael Naas, David Pellauer, Franklin Perkins and Peter Steeves. A special word of thanks goes to my friend and colleague Elizabeth Rottenberg for her wisdom and much needed perspective. David Krell has been a pillar of support since my arrival at DePaul and was gracious enough to comment on this book and to provide generous proofreading assistance. He, more than anyone, buttresses my faith in the power and value of conversations and collaborations. I also owe immense gratitude to Edward Freeman, who has supported this project since its inception and never ceases to inspire me through the way in which he lives the academic life.

I am in the fortunate position to have been brought up as someone who thrives on conversation, debate, and mediation. For that, I have my father, mother and my two brothers to thank. Submitting to the force of the better argument has never come easy for any of us, but, as I have come to appreciate from an early age, it has its own worthy rewards. To a great extent this exposure to the cut and thrust of the debate made me and continues to make me who I am, and informs everything I do and write.

I am particularly grateful to my husband, Arno Morland, who has had to live with the anxieties that my multiple conversations precipitate, and continues to love and support me regardless. He is the one person who has read every single word I have ever written. He is also someone who believes that there is no formulation that is beyond improvement. As such, he has inspired me to work even harder at conveying my thoughts in writing. As language editor of this book, he smoothed out many of the rough patches that is the inevitable consequence of my simultaneous participation in so many widely disparate conversations. For his hours of work and his tenacious support I can never thank him. For who and what he is I do love him and dedicate this book to him.

1 | Introduction: the dissociation of ethics from practice

Ethics talk has never been more prevalent than in the first few years of the twenty-first century. Corporate scandals have shaken the international business community over the last few years and seem to have reanimated many people's interest in ethics. As a result, codes of conduct, ethics management programs and ethics offices are being created with breathless haste. Even skeptical corporate executives are beginning to acknowledge that there may be more to ethics than "motherhood and apple pie." Many have even come around to the idea that ethics is something that has to be institutionalized, resourced and managed. To the extent therefore that they are interested in keeping their organizations out of trouble and limiting their potential liabilities, these "upright" captains of industry now stand ready to invest time, effort and money in the promotion of ethics. In the face of this wave of unprecedented interest, many business ethicists have concluded that the business community no longer sees business ethics as an oxymoron. In fact, an investment in business ethics has become a prerequisite for an organization's continued participation in formal business networks.

Given these conditions, one would expect this to be a good time to be a business ethicist. In some respects, however, it is both the best of times and the worst of times. It is the best of times in that business ethics and corporate governance are becoming standard features in both tertiary curricula and corporate training budgets. All of a sudden, everyone seems to have awoken to the importance of teaching people ethics. The assumption is that teaching ethics builds integrity, encourages responsible behavior, and generally puts moral considerations on the business agenda. There are also benefits, such as enhanced employee morale, lower staff turnover, and enhanced corporate reputations that are associated with ethics training.

In other respects, however, this is the very worst of times for business ethics. Many corporate ethics programs have become no more than "insurance policies" against corporate liability and are implemented and managed with an indiscriminate "checkbox" mentality. Having an

1

organizational ethics program is begrudgingly accepted as a "must-have" check on business practices. As such, it is conceived of as something quite separate from what business is actually focused on. In fact, such consideration as ethics does receive is perceived as time spent on "soft issues," i.e. matters that distract from "business as usual."

The approach to business ethics that is currently being extolled in many business and academic forums may implicitly be contributing to the dissociation of ethics with business practice. Ethics is portrayed as a set of principles that must be applied to business decisions. In this conception, ethics functions as a final hurdle in a deliberate decision-making process. The questions that inform this process are usually something along the line of: "May we do this?" or even more cynically: "Can we get away with this?" When approached in this way, ethics becomes something that people consider *after* they have interpreted events and determined what they want to do. When ethics functions as an integral part of business practice, however, it informs individuals' perceptions of events from the start and plays an important part in shaping their responses. This kind of ethics is not based on the deliberate application of general principles, but draws instead on tacit knowledge and individual discretion. The kinds of questions that ethics as practice would have us ask are of a decidedly different order. It asks us to consider: "How do we want to live?" and: "Who do we want to be?" When an organization's investment in business ethics becomes a mere insurance policy, really meaningful and significant questions such as these are never raised or addressed.

In itself, the claim that ethics and business practice are becoming dissociated may not seem particularly controversial. There are many business ethicists who would not only readily agree that such a thing is happening, but would also welcome it. Some would argue that ethics as practice is disappearing because it is an outdated notion. It is true, of course, that the association of ethics with practice is a very old idea. It is based on the ancient Greek concept of *phronesis*, or practical wisdom. Those who are critical of this view argue that it is more suited to the kind of small, ancient communities within which it was conceived than the complex contemporary world that we now inhabit. To think of ethics as part of everyday practice, they argue, is to associate it too closely with the "messiness" of individual perception and contextual biases. It simply allows individuals too much discretion to ensure the orderly conduct of business. In small communities, where individuals knew one another personally, such trust may have been possible. However, within the context of an impersonal global economy, we need something more solid and reliable to protect our interests. In contemporary business and society, it is only the law that can ensure responsible behavior. Those who subscribe to this line of reasoning therefore invariably turn to stricter legislation, more exacting compliance measures and the threat of imprisonment to keep business practitioners in line.

Despite its widespread implementation, this legislative approach does not seem to be working as well as its proponents might have hoped. News of fresh business scandals continues to arrive at our doorsteps almost every morning. Judged on the basis of their performance, then, rules and legislation alone appear to be poor substitutes for the kind of practical wisdom that is inscribed in the notion of ethics as practice. In fact, efforts to formulate unambiguous normative guidelines for the conduct of business may paradoxically cause us to neglect those very aspects of human life that both legality and morality attempt to protect.

Both legality and morality are concerned with establishing criteria for acceptable behavior. Both make these judgments on the basis of existing social norms and values. These norms and values are expressions of those things that the members of a particular community consider important enough to protect and nurture. The protection of our lives and property, for instance, is guaranteed by law. Naturally these primary security needs are exceptionally important, but there are things that speak to the very core of our self-understanding as human beings that we don't necessarily want to secure through legislation or regulation. Consider, for instance, the implications of legally enforcing things like fidelity, trust, responsibility and care. The world would be a sad place indeed if we felt compelled to adopt a law to ensure that friends cared for one another and trusted each other. However, it would be an even sadder place if we didn't think these things important at all. Ethics is, in a sense, the practice of such things in everyday life.

Ethics in business is about the capacity to respond appropriately to the many competing pressures and expectations that push and pull individuals in the course of their daily participation in complex organizational and business networks. It requires an intuitive and continuous balancing act, in which an individual's character, values, and relationships all register in significant ways. This is precisely why the law cannot adequately serve ethics as practice. Practical wisdom is not simply the ability to identify and apply relevant rules. It is the capacity to make decisions in situations where there are no regulatory parameters to defer to, or where the rules are of such an imprecise, ambiguous nature that they require the exercise of discretion. To act with this kind of wisdom is simultaneously to be responsive to others, true to oneself and decisive in the absence of certainty. As such, it is not dissimilar to the kind of insight and skill that is required for any important practical decision in today's complex business environment.

Business ethics is supposed to be as much about business as it is about ethics. As self-evident as this may seem, business ethicists are often guilty of not paying enough heed to the complex dynamics of contemporary business life in the way that they approach the subject. This may be due, at least in part, to the fact that many still subscribe to the view that normative imperatives should be unchanging, irrefutable standards that define what is acceptable in business behavior. Morality, from this perspective, should be defined "objectively." That is to say that moral imperatives have to be articulated independently from the pressures and expectations that inform people's experiences and perceptions in particular situations, relationships and contexts. Proponents of this view believe that it is only once normative imperatives have been formulated in this way that they can be brought into relation with, or "applied," to specific cases. It is not hard to see why so many people continue to think this way about morality. We prefer not to have the messiness of the real world interfere with our sense of "right" and "wrong." To have to constantly rethink or renegotiate those norms on which we rely for guidance is disorientating and undermines our sense of certainty. It seems to open a door to the kind of relativism and moral subjectivism that renders ethics meaningless. It is tragic to note, however, that, because of our lack of nerve, the kind of moral responsiveness and personal discretion that is such a key feature of ethics as practice is slowly and systematically being suppressed in business life. While some business ethicists have been occupying themselves at the top of their academic ivory towers with the philosophical reinforcement of ostensibly immutable normative principles, those who make their living in the corporate jungle around them are making up their own rules for the game. If business ethicists are unable to appreciate this game, and are unable to participate in the dynamics that shape business practitioners' moral sensibilities, the association of ethics with practice will continue to weaken until it effectively ceases to exist.

The tendency to dissociate ethics with particular situated practices often undermines the meaningfulness of business ethics interventions.

Business ethicists who support the abstraction and generalization of ethical imperatives often develop standardized ethics management models that are intended to serve as a vehicle for interventions in any organization. However, because it is mostly large corporations that can afford to implement such models, they are often designed with these organizations in mind. In the process, not enough consideration is given to the fact that small and medium-sized businesses, as well as "not-for-profit" organizations often do not have the resources to implement and manage such programs. These enterprises are simply left to forge ahead without much attention to the moral dimensions of their business practices. A tacit sense of normative propriety nevertheless develops among the employees of such organizations and as they grow and expand it becomes increasingly difficult to change or alter entrenched perceptions and expectations.

In addition, pre-packaged business ethics strategies often rely on the institutionalization of standardized codes and compliance procedures. These codes and procedures are not tailored to reflect the unique sensibilities that may have developed within a particular organization or the expectations and dynamics that exist within specific industries. This limits their relevance and ability to effect change.

There are many who believe that ethics officers and ethics offices play an important role in making ethics a central concern amongst an organization's workforce, but often little consideration is given to how a small minority of individuals are supposed to shape and transform the cultural dynamics of a complex organizational system. Ethics surveys and climate studies are regularly employed, but are mostly incapable of detecting or describing the tacit, unwritten rules that are the primary source of moral orientation in many organizations. No expense is spared in the internal communication of an organization's moral commitments and ethical standards, but these efforts often do little to change the perception among ordinary employees that ethics is simply the latest in a succession of temporary management obsessions. In ethics training initiatives employees are taught to use ethics "quick tests." Case study analyses are employed to hone the moral reasoning skills of workers who are unlikely to be given sufficient discretionary freedom to use them.

In all of this, individuals are never asked to reconsider fundamentally who they are, what they really care about, and how they can leverage these beliefs to make their workplace a better environment.

When one considers the practical effect of ethics' dissociation from practice on each level of a typical ethics program, one begins to appreciate why it is so important to address and reverse it. If we are willing to revisit our most basic assumptions about ethics in organizations, it may be possible to infuse our theory and practice with some much needed new perspectives. In what is to follow, I will briefly consider the main elements of organizational ethics programs, and point out some of their limitations. The goal of this analysis is to identify where we should focus our attention in re-establishing ethics as an everyday part of business practice.

The typical ethics management process and its limitations

The Federal Sentencing Guidelines for Corporations includes a description of seven steps that should be taken in the establishment of an ethics and compliance program.[1] The Guidelines include elements of best practice ethics management techniques, such as the development of a code, the implementation of ethics training, setting up reporting channels, ensuring proper communication of ethical standards and raising ethical awareness, as well as the enforcement of discipline.[2] These elements are typical of most ethics programs and can, for the purposes of our discussion here, be meaningfully divided into three basic elements or phases, namely: *motivation, formulation* and *integration*. These are summarized in Table 1.1, and discussed in greater detail in the rest of this chapter.

The first of these has to do with the process of establishing a rationale for an ethics program within an organization. Ethical risk assessments are often employed to this end. The *formulation* phase of an ethics program typically includes the establishment of some source of normative orientation. This is mostly done by means of an organizational code of conduct. In most cases, the *integration phase* of an ethics program is a

---

[1] The FSG's seven steps include (1) formulating compliance standards and procedures such as a code of conduct or ethics; (2) assigning high-level personnel to provide oversight (e.g., a compliance or ethics officer); (3) taking care when delegating authority; (4) effective communication of standards and procedures (e.g., training); (5) auditing/monitoring systems and reporting mechanisms, whistle-blowing; (6) enforcement of disciplinary mechanisms; and (7) appropriate response after detection.

[2] For a more detailed analysis of the various elements of an ethics management program, see: Dawn-Marie Driscoll and W. Michael Hoffman, *Ethics Matters: How to Implement Values-driven Management* (Bentley College Center for Business Ethics, 1999).

Table 1.1 *Phases and elements of a typical ethics management program*

Motivate	Formulate	Integrate
Identify ethical risks Get Board and leadership commitment	Identify existing and desired values Formulate codes of ethics and codes of conduct	Train Communicate Assign responsibilities for ethics
	Evaluate	

multifaceted process that includes the appointment of an ethics officer, the roll-out of a training and communication program, the establishment of reporting channels, the enforcement of rules and regulations through the implementation of disciplinary procedures against offenders, and doing regular audits.

Ethics programs typically also include a fourth element, namely, "evaluation." However, various forms of evaluation are typically included as part of the motivation, formulation and integration of such programs in organizations. As such, they are more meaningfully discussed within the context of each of these three aspects of a typical ethics program. The motivation phase of an ethics program, for instance, typically includes an assessment of the ethical risks that are present within an organizational environment. To formulate meaningful points of normative orientation for the members of an organization, some sort of evaluation is usually done to find out what they value and believe. As part of the process of integrating ethics into the life of an organization, it is usually necessary to establish how values are reflected in formal and informal systems and how they are integrated across organizational functions and silos. Evaluation is also part of how an organization reports on its activities.

Motivation: fear of penalty and ethical risk

One of the main challenges for practitioners in the ethics and compliance field is to motivate the leadership of organizations to invest money, time and effort in ethics. The fact that the collapse of companies like Enron and WorldCom could be directly attributed to unethical behavior, have, of course, made their task a little easier of late. The introduction of stricter legislation and other forms of regulation have imposed new parameters on business activities and have bolstered the case for ethics interventions in organizations. In the US, for example, it has become easy to use compliance with the Federal Sentencing Guidelines (FSG), the protection of an organization against lawsuits and liability, or the new SOX requirements[3] as a rationale for ethics programs.[4]

From a business ethics perspective, the fact that the US Sentencing Commission provided parameters for federal judges to follow in their sentencing of business organizations is not its most significant contribution. More important is the Federal Sentencing Commission's introduction of guidelines that incentivize business organizations to proactively fight corporate misconduct by implementing structured ethics and compliance programs. According to the FSG, if a business organization charged with corporate misconduct has these elements in place and cooperates fully with investigating authorities it might be given a reduced fine, or even avoid prosecution altogether. Many organizations did the math and realized that investing in an ethics program would probably cost them less than they stand to lose in the event of a lawsuit. The problem, of course, is that when ethics programs are motivated by this kind of logic, they can end up being no more than relatively cheap insurance policies against costly lawsuits. There are unfortunately many such corporate ethics programs that look good only on paper. This is hardly the kind of commitment to ethics that the Federal Sentencing Commission hoped to encourage in organizations.

The spate of corporate scandals that followed the initial introduction of the Federal Sentencing Guidelines in 1991 compelled the Federal Sentencing Commission to reassess the compliance-driven approach that it had initially adopted. In the process, the members of the Commission became convinced that an important element was missing from business organizations' compliance programs. In 2004, the Commission decided literally to replace every reference to "compliance" in the

---

[3] Joshua Joseph, "Integrating Business Ethics and Compliance Programs: a Study of Ethics Officers in Leading Organizations," *Business and Society Review*, 107 (3) (2002), 309–347.

[4] Paula Desio, "An Overview of the Organizational Guidelines" in *An Overview of the United States Sentencing Commission and the Federal Sentencing Guidelines* (Online at www.eoa.org, 2005).

1991 Guidelines with "ethics and compliance." In the new Guidelines, the criteria for effective compliance and ethics programs are discussed separately (in guideline §8B2.1), underlining the importance that the Commission attaches to such programs. The Commission also elaborated on these criteria, generally introducing greater rigor and assigning significantly more responsibility to the governing authority (e.g., the Board of Directors) and executive leadership of an organization. To meet the new standards, an organization must demonstrate that it has exercised due diligence in fulfilling the Guidelines' requirements. In addition, it has to show that it has promoted "an organizational culture that encourages ethical conduct and a commitment to compliance with the law." As Ed Petry points out, other agencies, like the SEC, the New York Stock Exchange, Congress, the Department of Justice, and various rating agencies have all joined the Sentencing Commission in weighing in on the issue of corporate culture.[5]

As a result of these developments, the interest in measuring various dimensions of organizational culture has grown. In fact, it could be argued that in the US today, "managing organizational culture is the new compliance." This has lead some organizational theorists to argue that the current interest in organizational culture is a mere continuation of the managerialist strategies initiated by Frederick Taylor early in the twentieth century. From this perspective, the current obsession with corporate culture is just a veiled form of the managerial impulse to exercise control over employees.

Although the interest in assessing and managing organizational culture has gained new momentum in the last few years, it pre-dates the new Federal Sentencing Guidelines. In fact, organizational culture became a buzzword as early as the 1980s. Some of the key texts that played a role in the theoretical development of the concept of organizational culture, are Peters and Waterman's *In search of Excellence*, William Ouchi's *Theory Z* and Deal and Kennedy's *Corporate Cultures* (1988).[6] Martin

---

[5] Ed Petry, "Assessing Corporate Culture Part 1," *Ethikos* 18(5) (March/April, 2005).

[6] Thomas J. Peters and Robert H. Waterman, *In Search of Excellence* 1ˢᵗ edition, (New York: Harper & Row, 1982); William G. Ouchi, *THEORY Z* (Reading, MA: Addison-Wesley, 1981); Terrence E. Deal and Allan A. Kennedy, *Corporate Cultures* 1ˢᵗ edition, (Perseus Books Group, 2000). Some argue that the notion of organizational culture emerges from the interest in "organizational climate" that preceded it. Organizational climate has been used to refer to a broad array of organizational and perceptual variables that have

Parker criticizes these three texts for their "self-help tone" and the fact that they promise to deliver efficiency, job satisfaction and a number of other benefits through management-driven cultural interventions.[7]

Whatever lies behind the current widespread interest in organizational culture, it has resulted in a proliferation of new survey instruments. The interest that business ethicists have in measuring corporate culture is related to the belief that insight into an organization's culture would allow corporations to manage their ethical risks proactively. Ethics consultants and ethics officers therefore often use ethical risk analyses to substantiate their proposals and requests for ethics interventions and programs. There is nothing that motivates a board of directors like a statistical analysis that clearly demonstrates employees' and other stakeholders' negative perceptions of an organization. Such an analysis typically includes some form of interaction with an organization's internal and external stakeholders, as well as an assessment of its compliance environment and a survey to gain insight into its employees' beliefs and expectations.

In many cases, general quantitative surveys are employed to this end. These surveys are called by many different names, such as "Climate studies," "Organizational culture surveys" and "People's surveys." They typically serve multiple purposes. Some include questions that are specifically formulated to gauge the ethical orientation of an organization's employees. They may, for instance, probe things like employees' willingness to report misconduct, the number of incidents of unethical conduct that they had witnessed, and their perceptions with respect to their organizational leadership's commitment to ethics. However, most

the ability to reflect what happens in individual and organizational interactions, and that can also affect behavior in organizations. On the more specific topic of ethical organizational climate, Victor and Cullen's (B. Victor and J. Cullen, "The Organizational Bases of Ethical Work climate," *Administrative Science Quarterly*, 33[4] [1988], 101–125) definition is also widely used. They define ethical climate as: "the prevailing perceptions of typical organizational practices and procedures that have an ethical content." Since it owes its existence to psychological research, the notion of "organizational climate" faced a series of difficulties. For example, a debate ensued around what the unit of analysis should be – should the individual, organization, or various subunits within an organization be studied? It was also argued that climate studies overlaps with most constructs in organizational behavior and lacks the clear focus that would allow it to function as a viable theoretical construct.

7 Martin Parker, *Organizational Culture and Identity: Unity and Division at Work* (London: Sage, 2000), p. 15.

surveys are also used to gather basic information about an organization's human resource environment, such as staff turnover, performance systems and procedures, and even the strength of an organization's brand. It is believed that though such surveys include questions that are not explicitly directed at ethics, they can provide important insight into an organization's ethical risks.

As instruments employed as part of "ethical risk assessment" proliferated, debates on how the "organizational culture" should be defined ensued. According to Hofstede, Neuijen, Ohayv and Sanders, there is no commonly accepted definition of organizational culture. They argue, however, that there are a number of characteristics that are common to most authors' conception of organizational/corporate culture.[8] They describe organizational/corporate culture as holistic, socially constructed, historically determined and difficult to change. It is a "soft" construct among anthropological concepts. According to Hofstede *et al.*, organizational/corporate cultures may be meaningfully divided into four categories, namely: symbols, heroes, rituals and values. For Trevino, Butterfield and McCabe, organizational culture is both the medium and the outcome of social interaction.[9] From this perspective, ethical culture is viewed as a subset of organizational culture, which reflects the multidimensional interplay between formal and informal behavioral control within organizations. Culture signals the boundaries between what is legitimate and what is unacceptable within a particular social setting. In this definition, "organizational culture" is a characteristic of an organization and therefore something that can be assessed, described and managed. This understanding of culture may contribute to the idea that "an ethical culture" can be a helpful tool in managing ethical risks.

Trevino *et al.* have also commented on the relationship between organizational climate and organizational culture. They point out that the two multidimensional constructs of ethical climate and ethical culture were developed more or less independently and were based on different theoretical points of reference and assumptions. They cite research that attributes the differences between the concepts of

[8] Geert Hofstede, Bram Neuijen, Dense Daval Ohayv and Geert Sanders, "Measuring Organizational Cultures: a Qualitative and Quantitative Study across Twenty Cases," *Administrative Science Quarterly*, 35 (1990), 286–316.
[9] Linda Klebe Trevino, Kenneth D. Butterfield and Donald L. McCabe, "The Ethical Context in Organizations: Influence on Employee Attitudes and Behaviors," *Business Ethics Quarterly*, 8(3) (1998), 447–476.

"climate" and "culture" to differences in theoretical roots, as well as preferred research methodology and perspective, rather than to substantive differences. Trevino *et al.* concur with these findings and argue in favor of an integrative approach. They utilize organizational climate constructs in addition to ethical culture variables in evaluating the ethical context of organizations.

Though the idea of organizational climate encompasses all the various qualities and conditions that may affect individuals' feelings and perceptions about the organizational system in which they participate, it is unclear what effect it has on their behavior. The concept of organizational "culture," on the other hand, is associated with the rules, rewards, codes, leadership, rituals and stories within an organizational system. Since the idea of a "culture" characterizes an organization more clearly in terms of its formal and informal structures, Trevino *et al.* argue that "organizational culture" is likely to have a more pronounced effect on behavior. In developing their more integrative approach, Trevino *et al.* drew on Victor and Cullen's ethical climate questionnaire and focused on five climate types that were validated by means of a series of survey studies.[10] Despite these efforts, they found it difficult to establish a conclusive relationship between different types of organizational climate and the ethical or unethical behavior of those who are exposed to it. To address this problem, Trevino *et al.* developed an instrument that combined nine theoretical dimensions of climate with items that are thought to be indicative of ethical culture. The "culture" items in their instrument include the measurement of peer behavior, the extent to which norms support ethical conduct, the extent to which ethical behavior is rewarded and unethical behavior punished, the degree to which people are exposed to ethical role models, reporting behavior and the extent to which those in authority allow their actions and decisions to be challenged by their subordinates.

The integrative approach that Trevino *et al.* propose has its advantages in that it acknowledges the impact that informal and formal structures have on organizational values and practices. However, as in the case of many other researchers that focus on culture, they seem to

---

[10] Victor and Cullen identified specific normative climate types, such as "benevolence climates" versus "egoistic climates." Other climate types such as "independence climates," "instrumental climates," "rules climates" and "caring climates" reflect the level of behavioral guidance that is offered in an organizational setting.

believe that these structural elements can give us a relatively stable understanding of organizational culture as an object of study. The question is whether this understanding of culture can accommodate the fluidity of the ongoing processes by which meaning is created and circulated within organizations.

Hofstede *et al.* see organizational cultures as gestalts, or organized wholes that are more than the sum of their parts. As such, they argue, organizational cultures can only be appreciated by insiders, or by empathetic outsiders. A qualitative orientation is therefore needed in their assessment. However, for Hofstede *et al.*, qualitative analysis should be complemented by quantitative verification. Hofstede and his team used interviews to gather qualitative data. They used this data to develop an empathetic gestalt description of the organizations that they were studying, and then employed a questionnaire to analyze values and practices in these organizations. Their study tried to gauge what they saw as the basic elements of culture, i.e. values and practices. Understanding practices, in their view, requires an analysis of symbols, rituals and heroes. Their analysis of values included questions about people's work goals and general beliefs. They also looked at how promotion and dismissals were dealt with and how time was managed in these organizations to get a sense of the nature of their internal practices.

Like Peters and Waterman, who place "values" at the core of organizational culture, Hofstede *et al.* initially hypothesized that values are central to corporate culture. They defined values as "broad, nonspecific feelings of good and evil, beautiful and ugly, normal and abnormal, rational and irrational – feelings that are often unconscious and rarely discussable, that cannot be observed as such but are manifested in alternatives of behavior."[11] Interestingly, Hofstede *et al.*'s findings suggested that it is shared perceptions about the daily practices of an organization, rather than values that are at the core of corporate culture. Hofstede *et al.* argue that practices may also be thought of as "conventions," "customs," "habits," "mores," "traditions" or "usages." It is important to note how Hofstede *et al.* view the relationship between values and practices. Their study found that even though a group of individuals may subscribe to the same values, they may develop completely different practices. The reason

[11] Hofstede *et al.*, "Measuring Organizational Cultures," 291.

for this, according to Hofstede *et al.*, is that values are formed early in life, while organizational practices are developed through socialization within an organizational context.

Hofstede *et al.* argue that even in cases where strong leaders' values inform an organization's culture, employees do not simply adopt their leaders' values. What happens instead is that these values are translated into organizational practices, which ultimately inform individuals' behavior. They argue that in studies of organizational culture, a distinction is usually made between the phenomenal, or observable manifestations of culture, and its more ideational elements, such as deeper level values, assumptions and beliefs. This is because it is generally recognized that there are patterns of underlying values, beliefs and assumptions that significantly inform the behavior of those who participate in an organizational system. Hofstede *et al.* seem to see values as relatively fixed, circumscribed normative orientations that are unlikely to change. Though their observations with respect to organizational practices are helpful and important, these views are more problematic. For them, normativity within an organization appears to be something that is separate, deeper, and more unchanging than practices. As such, their views on values may implicitly lend support to the dissociation of ethics from practice in organizational life.

It is very difficult to gauge accurately those elements of organizational culture that inform ethical behavior. The problem with many of the instruments that have been developed to study organizational culture, is that there are aspects of people's experience of working in an organization that defy clear conceptualization and articulation. It is very difficult for researchers, who are not participants in an organizational system and who may subscribe to worldviews and beliefs that differ significantly from those of their subjects, to come to terms with the tacit elements of an organization's cultural dynamics. Callahan[12] has given a good description of the difficulties that researchers face when they try to gain insight into an organizational system's cultural dynamics. He offers an explanation for why so many qualitative and quantitative studies fail to give meaningful accounts of the cultural dynamics of organizations. Callahan explains that it is impossible for a researcher to lay claim to people's knowledge without their acquiescence. The best that a

---

[12] Shaun Callahan, "Our Take on 'How to Talk about Knowledge Management'," *Anecdote Whitepaper*, 6 (March, 2006), 3–4.

researcher can do is to try to encourage people to voluntarily share what they know. What complicates things even more is that people invariably know more than they can tell, and always tell more than they can write. Human knowledge is deeply contextual and is triggered by circumstance and need. This means that people only access and use what they know when they need to. According to Callahan, knowledge is "sticky," i.e. it does not flow easily across organizational boundaries. People are reluctant to share the information that they have secured in organizational silos, and they are even more reluctant to share it with outsiders. Trust is therefore essential in the process of knowledge sharing and gathering. However, the need to establish relationships of trust in the gathering of information is somewhat difficult to reconcile with the notion of researcher objectivity. The kind of tacit knowledge that informs the beliefs and behavior of those who participate in complex organizational systems may, in any event, not lend itself to objective, clear and concise formulation.

Martin Parker has drawn attention to another aspect of organizational culture that most studies overlook or underestimate. Parker points out that, etymologically speaking, the words "culture" and "organization" are both associated with processes, rather than with objects.[13] In other words, neither word denotes something that has assumed a final, stable or readily recognizable form. According to Parker, the word "culture" refers to a process of cultivation and of tending natural growth. "Organization" literally refers to the process of making tools. The word "organization" is therefore more properly understood as a verb, than as a noun. The point that Parker is making is that researchers, in their attempts to offer accurate statistical descriptions of an "organization" and its "culture," often overlook the fact that they are studying complex interpersonal dynamics within a perpetually shifting system of relations rather than fixed behavioral patterns in a circumscribed organizational structure. For Parker, organizational culture is a process which is locally produced by people. As a process, it is something that has certain effects on people. As such, it is both a verb and a noun.[14] The problem is that most studies of organizational culture ignore its process character. It is impossible to point to a process as if it were an entity with a recognizable form that could be readily observed and identified. What this

---

[13] Parker, *Organizational Culture and Identity*, p. 81. [14] *Ibid.*, p. 83.

means is that organizational culture, as process, can only be studied across various iterations and enactments. As such, it is not possible to claim, on the basis of an empirical study, that a particular organization *"possesses an* ethical culture."

It is also extremely difficult to gauge the various cultural iterations that are continually manifesting and morphing within an organizational system by means of a single survey instrument. In their daily activities at work, some individuals may shift between various constructions of meaning. Organizational systems do not function in isolation. They respond creatively to their stakeholders and environments. Because of these complex dynamics, an organizational system may be experienced in many different ways, both by those who participate in it and by those who observe its various concrete iterations. Little wonder then that when people are asked about their perceptions and experiences of organizational culture in surveys, they often feel compelled to initiate their responses with a qualification such as: "Well, it depends ... "

In conducting surveys on organizational culture, researchers all too often assume that there are homogeneous cultures, or subcultures, within organizations, whereas the reality is infinitely more complex. According to Martin Parker, organizational cultures are often significantly fragmented. He points out that there may be many different kinds of cultural orientation within a single organizational environment. There may be various types of divisions within an organizational system that give rise to significant internal disputes in what may otherwise seem like a perfectly homogeneous organizational culture.[15] Parker identifies three variables that may contribute to the appearance of such divisions in an organizational system. The first of these has to do with forms of spatial or functional identification. What Parker has in mind here is the way in which people sometimes identify more closely with a particular group of colleagues in their work environment because of the fact that they work in the same office space or organizational department. It is the old "them over there, us over here" mindset. Divisions may also be caused by generational differences. That is, people may identify more with the outlook of those of their colleagues that are of the same age as they are, or with whom they have shared the various vicissitudes of a particular historical period. Here it is a question of "them from that time, us from this time."

[15] *Ibid.*, p. 188.

Occupational or professional differences may also play a role in the appearance of divisions within an organizational system, i.e. "them who do that, us who do this."[16] In his study of organizational culture, Parker found that clear differences and even antagonism often lay behind the "team" rhetoric that was vaunted by the organization's management. In the case of one manufacturing company, the divisions were mainly along departmental, geographical, and historical lines. Whereas this company's upper management had cozy, homey offices, the factory managers' offices were impersonal and functional. In addition, the upper management was relatively "new" to the company, whereas the old-timers down in the factory had been part of the "family" all along. The company's "family" rhetoric therefore turned out to be no more than nostalgia for "the way things used to be." It did not accurately reflect the reality of a fragmented company culture.[17]

The fact that organizational cultures are often fragmented does not mean that there are no meaningful points of common orientation and identification in organizational systems. However, it is important to note that, even though there may be ideas and expectations that inform the perceptions and behavior of all the participants in an organizational system, they may find many different behavioral expressions in the conduct of an organization's various agents. The fact that there is no agreement, consensus or identifiable "core values" in an organizational system does not mean that its culture is "weak." Divisions only become intelligible and significant within the context of some wider form of common identification. As systems of meaning, organizations are capable of accommodating both agreement and dissent. The meaning and moral significance that participants in an organizational system attach to particular actions and decisions are informed by the intricate interplay of dissent and agreement to which they are party in their daily interactions with colleagues. This makes it very problematic indeed to use the existence of some sort of deliberately expressed formal moral consensus in an organizational system as an indication of a "strong ethical culture."

---

[16] *Ibid.*, p. 108. Parker illustrates how managers and doctors working within the same hospital have different perceptions on what the organization stands for and how it should operate. This is due not only to their occupational differences, but also to the introduction of new information technology that the doctors failed to see the need for within the context of their daily functions.

[17] *Ibid.*, p. 154.

The work of Joanne Martin[18] has been influential in shedding light on theoretical disagreements regarding the nature of culture, and the implications that these debates have for studying and measuring it. Martin distinguishes among three approaches to culture, namely the *integration* approach, the *differentiation* approach and the *fragmentation* approach. Proponents of the integration approach argue that cultures are homogeneous wholes within which collective-wide consensus exists around certain deep-seated beliefs. The differentiation perspective highlights the existence of certain subcultures. These subcultures are often in conflict, but can also operate in harmony or display indifference towards one another. The fragmentation view, which Martin seems most drawn to, views culture as invariably characterized by ambiguity. As a result of persistent tensions, irony and paradoxes that are often irreconcilable coexist. Martin insists that these three views of culture are not mutually exclusive and that they should be combined in a "three-perspective" view in order to analyze the various aspects of an organization's cultural dynamics.

Martin's second major work on culture, entitled *Organizational Culture: Mapping the Terrain*, contests the boundaries that are typically associated with culture.[19] The way in which the term "culture" is employed tends to assume a certain physical location, an embodied manifestation of shared beliefs, and/or certain job-related similarities. Martin questions all of these assumptions and argues that as a result of the socially constructed nature of cultural boundaries, they remain blurred, permeable, fluid and moveable. Martin also points out that the existence of diverse stakeholders renders the drawing of an organization's cultural boundaries problematic. This insight is extremely helpful in understanding the difficulties in studying the ethical aspects of organizational culture. The inclusive kind of stakeholder engagement model that many business ethicists insist upon makes it nearly impossible to know where the boundaries of "the organizational culture" lie.

Martin also rejects the boundaries that are often erected between the public and private spheres. She argues that individuals are part of overlapping cultures and that each individual engages in subjective

---

[18] Joanne Martin, *Cultures in Organizations: Three Perspectives* (New York: Oxford University Press, 1992); Joanne Martin, *Organizational Culture: Mapping the Terrain* (London: Sage, 2002).
[19] Martin, *Organizational Culture*, p. 325.

boundary-drawing processes on an ongoing basis. These insights have significant implications for the ability of researchers to measure cultural change and hence for management to know and understand organizational culture. If the cultural production of boundaries is in fact based on social constructions, it becomes impossible ever to get a satisfactory "picture" of organizational culture. Measuring the success of an ethics program in terms of the "creation of a certain culture" becomes equally complicated, if not impossible.

Since it is so difficult (and perhaps inappropriate) to try to measure the effect that ethics programs have on organizational culture, some ethics practitioners have tried to offer other forms of justification for the money that is spent on such initiatives. Studies have, for instance, been done that try to establish a positive relationship between ethics programs, financial performance and investor confidence. In many cases, these attempts were successful. For example, Curtis Verschoor found that the MVA (market value added) of companies with a stated commitment to ethics is three times that of companies without such a commitment.[20] Verschoor also found that companies' non-financial performance, which influences their reputation score, is 6.7 percent higher for companies with an extensive stated public commitment to ethics and 4.7 percent higher for those that have a Code of Conduct. Non-financial performance is based on criteria such as innovation, an organization's ability to contract, develop and keep talented people, the quality of its management, the quality of the goods that it produces, and the extent to which its members assume responsibility for their community and environment. There are, however, those who argue that there is no significant difference between what investors are willing to pay for the shares of a company with a stated commitment to ethics and what they are willing to offer for stock in organizations that merely meet basic governance requirements.

The debate on whether there is a definitive relationship between ethical performance and financial results continues. Margolis and Walsh looked at ninety-five studies over thirty years and concluded that, though

---

[20] Curtis Verschoor, "Corporate Performance is Closely Linked to a Strong Ethical Commitment," *Business and Society Review*, 104 (1999), 407–415. Also: Curtis Verschoor, "Does Superior Governance Still Lead to Better Financial Performance?" *Strategic Finance*, 86 (2004), 13–14, and Curtis Verschoor, "Is there Financial Value in Corporate Values?" *Strategic Finance*, 87 (2005), 17–18.

there seem to be enough indications of a positive relationship between social (ethical) performance and financial performance, questions remain about the validity and diversity of the measures that have been used to assess social performance.[21] Surveys often fail to make clear exactly what "social performance" is. It could, for instance, refer to corporate social responsibility, but it could also be associated with good governance or internal ethics management. Social performance might also be interpreted as a combination of all of these.

What is often not adequately considered is the fact that some companies may have a sound corporate social responsibility program, but nevertheless condone or encourage ethically questionable behavior by the way they manage their internal organizational environment. Enron is a case in point. They won various awards for their corporate social responsibility efforts, but lacked the most basic elements of good governance and ethics management.

Justifying the cost of ethics programs by reference to their perceived benefits is also complicated by the fact that the effect of ethical sensitization on aspects of organizational life such as employee morale, motivation, work ethic and staff turnover cannot always be measured. The wisdom of using statistical data to justify ethics programs to the members of corporate boards has to be fundamentally questioned. The way in which these empirical surveys are designed and carried out creates an impression of the role and nature of ethics that further contributes to its dissociation with everyday business practice. The goal of corporate business ethics interventions should be to effect a meaningful integration of ethics with core business concerns. By portraying ethics as no more than a useful instrument in the pursuit of the real financial goals of business, business ethics practitioners miss the whole point of the process they are trying to initiate in an organizational system. It also sends a counterproductive message to internal and external stakeholders. It suggests that ethics is only important insofar as it serves to facilitate the pursuit of profit. Ethics programs should not be checks on what can be done in the process of making money. A truly worthwhile ethics program is one that informs the way in which participants in an organizational system go about everything they do.

---

[21] Joshua Margolis and James Walsh, "Building the Business Case for Ethics," *Bridge paper by the Business Roundtable Institute for Corporate Ethics* (Charlottesville, 2006).

Gathering factual evidence about a company's ethical risks and quantifying the value of ethics in dollar terms to make a case for corporate ethics programs is misguided, not only in terms of process, but also in content. It is also directed at the wrong audience. Those who employ this strategy assume that it is primarily the board, corporate executives and shareholders of a company that have to be convinced of the value of ethics. What they fail to recognize is that all stakeholders need to be on board if ethics are to become a part of everyday business practices within an organizational system.

People participate in, and contribute to, things that they believe in and consider worthwhile. When the need to comply with legislation is the only motive behind a company's ethics programs, employees are compelled by fear and necessity to refrain from certain actions, instead of being drawn in, and moved, by something that they believe in and value. People are more likely to recognize the value of an ethics program if it is aligned with the values in their working lives. It is therefore important in the conception and implementation of an ethics program to consider what the various daily activities in an organizational system are directed at. When an ethics program supports and showcases the ideals that participants in an organizational system value, it becomes a source of company pride.

Formulation

The dissociation of ethics from business practice is also evident in the way that the value priorities that inform the normative sensibilities of those who participate in an organizational system are expressed in ethics programs. Those things that represent moral truths or ideals within an organization are often referred to as "core values." These values are usually organized and discussed in "values statements," "codes of ethics," or "codes of conduct." Typically, a "values statement" consists of a brief aspirational enumeration of the normative commitments that an organization makes to its stakeholders. One of the best examples of a values statement is Johnson & Johnson's Credo.[22] A code of ethics is normally slightly longer, but still aspirational rather than directive in tone. Codes of conduct, however, are directive in form and intent. Their

---

[22] The Johnson & Johnson Credo is available on the company's website www.jnj.com.

purpose is to provide employees with behavioral guidelines.[23] In many cases, these codes are supported by a whole hierarchy of policy documents and organizational procedures.[24] This array of documents has long been regarded as one of the most important elements of a successful ethics management program.[25]

The formulation of ethical commitments and compliance standards in codes of ethics and codes of conduct play a very important role in the Federal Sentencing Guidelines for corporations. Both the first and more recent version of the FSG insist that a document that commits a company to clear ethical standards be drawn up as part of its ethics and compliance program. In the revised guidelines, it is made clear that the mere existence of such a document does not in and of itself have any merit. The standards to which a company is committed should be communicated to all employees and care must be taken to ensure that it is translated into a culture of ethical compliance. The new emphasis that is placed on the institutionalization of codes in the latest version of the FSG is indicative of the cynically empty way in which many companies complied with the 1991 version's code provisions. The crucial question, as far as ethics management is concerned, is whether codes of conduct really have any effect on people's beliefs and behavior, or whether they have become no more than a mindless paper-exercise in compliance. Codes are often regarded with skepticism by both internal and external stakeholders. They are perceived as window-dressing, as public relations exercises that have no real effect on "business as usual." To the extent that there is merit in these charges, codes may actually contribute to the dissociation of ethics from business practice.

Doubts about the effectiveness of codes are regularly expressed in business ethics literature. Studies have yielded mixed results. Loe *et al.*,

---

[23] There are no generally accepted standards with respect to the names that are used to refer to various kinds of codes. There are many examples of shorter, aspirational documents that are nevertheless referred to as "codes of conduct," and brief value statements that are called "codes of ethics." Sometimes companies have a brief values statement that is fleshed out in more detail in a code of ethics and that is supported by a number of more specific codes of conduct. For an example of a very well developed hierarchy of documents, see the visual illustration of BHP Billiton's Charter, Codes and Policy documents at www.bhpbilliton.com.

[24] For a more detailed discussion of various types of codes and the advantages and disadvantages that are associated with them, see Deon Rossouw, *Business Ethics in Africa*, 2nd edition (Cape Town: Oxford University Press, 2002).

[25] See Driscoll and Hoffman, *Ethics Matters*.

for instance, found that in most of the seventeen empirical studies that they consulted, a positive relationship could be established between ethical codes and ethical behavior.[26] Schwartz, on the other hand, analyzed nineteen such studies, and could find such a positive relationship in only nine of these. There seems therefore to be no definitive evidence that codes have a significant effect on ethical behavior in organizations.

The objections that are raised against codes in business ethics discourses range from a critique of their intent and the implications of their promulgation, to realistic assessments of their use.[27] Researchers point out that since many codes are promulgated to comply with regulatory demands, or to reduce companies' legal risks, they induce only routinized compliance.[28] Codes that are primarily drawn up to limit a company's legal liabilities therefore tend to reflect little of what is really valued by, or expected of, those who participate in an organizational system. Schwartz concurs that codes are mostly inward-looking, i.e. aimed at behavioral conformity.[29] As such, they do little to stimulate moral discretion. In fact, the kind of behavioral conformity that they advocate discourages moral responsiveness by undermining individual autonomy. Kjonstad and Willmott make a distinction between restrictive ethics and empowering ethics. The former is concerned with formulating and operationalizing codes of conduct, the latter with moral learning and development. They argue that moral reasoning should be less routinized and include intuitive sense-making. Codes offer instructions but are less capable of what Kjonstadt and Willmott call "reflective practical understanding of the normative organization of human interaction."[30] This kind of understanding requires an integration of intuition and compassion and an awareness of the relational aspects of our human reality.

[26] T. W. Loe, L. Ferrell and P. Mansfield, "A Review of Empirical Studies Assessing Ethical Decision Making in Business," *Journal of Business Ethics*, 25 (2000), 185–204.

[27] Mark Schwartz, "Why Ethical Codes Constitute an Unconscionable Regression," *Journal of Business Ethics*, 23(2) (2000), 173–184.

[28] Colin Fisher. "Managers' Perceptions of Ethical Codes: Dialectics and Dynamics," *Business Ethics: a European Review*, 10(2) (2001), 148.

[29] Alberetic Pater and Anita Van Gils, "Stimulating Ethical Decision making in a Business Context: Effects of Ethical and Professional Codes," *European Management Journal*, 21(6) (2003), 764.

[30] Bjorn Kjonstad and Hugh Wilmott, "Business Ethics: Restrictive or Empowering?" *Journal of Business Ethics*, 14(6) (1995), 445–464.

Codes may also have unintended negative effects on employees' commitment to ethical standards. Fisher interviewed forty-five financial and human resource managers in order to engage them in a dialogue on how they perceived the meaning of ethical codes within their organizations.[31] Respondents indicated that they paid little attention to codes because they considered them banal and unnecessary. They also felt that codes undervalued their experience, stated the obvious and insulted their moral intelligence. Some also commented that they felt as though their honesty and integrity were being called into question when they were required to sign certificates to confirm their willingness to abide by a code. Schwartz goes so far as to argue that codes alienate employees from their innate morality.[32] A study by Pater and Van Gils seems to lend support to this idea. They found that the presence of an ethical code had a negative effect on individual ethical decision making.[33] Their explanation for this counter-intuitive finding is that the existence of control mechanisms and rules don't affect the ethical attitudes that actually inform behavior. The fact that code content is often commonsensical may indeed insult employees' intelligence. Providing more detail in codes of conduct may also be counterproductive, as it leaves no room for individual discretion. In fact, a heavy reliance on rules and policies may bring individuals to the conclusion that if something is not strictly forbidden, it is permissible. There are various other authors who attribute the indifferent attitudes of employees to codes to the fact that people believe themselves capable of distinguishing right from wrong without the guidance of a code.

Many also believe that an individual's moral sensibilities are shaped early on in life and that they are therefore not something that can be taught or acquired at work. Some organizations' preoccupation with ethical compliance creates an impression among their employees that they need not assume any direct or personal responsibility for what happens in their work environment.

A further problem regarding codes relates to the way in which they are used. Research has shown that though a very large percentage of organizations have codes, a much smaller percentage of employees are aware of their existence and an even smaller number are versed in

---

[31] Fisher, "Managers' Perceptions of Ethical Codes," 146–147.
[32] Schwartz, "Why Ethical Codes Constitute an Unconscionable Regression," 176.
[33] Pater and Van Gils, "Stimulating Ethical Decision making," 762–772.

their content.[34] This study also found that the existence of a code was unlikely to have an effect on an employee's decision to report observed unethical behavior.[35]

In a sense, codes exemplify the basic philosophical challenge of bridging the gap between theory and practice. Codes are often perceived as theoretical exercises, which are embarked upon for instrumental reasons. Little wonder that they are so often treated as no more than theoretical encumbrances in the practical realities of everyday business practice. The problem with codes then, is that they seldom contribute, or speak to that which people really believe and value in their work.

Many authors argue that codes are only effective insofar as they are enforced and communicated via effective ethics training programs.[36] These authors believe that the relevance of codes may be demonstrated through the practical case study discussions that are part of many ethics training programs. Whether this strategy really succeeds in bridging the gap between theory and practice remains questionable, however. Nevertheless, training programs remain central to most companies' ethics and compliance efforts and it is to a careful consideration of the way in which they are used that we turn next.

Integration

Ethics training and communication
The Federal Sentencing Guidelines have effectively made ethics training programs compulsory in companies' ethics and compliance programs. Because of this, they have become a standard feature of most organizations' ethics and compliance functions. Service providers have developed multiple training modules and products that can meet the needs of any size company, in any industry and of every nationality. Though these training modules may often be tailor-made to meet specific corporate needs, and despite the variety of ways in which they are

---

[34] See surveys done by the Ethics Resources Centre at www.ethics.org and the Business Ethics South Africa survey at www.ethicsa.com.

[35] Mark John Somers, "Ethical Codes of Conduct and Organizational Context: a Study of the Relationship between Codes of Conduct, Employee Behavior and Organizational Values," *Journal of Business Ethics*, 30 (2001), 185–195.

[36] Thomas R. Wotruba, Lawrence B. Chonko and Terry W. Loe, "The Impact of Ethics Code Familiarity on Manager Behavior," *Journal for Business Ethics*, 33 (2001), 59–69.

implemented, they all seem to follow the same basic approach. Typically, these modules convey information about a company's stated values, initiate employees in the principles of deontology, teleology, or virtue-ethics to enhance their ethical decision-making skills, and then create opportunities for participants to practice their newly acquired skills via case study exercises.

Many of those who write about ethics training stress the importance of demonstrating how corporate values inform everyday behavior on the job, as well as the applicability of ethical thinking in every aspect of corporate decision making. This seems a reasonable enough approach. The problem, however, is that there is little evidence to suggest that these training programs really affect the behavior of those who participate in organizational systems. It seems then that ethics training, in the form that it is currently being offered, may have some serious limitations. To gain an understanding of the nature of these limitations, it is necessary to consider what has become the conventional model for ethics training, in terms of its *content*, its *mode of delivery* and the *frequency* with which people are exposed to it.

The first and most basic question to be asked about ethics training is, of course, whether "ethics" can be taught. It is only once one has been able to give an affirmative answer to this question that it becomes possible to think about the content of ethics training. This question has preoccupied many ethicists and rightly so, since it concerns the very basis of many teaching and consulting careers.

Michael Hoffman, one of the fathers of the business ethics movement in the US, has argued that ethics training enhances people's ethical awareness by making them aware of their organization's values and the moral dilemmas that they may be confronted with as result of their commitment to these values.[37] He also insists that exposure to some of the philosophical approaches that may be employed in ethical reasoning helps people to think through moral dilemmas. Hoffman also believes that case study discussions assist people in the practical application of philosophical reasoning skills. Through this developmental process, participants progress through the phases of basic moral awareness, to employing philosophical reasoning skills, to the ability to apply

---

[37] Dawn-Marie Driscoll and W. Michael Hoffman, *Ethics Matters: How to Implement Values-Driven Management* (Waltham, MA: Bentley College Center for Business Ethics, 2000).

principles to practice. Hoffman contends that moral development culminates in ethical leadership. Hoffman's approach, like that of many other business ethicists, relies on a linear model of moral development. Lawrence Kohlberg's theory is emblematic of these ideas about moral development.[38] Kohlberg's research led him to conclude that an individual's moral sensibilities develop progressively, through stages, as he/she learns to think about moral issues, first in a "pre-conventional," then in a "conventional" and finally in a "post-conventional" way. In the pre-conventional phase, the individual (at this stage he/she is likely to still be a child) is concerned with self-interest. An individual in this phase of moral development is primarily concerned with eliciting praise or avoiding punishment. In the conventional phase, the individual develops a concern for enduring personal relationships. Because of this, the individual begins to balance his/her self-interest with the interests of those by whom he/she is surrounded and develops a concern for law-abidingness. In the post-conventional phase, the individual finally masters principled thinking. This, Kohlberg insists, allows the individual to think through moral dilemmas independently and thus make objective, rational decisions based on moral principles.

Kohlberg's theory has been criticized for a number of reasons. Feminist scholars, like Carol Gilligan, for instance, have criticized what they see as gender biases in Kohlberg's research.[39] Kohlberg's theory creates the impression that principled reasoning is the epitome of moral maturity. In the process, other forms of moral responsiveness, such as the ability to assume responsibility and to take care of others, are made to seem inferior. Gilligan points out that the ability to take care and a concern for sustaining relationships is primarily associated with the moral sensibilities of women. She argues therefore that to portray principled reasoning as the height of moral maturity, as Kohlberg seems to do, is sexist and discriminatory.

Objections such as Gilligan's seem not to have dissuaded the majority of business ethicists from making principled reasoning the focus and ultimate goal of all their training initiatives in corporate ethics programs. Interestingly, it is possible to detect what seems to be an implicit

[38] Lawrence Kohlberg, *The Philosophy of Moral Development* (San Fransisco: Harper & Row, 1981).
[39] Carol Gilligan, *In a Different Voice: Psychological Theory and Women's Development* (Cambridge, MA: Harvard University Press, 1982).

recognition of the limitations of principled reasoning in the proposals of some scholars. These limitations are, however, interpreted as something that can be compensated for by increasing the scope of principled considerations that are brought to bear on ethical problems. Scholars like Petrick and Quinn therefore encourage individuals to employ an array of ethical principles simultaneously in their consideration of ethical dilemmas. The rationale seems to be that, when employed together, these various forms of principled thought can compensate for each other's limitations.

Petrick and Quinn's integrity capacity construct includes a combination of four ethics theories (deontological, teleological, rights and systems development) with four legal theories (natural law, positive law, civic responsibility and social reform). They argue that individuals with high integrity capacity are capable of cognitively balancing the guiding principles of these theories when faced with a moral dilemma. Kulik has carefully considered Petrick and Quinn's proposals in relation to the collapse of Enron to try and ascertain whether this form of integrity capacity could have helped to prevent the ethical failures of those involved. His conclusion was that it probably wouldn't have made a difference.[40] Individuals may actually use the notion of "balancing" considerations to justify actions that may otherwise seem patently wrong. Enron's reporting practices, for instance, may, from the perspective of one set of principled considerations, have seemed simply dishonest to those involved. It is conceivable, however, that they could have reasoned that these principles needed to be "balanced" by other principled considerations. To this end they may have invoked a (mistaken) utilitarian understanding of the "greatest good" to justify their reporting practices as a measure that gave their shareholders the best possible advantage. They may also have thought it reasonable to "balance" the requirements of legal theories with the ability to go beyond "mere compliance" in considering their "creative" accounting practices. After all, those involved often argued that they were breaking new ground and that it was impossible to predict what would be legal in future. It seems then that ethical theories can be made to serve as self-deceiving justifications of corporate wrongdoing. They may be especially

---

[40] Brian W. Kulik, "Agency Theory, Reasoning and Culture at Enron: In Search of a Solution," *Journal of Business Ethics*, 59 (2005), 347–360.

vulnerable to this kind of cynical exploitation if they are only briefly explained in the most general of terms.

In large companies, information technology is increasingly being used in ethics training. This makes it possible to record the number of staff members who have completed an ethics training program, which is important in proving compliance with the FSG. Further advantages include cost-effectiveness, timeliness and expediency. However, these features of computer-based ethics training may also limit its value as far as having a real effect on people's beliefs, perceptions and behavior is concerned. In online ethics training, ethics is treated as though it comprises a fixed body of knowledge, which can be digitized and "downloaded" for easy consumption. As such, it is unlikely to have any meaningful effect on people's everyday behavior. Attempts have, however, been made to use information technology in more constructive ways. It has been employed, for instance, to create online chat rooms or to initiate interactive case study discussions. (See Chapter 6 for a closer consideration of these innovations.)

One of the challenges that ethics training programs face, is the fact that they compete with other job-related skills programs for time, attention and funding. Time consuming and costly face-to-face ethics training is therefore likely to be limited to annual or onc-off events. As such, ethics training remains low on the priority-list of both supervisors and staff.

The fact that so much emphasis is placed on deliberate, principled reasoning in ethics training programs limits its ability to insert ethics into the normal, everyday concerns of business practice. This preoccupation with deliberate, principled reasoning may be attributed to a number of important, though often largely unexamined assumptions. The first of these has to do with the nature of moral agency. Many business ethicists and practitioners uncritically assume that individuals are deliberating agents, who have the ability to consider objectively all the various contingencies that pertain to a particular situation before making a decision or taking action. A second, related assumption is that ethical learning takes place in a deliberate fashion. As I explain in Chapters 2, 3, and 4, these are highly questionable assumptions.

There is another important objection to the emphasis that is placed on deliberate, principled reasoning, however: it effectively enforces a separation between theory and practice. Many ethics training programs create the impression that morality is something that is properly contemplated in a state of rational detachment. That is to say, they encourage people to consider their ethical responsibilities "objectively," and not to allow their judgment to be "contaminated" by personal or contextual biases. Ethics thus becomes a matter of principle, rather than practice. This contributes to the impression that ethical considerations are *checks* on business practice, rather than a normal *part* of everyday business practice.

The ethics and compliance function

There are three moments within US corporate history that are of particular significance in the emergence of the ethics officer profession. Companies first employed ethics professionals as part of their response to the defense contracting scandals of the Reagan era. It was in these early years that the Ethics Officer Association (EOA) was established and based at the Centre for Business Ethics at Bentley College in Waltham MA. The profession was given additional impetus in the early 1990s when it was recommended, in the Federal Sentencing Guidelines for Corporations, that companies appoint designated officers to lead their ethics programs. A series of corporate collapses during the first few years of the new millennium precipitated a legislative and regulatory overhaul and revived many companies' interests in having an ethics officer on their staff.[41]

The revised version of the Federal Sentencing Guidelines that was introduced enhanced the stature of ethics officers by its new emphasis on ethics. However, it also precipitated a strong compliance drive among companies. The ethics officer profession had no choice but to respond to the new regulations' extensive compliance provisions and standards. The Ethics Officer Association's name was changed to the Ethics and Compliance Officer Association (ECOA). This name change is indicative of the significant changes that the profession has undergone over the past few decades. The fields of ethics and compliance have become inextricably linked within the US corporate environment. Even organizations that had previously focused exclusively on compliance have now begun to recognize the need to pay attention to ethics. The Health Care Compliance Association (HCCA), for instance, recently established a

---

[41] Nikki Swartz, "The Rise of the Ethics Officer," *The Information Management Journal* (2003).

new organization, called the Society for Corporate Compliance and Ethics (SCCE). The intimate relationship that now exists between ethics and compliance has both advantages and disadvantages.

It can be argued that these developments have created a US corporate environment in which compliance takes precedence over ethics. In fact, the heavy emphasis that is placed on compliance in the US has significantly colored many people's perception of the value of ethics and has left it with a very narrowly circumscribed role. Nearly three-quarters of surveyed US ethics officers said that their program was initially developed to satisfy a limited set of compliance priorities, such as meeting legal and regulatory requirements, minimizing risks of litigation and indictment and improving accountability mechanisms.[42] However, research shows that the priorities that organizations pursue in their ethics and compliance programs sometimes broaden over time. Joshua Joseph conducted interviews with a number of ethics officers of Fortune 500 companies and other leading organizations in order to determine the justification, priorities and structure of their ethics programs.[43] More mature programs tend to focus on ethical values, maintaining a company's brand and reputation, recruiting and retaining desirable employees, and helping to unify and guide a global workforce. Whereas it may seem more challenging and interesting to try to encourage relationships of trust through an ethics program, it is much more difficult to realize goals of this order in practice. In a compliance-driven environment preoccupied with measurement, it is much easier to focus on complying with legal and regulatory requirements than it is to engage with the nebulous relational complexities of an organizational system's cultural dynamics.

Ed Petry has specifically looked at the role that ethics officers play in promoting a culture of ethical compliance in organizations. He questions whether ethics officers have the resources and the clout to have a real impact on an organizational system's cultural dynamics.[44] To address potential problems in an organizational system, for instance, ethics officers have to describe and assess its cultural dynamics. However, the kind of information that is required to do so is difficult to obtain and interpret. Furthermore, there are no paradigmatic benchmarks to guide and assist ethics officers in the identification and evaluation of relevant

[42] Joseph, "Integrating Business Ethics," 317.   [43] *Ibid.*, 311.
[44] Petry, "Assessing Corporate Culture," 10.

information. Peer-to-peer exchanges could provide very useful points of reference in this process, but they require sustained effort over a long period of time. The nature of the task and the material is such that general benchmarks are likely to be elusive anyway. Since every organizational system's cultural dynamics are likely to be informed by a unique and ever shifting combination of personal and contextual contingencies, it probably would not make sense to try to develop a generally applicable model or standard for organizational culture. As such, it is not difficult to understand why most ethics officers continue to focus their efforts on complying with the seven steps of the Federal Sentencing Guidelines.

In reality, the task of an ethics officer goes far beyond compliance. Even in the management of a conventional ethics program, considerable imaginative and integrative competencies are required. An ethics officer is the custodian of an organization's code of ethics, the planner and executor of its ethics training, the ear behind its ethics help-line, the mind behind the formulation of its policies and, in some cases, even the driving force behind their enforcement. Ethics officers also play an important role in maintaining an organization's relationships with internal and external stakeholders. To do his/her job well, an ethics officer should possess the kind of sophisticated interpersonal skills that allow him/her to interact comfortably with almost everyone who participates in an organizational system. He/she should also be capable of building meaningful relationships with the members of an organization's board, individuals at senior and middle management level, and ordinary employees. According to PricewaterhouseCoopers' CEO, Sam DiPiazza, the ethics officer must be the first to identify ethical issues within business practice, and must then be able to mobilize the necessary resources to address them. He/she must be able to gather subject experts to talk through the issue on a real-time basis and find a way to respond to the issue in an ethical manner.[45]

The range of tasks assigned to ethics officers tends to be very broad. According to Joseph, ethics officers' responsibilities typically include the following: overseeing an organization's ethics function, collecting and analyzing relevant data, developing and interpreting ethics-related policy,

---

[45] Samuel A. DiPiazza, "The Value of the Corporate Ethics Office. Musings from the 'Other' CEO," *Vital Speeches of the Day*, delivered at the Conference Board Conference in New York City (May, 2001).

developing and administering ethics education and training materials, and overseeing ethics investigations.[46] Though Joseph's survey showed that not all ethics officers were involved in investigations and disciplinary procedures, it did indicate that most companies' ethics office tends to work closely with departments such as human resources, auditing, legal and security. A recent study by the Ethics Resource Center depicts the ethics and compliance officer as being responsible for: the assessment of areas of risk for noncompliance and misconduct; the establishment of objectives for the organization's ethics and compliance programs and the management of such programs; implementing initiatives to foster an ethical culture throughout the organization; supervising ethics and compliance staff throughout the organization; frequently informing the board and senior management on the functioning of the program; implementing measurements to monitor the program and overseeing periodic measurement of its effectiveness.[47] The Ethics Resource Center report further states that ethics and compliance officers require management experience, the ability to work at executive level, strong knowledge of the business, knowledge and passion for ethical conduct and compliance, plus strong character and a commitment to integrity.

Ethics officers often have to contend with contradictory demands. In cases of misconduct, for instance, ethics officers have the unenviable task of having to be both the trusted confidant of employees, and the strict disciplinarian that protects an organization's interests. In most cases, he/she has to adopt a "both, and" approach, rather than an "either, or" attitude to balance successfully such divergent expectations. He/she might therefore try to make the investigative process that follows a report of misconduct more fair and transparent in the eyes of employees, while also taking care to protect an organization against misconduct. As is the case with all professions, an ethics officer has to acquire specialized knowledge and skills, maintain independence, and adhere to certain standards of professionalism.

[46] Joseph, "Integrating Business Ethics," 325.
[47] Ethics Resource Centre (ERC), *Leading Corporate Integrity Report* (Washington, DC: Ethics Resource Center, 2007). Working group Co-chairs: Scott A. Roney and Patricia J. Harned. Along with ERC, representatives of the Business Roundtable Institute for Corporate Ethics, the Ethics and Compliance Officer Association (ECOA), the Open Compliance and Ethics Group (OCEG), and the Society of Corporate Compliance & Ethics (SCCE) came together in an ERC Fellows Program working group.

The need to maintain a certain professional independence sometimes places ethics officers in a precarious position. This is because ethics officers must also become "insiders," within an organizational system, with intimate knowledge of its issues and activities, in order to maintain the trust and confidence of employees and management. In some respects then, ethics officers have to perform the same precarious balancing act between loyalty and independence as internal auditors.[48] The ability to deal with paradox and ambiguity, and to "navigate the grey" is essential in an ethics officer's job, but it is not something that is easily acquired. Ethics officers are often drawn from the legal, auditing and human resources fields and are thus not always equipped with the full range of competences that are required to do an ethics officer's job.

Most successful ethics officers attribute their achievements to the fact that they have a direct line to the CEO of their organization, or are able to report directly to the board. The more senior the position of an ethics officer within the management hierarchy of an organization, the easier it is for he/she to bring matters of concern to the attention of those at the highest levels. However, it is by no means clear that an organization's ethics officer should be part of its executive management team. From the perspective of Sam DiPiazza, the CEO of PricewaterhouseCoopers (PwC), it is not the task of an ethics officer to assist the executive leadership of an organization in the running of a business. He does, however, expect an ethics officer to be part of the governance process in an organization, and hence PwC's ethics officer has a direct reporting line to the board and meets with them regularly.[49]

What complicates this issue is the fact that there are likely to be both advantages and disadvantages to whatever position an ethics officer is given in an organization's management hierarchy. If an ethics officer is not considered a senior member of an organization's management system, he/she may not get the kind of deference and respect from employees that is needed to have a real influence on the way people go about their daily business. Yet, if an ethics officer is given too senior a position within a corporate hierarchy, he/she might become so closely associated with management in the eyes of employees that

---

[48] Dove Izraeli and Anat BarNir, "Promoting Ethics through Ethics Officers: a Proposed Profile and Application," *Journal of Business Ethics*, 17 (1998), 1189–1196.

[49] DiPiazza, "The Value of the Corporate Ethics Office," 715.

they become reluctant to ask sensitive questions or share confidential information.

It is clear, then, that to fulfill the role of ethics officer, an individual must master a wide array of complex skills. The kinds of information that ethics officers need to do their jobs are hard to come by, the relationships that they must sustain are fluid, and the roles that they have to play are sometimes contradictory. To associate ethics officers too closely with the cause of compliance is therefore to seriously underestimate the complexity of their role in organizational practice.

Evaluation

Ethics and performance management systems

The practice of rewarding employees based on their performance is common in the corporate world. Organizations have certain goals, and would like to ensure that their employees pursue them faithfully and with appropriate vigor. Incentives like bonuses and other performance-based rewards are often used to effect an appropriate alignment between individual and organizational goals. There are many types of organizational incentives, such as bonuses, stock options, cash or prizes. In some cases, all employees are rewarded for organizational success (e.g., profit-sharing schemes, or across-the-board bonuses based on revenue growth). In other cases, individuals are singled out for outstanding performance through merit-based bonuses or salary increases.[50] Rewarding employees across the board for organizational success is perceived as less ethically problematic than the latter, as it is generally accepted that employees should be allowed to share in an organization's accomplishments. When employees are rewarded on an individual basis, there is always the risk that it may encourage self-interested behavior, unwillingness to share information, and ruthless competition. Organization-wide rewards, on the other hand, may create a common, groupthink-like fixation on profit maximization among employees, which could lead to the neglect of other crucial organizational priorities. The rule of thumb is therefore that performance incentives must never be structured in a way that entices employees to do harm to the interests of customers or other stakeholders.

---

[50] Peter K. Kensicki, "Are Performance-Based Incentives Unethical?" *National Underwriter* (September 10, 2001).

The spate of corporate scandals that rocked the business community during the early years of the new millennium provided a clear rationale for incentivizing ethical business practices. The Federal Sentencing Guidelines, for instance, suggest that a concern for ethics and compliance should be reflected in organizational performance management and disciplinary systems. As a result, the integration of ethics criteria into performance management systems has become a standard feature of most ethics management programs. Many theoretical justifications have been offered for this practice. "Reinforcement theory," for instance, suggests that an organization can induce ethical behavior among its employees by institutionalizing rewards and punishments for ethics. Empirical studies have attempted to illustrate that unethical behavior increases if the perception exists that an organization rewards such behavior. It has also been hypothesized that inconsistent rewards and discipline promote justifications or rationalizations of unethical behavior. Trevino and Youngblood have specifically studied the impact of organizational reward systems on ethical behavior.[51] The aim of their research was to try to establish whether unethical behavior is the result of "rotten apples," i.e. morally flawed individuals, or "rotten barrels," i.e. an immoral organizational ethos. Using what they call their "interactionalist" approach, they investigated the intricate relationships between individual moral development, locus of control, rewards, and ethical decision-making behavior. Their conclusion was that individual managers' cognitive moral development and locus of control does affect their decision making.[52] They argued that rewards play into this decision-making process by influencing individuals' outcome expectancies. However, Trevino and Youngblood were unable to establish a direct link between perceived reward system pressures and ethical decision making.

A recent study by Ashkanasy, Windsor and Trevino also explored the relationship between rewards and ethical behavior.[53] In this study, Ashkanasy *et al.* used aspects of social learning theory and cognitive

---

[51] Trevino and Youngblood, "Bad Apples in Bad Barrels: a Causal Analysis of Ethical Decision-Making Behavior," *Journal of Applied Psychology*, 75(4) (1990), 378–385.

[52] *Ibid.*, 382.

[53] Neal M. Ashkanasy, Carolyn A. Windsor and Linda K. Trevino, "Bad Apples in Bad Barrels Revisited: Cognitive Moral Development, Just World Beliefs, Rewards, and Ethical Decision Making," *Business Ethics Quarterly*, 16(4) (2006), 449–473.

moral development theories to look at the interrelationships between individual factors, rewards and ethical behavior. According to social learning theory, most learning takes place vicariously through the observation of peers, and the outcomes of others' actions.[54] The deeply held beliefs that people develop over years of social learning are factored into the Ashkanasy *et al.* study through the BJW variable, i.e. "belief in a just world." The study suggests that it is a combination of individual moral development, deeply held beliefs, and organizational cues that informs ethical behavior. Like Trevino and Youngblood, Ashkanasy *et al.* did not find a significant relationship between perceptions of ethical reward and ethical behavior.[55] In this study, the only group of people influenced by perceptions of reward was pragmatic managers, whose cognitive moral development was rated low by the researchers. It could be argued, however, that this is the profile of most business managers. If this is the case, then the results of Ashkanasy *et al.*'s study may be used to justify the inclusion of ethical priorities in performance management systems. However, the individual and contextual factors that shape and inform an individual's perceptions and behavior are by no means so clear-cut. What Ashkanasy *et al.*'s study points to is the complex and often unarticulatable relationship that exists between ethical development, deeply rooted beliefs and perceptions of reward.

The internal dynamics of the Enron Corporation prior to its catastrophic collapse is a good example of the role that an organization's human resource environment can play in shaping the behavior and priorities of those who participate in it. Enron's human resource management system was designed to foster innovation and included both formal and informal behavioral triggers. Enron recruited candidates whom they considered suitably "bold, hungry and creative." These were individuals who would not typically be interested in the Texas energy environment.[56] To make employment at Enron more attractive, the performance management system allowed employees seamless movement from one section to the next. This encouraged employee flows within the organization. In terms of work system design, Enron incentivized new business ideas by awarding its creators "phantom equity"

---

[54] *Ibid.*, 450.   [55] *Ibid.*, 465.
[56] Bert Spector, "HRM at Enron: the Un-indicted Co-conspirator," *Organizational Dynamics*, 32(2) (2003), 207–220.

even before their ideas began to yield profit. Once ideas did yield profit, their authors could exchange their phantom equity for real Enron shares. Enron was renowned for its lavish performance rewards and bonuses. Bonuses were paid once deals were completed and their potential future revenues booked. All of these performance management strategies created a short-term orientation among Enron's employees. Deals did not have to be sustainable over the long-term to put cash in employees' pockets. Enron was equally notorious for its "rank and yank" system. This system made provision for the annual dismissal of 15 percent of the organization's employees, based on their performance ranking. Systems such as these helped to create a pernicious, one-dimensional view of success within the organization. Though Enron's eventual demise cannot be directly attributed to its human resource systems, it seems clear that they contributed to the emergence of a particular way of thinking among the organization's leadership and employees. Some business ethicists hypothesize that the disjunction between what was happening inside of Enron and the values that its leadership were espousing to the world outside contributed to the collapse of the energy giant. Enron's leaders claimed that they were committed to integrity and respect, but these values played no role in the organization's performance review process.[57] It was not that Enron's performance system, in and of itself, or explicitly, sanctioned immorality, or dismissed values. Rather, these were the unintended effects of a system that was designed to reward creativity and innovation. These unforeseen consequences only become evident after the fact. Enron's performance management system reflected certain beliefs. This is also true of every other organization's performance system. The beliefs that are inscribed in performance systems create and sustain particular value preferences in an organizational system. In some cases, these preferences may create expectations that make it difficult for the members of an organizational system to act in ethically appropriate ways.

Some authors argue that the practice of encouraging ethical behavior by means of performance management systems is based on questionable assumptions. Primary among these is the assumption that there is a direct cause-and-effect relationship between rewards and behavior. As we have seen, there seems to be no factual basis for this assumption and "management control systems" are therefore often far less effective than

---

[57] *Ibid.*, 218.

people expect them to be. In fact, organizational reward systems have been shown to be inherently ambiguous. According to Rosannas and Velilla, Kerr's classical problem (i.e. "the folly of rewarding for A when hoping for B") is still very evident in organizational practices.[58] In many cases, employees are implicitly rewarded for attitudes and behavior that are at odds with the stated objectives of their organization's performance management system. In such cases, an organization's purposefully designed incentive system may only serve to perpetuate its management's illusions of control. Rosannas and Velilla draw on Hofstede's insights in their critique of management control systems. According to Hofstede, the use of such mechanistic control systems is complicated by the fact that objectives within an organization are often ambiguous, while activities are seldom repetitive.[59] Hofstede also points out that the measurement of these systems' outputs is imperfect and that the cause-and-effect relationships between rewards and behavior are by no means clear. Hofstede's observations suggest that management control systems that are designed and implemented without adequate regard for the complexity of human motivation and organizational practices are unlikely to have more than a superficial impact on the day-to-day realities of organizational life.

The use of performance management systems raises important questions about the way in which belief systems and organizational practices interact in the workplace. That this is no simple matter becomes clear when one considers the fact that even well-intended performance systems, in which ethics is explicitly rewarded and misconduct discouraged, sometimes have unforeseen negative effects. It seems that when performance management systems explicitly reward ethical behavior, it sometimes undermines employees' moral discretion by inducing minimalist compliance for the sake of self-interest. Rewards of this kind often also have the effect of undermining, rather than sustaining, relationships in an organizational system. The self-interested behavior that it tends to encourage, can, for instance, hamper teamwork. Group rewards may not be the answer either. The danger is that if employees are not individually held to account, they may feel and assume no personal

---

[58] Joseph M. Rosannas and Manuel Velilla, "The Ethics of Management Control Systems: Developing Technical and Moral Values," *Journal of Business Ethics*, (2005), 83–96.
[59] Hofstede *et al.*, "Measuring Organizational Cultures."

responsibility for how things are done, or what goes on, in an organizational system. It is under such conditions that the members of an organization resort to "passing-the-buck." It is unfortunately often the case that if everyone is responsible, no one takes responsibility.

Many business ethicists also stress the importance of punishing misconduct consistently. However, discipline and the enforcement of behavioral guidelines do not have unequivocally positive results. Disincentives or discipline may signal to employees that those who occupy positions of authority within an organizational system do not trust them. They create the impression that the leadership of an organization has so little faith in the integrity and discretion of their employees that they think it necessary and appropriate to introduce such "Pavlovian" control measures. They may even create a desire within some individuals to "beat the system" or "prove them right." In such cases, misconduct may amount to paradoxical, self-fulfilling prophecies.

When it comes to rewards and discipline, it is important to acknowledge the complex nature of human motivation. The interaction between an individual and the organizational system in which he/she participates plays a crucial role in shaping his/her perceptions and behavior. To therefore assume that there is a direct cause-and-effect relationship between organizational rewards and discipline, on the one hand, and the behavior of individual employees, on the other, is to seriously oversimplify the way in which these factors play out in practice. In Chapter 3, I will explore the intricate interplay of personal and contextual factors that inform behavior within a complex organizational system in more depth.

Willingness to report misconduct

The existence of a whistle-blowing or confidential reporting line has long been regarded as one of the basic elements of an ethics and compliance program. In the US, a Whistleblower Protection Act has been in place since 1989. In 2003, Section 301 of the Sarbanes–Oxley Act (SOX) compelled all organizations to institutionalize whistle-blower protections. A further US Senate bill made provision for the reinstatement of whistle-blowers and the payment of damages, thereby ensuring that federal employees would have the same kind of protection as private sector employees have under SOX. However, to have a whistle-blowing line is one thing, but to get people to use it is another. The usefulness of a whistle-blowing line depends entirely on employees' willingness to report misconduct. There may be a number of factors that play into this. According to Near and Miceli, there are both individual and situational factors that influence whistle-blowing.[60] Individual factors include the personal characteristics of the whistle-blower, complaint recipient, and wrongdoer. In each case, the individual's credibility and position of power vis-à-vis others in an organization play an important role. It is also more likely that an individual will report misconduct if whistle-blowing is perceived to be part of his/her role within an organization.[61] There are also situational factors that influence whistle-blowing. For instance, the nature of the transgression, the extent to which an organization's fortunes are likely to be affected by it, the availability of evidence, and the legal basis for the complaint, are all important. An organization's characteristics may also play a role.[62] Whistle-blowing may, for instance, be affected by the way in which an organization is structured. A less rigidly hierarchical bureaucratic structure is believed to encourage more open communication. If an organization succeeds in establishing clear and proper channels for the internal disclosure of unethical behavior, there may be no need for a designated whistle-blowing line.[63]

Attempts have been made to determine what influence organizational climate has on the effectiveness of whistle-blowing practices. Drawing on Victor and Cullen's research into different climate types, Rothwell and Baldwin have tried to determine whether whistle-blowing is more likely to occur in "independence" climates, "instrumental" climates, "caring" climates, "rules" climates, or "law and code" climates.[64] They found that none of the ethical climate types were consistently associated with employees' willingness to report misconduct. However, the same study also looked at whether an organization's size, the existence of policies that make reporting misconduct mandatory, or respondents'

---

[60] Janet P. Near and Marcia P. Miceli, "Effective Whistle-blowing," *Academy of Management Review*, 20(3) (1995), 679–708.

[61] Marcia P. Miceli and Janet P. Near, "What Makes Whistle-Blowers Effective? Three Case Studies," *Human Relations*, 55(4) (2002).

[62] Granville King, "The Implications of an Organization's Structure on Whistle-blowing," *Journal of Business Ethics*, 20 (1999), 315–326.

[63] *Ibid.*, 324.

[64] Gary R. Rothwell and J. Norman Baldwin, "Ethical Climates and Contextual Predictors of Whistle-blowing," *Review of Public Administration*, 26(3) (2006), 216–244.

supervisory status influenced people's willingness to blow the whistle. The researchers concluded that there were no conclusive relationships between most of the program elements that they included in their study and the use of whistle-blowing lines. Supervisory status was the most consistent predictor of whistle-blowing, while the existence of a policy that encouraged whistle-blowing also seemed to play a role.[65] This suggests that people are generally more likely to report misconduct if they feel that it is their responsibility to do so.

Research by Curtis has also shown that individual employees' propensities with respect to whistle-blowing may not be consistent over time. Individuals' willingness to report misconduct varies across mood states and is often influenced by relatively minor events.[66] Researchers also found that people with a negative view of the world were less likely to report misconduct. These findings suggest that belief structures and emotions may play a significant role in how people interpret their personal ethical responsibilities in, and towards, an organizational system.[67]

People are sometimes reluctant to report misconduct because of the negative experiences that they, or some of their colleagues, have had in calling their organization's ethics hotline. These negative experiences may be partly attributable to the fact that many organizations outsource their whistle-blowing lines to call centers. Alice Petersen, founder of a unique whistle-blowing service called "Listen-up," has identified a few basic problems with how whistle-blowing lines typically function.[68] According to Peterson, whistle-blowers generally respond very negatively to the scripted responses that are used in call centers. Call centers usually serve a wide variety of clients with divergent needs. It is for this reason that pre-prepared scripts are employed. They are designed to ensure that consultants respond to calls consistently, and they address all necessary and relevant issues in an appropriate way during the course of a consultation. Call center consultants are rarely instructed or trained to be spontaneously responsive, or to establish a relationship of trust with callers who have sensitive information. Instead, scripted responses are

---

[65] *Ibid.*, 235.
[66] Mary B. Curtis, "Are Audit-Related Ethical Decisions Dependent Upon Mood?" *Journal of Business Ethics*, 68 (2006), 191–209.
[67] *Ibid.*, 206.
[68] Interview with Alice Petersen at the Listen-up head offices, Chicago, January 2005. Rothwell and Baldwin, "Ethical Climates and Contextual Predictors of Whistle-blowing," 216–244.

used to identify, as quickly as possible, the issue at stake and offer a standard solution or response. Whistle-blowers tend to take this as evidence that the organization does not take their unique situation seriously, or that it simply seeks as expedient a solution as possible to the problems that they raise. By sanctioning, or insisting on, the use of such standardized procedures, companies create the impression that they do not consider themselves accountable *to* the caller or the various other stakeholders that may be involved, but rather seek to limit their own liability *for* anything that might have gone wrong. Instead of adopting a relational perspective and recognizing that whistle-blowing is an act of loyalty, these organizations place the whistle-blower in opposition to themselves.

Petersen's firm developed an alternative service that allows for more responsive interactions with whistle-blowers. Those who answer whistle-blowers' calls are trained to acknowledge the problem that is being reported and to show proper appreciation for the fact that it arises in, and from, a unique set of circumstances and relationships. Agents are also encouraged to demonstrate appropriate concern about what is being reported and about the possible implications that it may have for everyone involved. Calls are treated with the utmost confidentiality and the problems that are raised receive immediate attention. By treating whistle-blowers in this way, Peterson's staff gradually builds the trust and confidence that is necessary for such a system to function effectively.

Trust in such systems may be undermined, however, if a whistle-blowing line is used inappropriately. In some cases, the allegations that are made through a whistle-blowing line are malicious, or strategic. People may, for instance, use a whistle-blowing line in an attempt to effect a reconfiguration of the power relationships within an organization. Those who are interested in maintaining the status quo within an organization may be tempted to use it to discredit dissenting individuals.

Whistle-blowing lines are communication vehicles that allow an organizational system to consider both the legality and appropriateness of its members' actions and decisions. Unfortunately, this is not always how it is perceived. If an organization's whistle-blowing line comes to be perceived as a control instrument, people are unlikely to use or support it.

Whistle-blowing can create an environment in which individuals feel as though they are constantly being watched by their colleagues and superiors. In such an environment, colleagues may find it hard to trust one another. In some cases, employees may internalize the fear of being constantly watched by others to such an extent that they begin to police themselves (i.e. the so-called "panopticon effect").[69] Managers who are interested in exercising control over their subordinates may welcome this effect, but it is not conducive to a healthy organization environment. Studies into the effects of social monitoring mechanisms, such as email monitoring, have shown that this form of internalized control may have all sorts of counterproductive side-effects.[70] The feeling of "being watched," for instance, may breed paranoia, which has a disempowering effect on an individual. The "anticipatory conformity" that it induces also hampers creativity and causes a loss of autonomy.[71] In general, monitoring conveys the message to employees that they are not trusted. In consequence, some of the basic elements of healthy organizational relationships, like respect for others' privacy and trust amongst colleagues, may be sacrificed.

It is clear then, that if an organization's whistle-blowing system works, it is not because of the institutionalization of deliberate processes or systems, or because of its climate, or structures. People will report misconduct only if they trust their colleagues and superiors, when the power dynamics within an organization allow it, and when they feel so inclined. These are not the kinds of factors that are usually addressed in compliance programs.

Reporting practices

Many organizations are primarily motivated to invest in ethics programs for the sake of legal compliance and reputation management. It is not surprising then that they would use their public reports to give an account of the nature and extent of their compliance efforts. In recent years, more and more companies worldwide have begun to adopt the practice of preparing sustainability reports, also called "corporate social responsibility reports," "social environmental reports," "triple bottom-line reports," or "reports to society." However, many of these reports initially focused mainly on environmental concerns. Formal efforts at

---

[69] See Michel Foucault, *Discipline and Punish: the Birth of the Prison* (New York: Random House, 1975).
[70] Christopher Sprinkle, "Surveillance in America. An Interview with Christian Parenti," *American Behavioral Scientist*, 48(10) (2005), 1375–1382.
[71] Kirsten Martin and Edward R. Freeman, "Some Problems with Email Monitoring Part 1," *Journal of Business Ethics*, 43(4) (2003), 353–361.

standardized corporate responsibility reporting began in the early 1990s.[72] In 1991, seven companies had published sustainability reports. This reporting trend has since gained momentum and changed in form and content. In recent years, reports have come to address not only environmental issues, but also economic and social performance, hence the designation "triple bottom-line" reporting. In the last fifteen years, the number of corporations worldwide that document their social behavior has grown exponentially. As of October 2005, 714 firms report in accordance with, or with reference to, the Global Reporting Initiative; and more than 2,500 firms worldwide publish some type of stand-alone report on citizenship, sustainability, environmental and/or social concerns. The number of standards and initiatives against which these reports can be judged has topped 200.[73]

Unfortunately, the positive trend towards reporting on organizations' "non-financial" performance stands in stark contrast to the many unethical practices that have recently come to light in the area of financial reporting. There have been many incidents of fraudulent financial reporting, and many companies have been forced to restate their financial results. Incidents such as these belie an organization's publicly proclaimed ethical intentions. It seems as if a double standard is being employed – impressive non-financial reports, but financial reports that lack transparency and accuracy. This double standard is also evident in the fact that very few companies really incorporate their financial reporting within an integrated sustainability report. In most cases, annual financial reports are still being published separately from the company's corporate social responsibility report. These reports are generally considered less important and therefore command less attention in the business media than an organization's annual financial reports. As such, ethics remains on the fringes of the business community's concerns. If triple bottom-line reporting is treated as just another reputation enhancing, "check-the-box" exercise, conducted in isolation from the organization's "real business," it will remain entirely inconsequential.

The content of triple bottom-line reports also remains an area of concern. The Global Reporting Initiative has developed specific performance

---

[72] Laura Hartman and Mollie Painter-Morland, "Exploring the Global Reporting Initiatives' Guidelines for Triple Bottom-line Reporting," *African Journal of Business Ethics*, 2(1) (2007), 45–57.
[73] UN Commission on Human Rights, 2005.

indicators, which guide organizations in what to include in a triple bottom-line report. However, the GRI indicators do little to facilitate the integration of ethics into day-to-day organizational practices. Both the 2002 Guidelines and the G3 Guidelines, for instance, pay little attention to ethics management practices and good governance in general. In the G3 guidelines, there is only a brief reference to codes under Section 4 of Part 2 entitled "Governance, Commitments and Engagement." It requires that organizations disclose "internally developed mission and values statements, codes of conduct and principles relevant to economic, environmental and social performance and the status of their implementation." Organizations typically respond to this requirement by including a brief statement in their reports that confirms the existence of a code of conduct. However, they rarely provide information about the content of their codes, or the way in which they are disseminated and institutionalized. Merely compelling companies to check-the-box in their reporting on codes and other policy documents does not allow stakeholders to judge the validity of an organization's ethical claims.

This may be partly attributable to the fact that there have been no adjustments in the G3 requirements to parallel the new emphasis on efficient ethics and compliance programs and on executive and board responsibility in the revised United States Federal Sentencing Guidelines. Information about the way in which the organization responds to its various stakeholders could have been included in the information that the GRI requires organizations to present as part of their sustainability report. If information about the cultural dynamics within an organizational system were required by the GRI performance indicators, crucial information, which is not currently included by organizations in their reports, would be made available. Including more guidance on what organizations should report on in terms of ethics and good governance might also have gone a long way in encouraging organizations to integrate their corporate social responsibility initiatives with their internal ethics programs. This oversight by an influential organization like the Global Reporting Initiative shows that the integration of all those aspects of organizational life that pertain to ethics is yet to be accomplished. Sustainability issues and ethics management are still being addressed in organizational silos. This makes it difficult, if not impossible, to effect a meaningful alignment between an organization's value orientation and its core business. As such, it perpetuates the dissociation of ethics from business practice.

Table 1.2 *Limitations of ethics programs within organizations*

Self-assessment and risk analysis	Typically done by means of checklist surveys that gather little qualitative data	Motivate
Ensure leadership commitment	Leadership's primary motivation is their fear of legally imposed financial penalties	
Formulate compliance standards and codes	Codes are no more than glossy paper documents, or plaques on the wall	
Training and communication	Training is a compliance exercise that is primarily directed at informing people about an organization's rules and policies. Communication is one-directional	Formulate
Establish an ethics and compliance office	Compliance, and not ethics, has become the primary focus of organizations' ethics function. Ethics management and CSR are not integrated, but rather isolated in their own organizational silos	
Reinforcement through discipline and reward	Managerial control through punishment and reward instead of support for what is already valued by employees	Integrate
Whistle-blowing	Whistle-blowing lines are outsourced to call centers, where agents' responses are pre-scripted and standardized	
Audits, reporting and realignment	Reporting is a compliance or public relations exercise	

Table 1.2 presents a summary of the limitations of typical ethics management programs.

Responding to the current state of organizational ethics programs

Perhaps part of the reason why so many business ethics models prove ineffective in making ethics part of everyday business practice is that not enough consideration is given to the basic philosophical assumptions on which they are based. A good way to start addressing the problems associated with ineffective business ethics interventions is to carefully unpack and scrutinize these unexamined assumptions. If business ethics interventions are to be reconceived and secured on a well-considered philosophical footing, we have to begin by considering anew the nature of a business organization and its agents. We also have to revisit how ethical decisions are made, both individually and collectively. In what is to follow then, I will examine how a reliance on certain philosophical assumptions continues to define the way in which many contemporary business ethicists approach morality in business, and how this undermines the notion of ethics as practice. It is only once these assumptions have been thoroughly challenged that an alternative approach can begin to be conceived, and it is ultimately to this end that this book is devoted.

   In what follows I attempt to provide an alternative perspective on the way in which ethics programs or initiatives are motivated, formulated and integrated within organizations. In Chapter 2, I consider the various views of moral decision making that typically inform ethics programs in organizations and argue that they misconstrue the nature and dynamics of morality in complex organizational environments. Furthermore, I will argue that the business ethicists' preoccupation with establishing immutable rational protocols to guide moral reasoning perpetuates the dissociation of ethics and business practice. The processes of rational deliberation that these approaches rely on does not speak to the tacit sense of normative propriety that guides everyday practice. Chapter 3 will deal with the issue of moral agency. In most ethics programs, little consideration is given to the complex interplay of personal, contextual and relational factors that inform individuals' perceptions, beliefs and behavior in an organizational system. In this chapter I therefore consider what it is that really motivates those who participate in an organizational system to behave in an ethically appropriate way. In the process, I address questions such as who the moral agent is and how a more comprehensive understanding of agency may affect the way in which ethics in organizations is conceived. If we want to challenge people to be morally responsive in their everyday interactions, we have to understand how value priorities come into existence. Chapter 4 provides an alternative perspective on the processes that shape people's beliefs about ethics and considers the role that such beliefs play in individuals' sense of normative orientation and behavior. These alternative views of moral agency and values compel us to reconsider organizational ethics programs and initiatives. Chapter 5 considers the ways in which the notion of ethics as practice challenge our understanding of leadership and accountability. In the last chapter, I will take a look at the potential practical implications of these considerations for institutional business ethics interventions. After all, when all is said and done, it is in the everyday business of business that the reconception of business ethics as practice has to prove its worth.

2 | *Reconsidering approaches to moral reasoning*

Many business ethicists seem to work from the assumption that individuals' behavior is informed by deliberate moral decisions. Their efforts are therefore often directed at helping people make better moral decisions by teaching them appropriate reasoning skills. Ethics training courses and university curricula therefore typically introduce people to philosophical paradigms, in which "rational" principles or "objective" procedures form the basis of morality. The role that these paradigms continue to play in people's perceptions and understanding of ethics is problematic, because they effectively enforce a distinction between theory and practice. This contributes significantly to the dissociation of ethics from business practice.

The distinction between theory and practice that is evident in many business ethicists' understanding of morality has a long history. One can argue that it has its origins in the seventeenth century, when philosophers began to explore various forms of universalism and instrumentalism in moral theory. At the dawn of the Enlightenment, slogans like "*Aude sapere!*" or "dare to know!" carried the day. Individuals were encouraged to use their capacity for reason in the formulation of moral rules, instead of simply deferring unthinkingly to the authority of the church or state. Some seventeenth-century moral philosophers came to see ethics less as a responsive sort of practical judgment, and more in terms of an effort to rationally formulate and objectively apply universal, *a priori* principles. Others argued that ethical decisions had to be based on a rational, unbiased assessment of the anticipated effects of all available courses of action. In the process, ethics became a discipline devoted either to the objective formulation of universal truths or the rational optimization of human utility.

Most of the ethical approaches that have subsequently been developed by business ethicists correspond, in one way or another, to two basic points of departure. These may roughly be described as either non-consequentialist or consequentialist in orientation. A form of consequentialist reasoning, for example, characterizes utilitarianism. Deontology, on the other hand, is perhaps the most important non-consequentialist approach to ethics. The German philosopher Immanuel Kant is considered the father of deontology. John Rawls, with his understanding of justice as fairness, also made significant contributions to furthering a balance between non-consequentialist and consequentialist approaches to ethics.

Both consequentialist and non-consequentialist approaches to business ethics find their philosophical justification in a specific worldview and anthropology. They both proceed from the implicit general assumption that the world is governed by an orderly system of rules and principles. Scientific enquiry and analysis supposedly allow us to identify and describe the immutable cause-and-effect relationships between the different elements and aspects of the world. If this is the case, it is within our power to anticipate accurately the likely outcomes of particular courses of action. In this paradigm, the moral agent is a rational individual, capable of formulating and applying moral principles with universal validity, or of securing a morally defensible balance of pleasures over pains.

The prominent role that consequentialist and non-consequentialist moral theories have come to play in business ethics has serious implications for the discipline. Jones, Parker and ten Bos, for instance, criticize what they see as the "foreclosure of philosophy" in business ethics.[1] They point out that though many important twentieth-century philosophers have had a lot to say about ethics, business ethicists have generally ignored these insights. Most prominent business ethics texts still draw almost exclusively on Aristotelian virtue-ethics, utilitarianism and deontology. Jones *et al.* are also critical of the general "foreclosure of the meaning of ethics" in the field of business ethics. They argue that business ethics texts treat Aristotelian, utilitarian and deontological ethical approaches in a way that creates the impression that some sort of common understanding of "ethics" exists. This is problematic, not only because of the various philosophical perspectives that are excluded from consideration, but also because there are significant differences among Aristotelian, utilitarian and deontological conceptions of ethics. Jones *et al.* propose a more relational approach to ethics, one that is more attuned to the singularity of events, experiences and perceptions.

[1] C. Jones, M. Parker and R. ten Bos, *For Business Ethics: a Critical Approach* (London: Routledge, 2005).

To acknowledge the irreducible singularity of individual experience and perceptions is to recognize the precariousness and unpredictability of human relations. Jones *et al.* argue, however, that ethics should not be employed in an effort to reduce this uncertainty. Instead, ethics should encourage people to recognize the precarious nature of all ethical decisions.

In what is to follow, it will be argued that the philosophical presuppositions that inform many business ethicists' and practitioners' understanding of, and approach to, business ethics contributes to the dissociation of ethics from practice. Many business ethicists are, for instance, committed to the idea of a "free," or independent, moral agent, who makes decisions in an objective and impartial manner. Since moral imperatives have to be articulated in "objective" terms, their general or universal validity has to be established beyond doubt. Because it is believed that they would introduce an unacceptable form of subjective bias to the process of objective moral deliberation, care is taken to exclude from consideration the singular contingencies and dynamics that pertain to particular relationships and situations. Ethical imperatives are thus treated as if they were immutable truths, the validity of which remains unaffected by the particularities of personal, interpersonal and contextual variables. From this perspective, it is possible to distinguish right from wrong "once and for all." Little consideration is given to the need to act appropriately within the context of particular relationships, situations and contexts. Morality is thus elevated to a realm of objective rational deliberation that is kept free from the "contaminating" perceptions and experiences that inform particular business relationships and incidents. It is here that the separation of ethics from business practice is effected. As we shall see, many of the ethical approaches that are conventionally employed by business ethicists contribute to this problem in some way.

Utilitarianism

The notion of "utility" or usefulness is central in the utilitarian approach to morality. The willingness of utilitarians to embrace "whatever works best" generally serves them well in the business environment. Most business practitioners are already familiar and comfortable with the kind of cost–benefit analysis that utilitarians employ in their moral reasoning. The two most prominent historical exponents of utilitarianism are

Jeremy Bentham and John Stuart Mill. Bentham's approach is based on the general association of morality with those acts and practices that maximize the balance of pleasures over pains in any given situation. When confronted with a moral dilemma, moral agents have to determine what course of action is most likely to bring about the optimal outcome in these terms. Some commentators have described Bentham's pleasure–pain calculus as a form of hedonism.

Mill's articulation of utilitarianism's principles makes it clear, however, that there is much more to this approach than the simple pleasure–pain calculations that are often associated with it.[2] Mill set about countering the charge that utilitarianism is hedonistic in orientation by making a distinction between the different kinds of pleasures that people experience. Some pleasures, argued Mill, are qualitatively better than others. For instance, the pleasures associated with intellectual activities may, in Mill's estimation, be considered superior to those that are obtained from the consumption of food. Mill's version of utilitarianism emphasizes that the benefit to the individual must always be such that it also serves to maximize the well-being of the broader community. Because of this, Mill's utilitarianism has been described as "social welfare utilitarianism."

Mill's utilitarianism required a rational, objective measure to rank pains and pleasures. He therefore proposed that "competent judges" who had experience of various kinds of pleasures should establish a hierarchy of pleasures. What Mill did not adequately recognize or consider, though, is the fact that individuals' consideration of pains and pleasures is likely to reflect their personal tastes, preferences and values. It is also unlikely that any mortal should have had experience of all possible pleasures. This means that there is simply no way that an "objective" criterion could be set up to establish what constitutes an optimum balance of pleasures over pains for everybody under all circumstances.

With its instrumental moral orientation, utilitarianism always runs the risk of objectifying people, as well as the various creatures and phenomena with which humans share the world. Utilitarian reasoning allows business practitioners to justify rationally some of the harmful consequences of their actions by simply out-balancing it with other perceived benefits. The belief that ends can justify means often serves to rationalize unethical behavior. Misrepresentation in financial

---

[2] John Stuart Mill, *Utilitarianism* (Montana: Kessinger Publishing, 2004).

reporting is a good example. Executives convince themselves and their colleagues that they are protecting the broader interest of employees and shareholders when they manipulate financial statements to create a false impression about an organization's financial prospects. They argue that, as long as they later reconcile the reality of their organization's assets with the promises in their public representations, no one needs to get hurt. With such nimble argumentative footwork, lying becomes acceptable, even good, but certainly not "wrong." Utilitarian calculations of this nature are often done at arm's length, so to speak, from those who stand to be affected by them. Because of this, stakeholders sometimes feature as little more than faceless, abstract entities in the analysis of a problem. The clinical procedures and formal logic of utilitarian calculations make it easy to forget that actual people stand to be affected in real ways by the decisions that are being considered.

When utilitarianism's instrumental principles are adopted by those who hold power, it not only allows them to objectify and treat others as if they were no more than means to their own ends, but also puts them in a position to act as arbiters of other peoples' pains and pleasures. It gives them the freedom, in a sense, to weigh and trade that which can only really be appreciated from the perspective of the one who experiences it. In the end, every person's reality is unique and each individual's experience singular. As such, the abstraction and prioritization of experience that is necessary for utilitarian calculations renders it incapable of adequately considering the meaning and significance of particular actions as experienced by those who are affected by them.

In the absence of a consensus about human priorities, the notion of a balance of pains over pleasures becomes meaningless. The compromises and trade-offs that we are prepared to undertake to achieve such a balance are indicative of our worldviews, lifestyle preferences, and all the other things we consider valuable and important. Because utilitarianism relies on the assumption that an "objective" balance of pleasures and pains can be achieved, its proponents often overlook the implicit assumptions and substantive value considerations that inform every act of calculation and compromise.

In a capitalist economy, for instance, business organizations are created to generate profit for their shareholders. This overriding capitalist imperative often functions like any other social priority. In the same way that things like honesty or respect for life act as points of moral orientation in social life, so "profit-maximization" becomes a value that informs and shapes the way people think and live in capitalist societies. This compels many business practitioners to perform a delicate, and often precarious, balancing act. Under circumstances where the state of an organization's bottom-line has become a value that competes with, and often outweighs, other, more openly acknowledged and celebrated societal values, it is difficult to maintain a utilitarian commitment to the notion of objectivity. To try to establish the relative weight of profit considerations in relation to other societal values in absolute terms only serves to exacerbate the unbearable tensions that many business practitioners already experience. As such, business ethics models that employ strict utilitarian principles run the risk of confirming the skeptical attitudes that some business practitioners have with respect to the relevance of ethics in business life.

Within a utilitarian cost–benefit analysis, all pains and pleasures are made commensurable in order to be able to calculate the overall pleasures and pains brought about by particular decisions. Abstract reasoning aimed at aggregating pains and pleasures allows utilitarians to avoid the specific experiences of those individuals who may be affected by their decisions. Furthermore, it is often impossible to gauge the potential effects on others over time. As a result, utilitarian calculations can't really accommodate unpredictable changes in context.

Non-consequentialist approaches

Non-consequentialist approaches to moral decision making are based on the belief that the morality of a particular course of action cannot be determined by its anticipated consequences. They encourage us instead to follow the directives of well-reasoned moral principles, irrespective of the consequences that doing so may have. Such rationally justified imperatives act as the foundation of all moral determinations in non-consequentialist ethical approaches. In this, non-consequentialist approaches are of a distinctly foundationalist nature. Those who are of a non-consequentialist orientation insist that moral imperatives should be formulated in an objective, rational and impartial manner. This orientation towards the universal is shared by two of the most important non-consequentialist moral theories: deontology, which is closely associated with the work of Immanuel Kant, and the rights-based approach of John Rawls.

Deontology

Those business ethicists who employ a deontological approach in their work base their understanding of ethics on a selection of readings from the work of Immanuel Kant. There are parts of Kant's first critique and his *Groundwork of the Metaphysics of Morals* that have become particularly influential, and which form the basis of many business ethicists' understanding of ethics. Jones, Parker and ten Bos are critical of this selective reading of Kant since it ignores the more complex nuances of Kant's broader oeuvre. They argue that business ethicists are employing the technical aspects of what Kant would describe as "theoretical philosophy." As a result, Kant's thought is interpreted as being primarily concerned with facts and the law-like relationships that govern them. What is ignored in the process is Kant's interest in "practical philosophy," which addresses the values of freedom, morality, beauty and sublimity.[3]

Business ethicists who draw on Kant's deontology are particularly intrigued by how moral imperatives are established by means of *a priori* reasoning. Deontology rejects consequentialists' careful consideration of the potential outcomes of their actions in their assessment of moral propriety. Kant was adamant that rational individuals shouldn't simply allow themselves to be guided by the moral directives of traditional authorities. In the true spirit of the Enlightenment, Kant encouraged individuals to act autonomously and formulate their own moral directives by utilizing their capacity for reason. Kant argued that rational individuals could reasonably identify the principles of morality and formulate moral maxims that could guide them in their decisions and actions. For Kant, a principle is a fundamental, objective moral law, grounded in pure practical reason.[4] By themselves, such principles cannot direct human behavior. This is why rational agents need maxims. A maxim is a subjective principle of volition, or rather, a principle that explains one's reasons for acting.[5] According to Kant, moral maxims have the character of synthetic, *a priori* statements. This is particularly important, because it helps to explain why Kant considered moral

---

[3] Jones, Parker and ten Bos, *For Business Ethics*, p. 42.
[4] Immanuel Kant, *Groundwork of the Metaphysics of Morals*, translated by Mary Gregor (Cambridge University Press, 1998).
[5] Frederick Copleston, *History of Philosophy*, Volume 6, Part II Kant (New York: Image Books, 1964).

maxims of this nature indisputable. An important aspect of Kant's thought is the balance that he attempts to strike between an appeal to the internal volition of individual moral agents and the need to formulate moral maxims with universal validity. Kant effects a kind of reconciliation between the two by appealing to the universal nature of reason. To the extent that individual rational agents share in the capacity for reason, they are united under the imperatives that it dictates. Because moral maxims are of a reasonable nature, all reasonable individuals are likely to submit to them of their own volition. It is in this logical reconciliation then that the categorical status, or universal validity, of moral maxims is secured in Kant's thought.

Kant's deontological approach is typically described in terms of two basic moral maxims, which he believed to be of such a self evidently reasonable nature that it would secure the acquiescence of all reasonable individuals. As opposed to hypothetical imperatives, moral duties are categorical imperatives. The categorical character of such imperatives gives them universal applicability and indisputable normative force. In identifying these maxims, Kant appeals to the rational nature of all human beings. He is convinced that something cannot be good if it cannot be the will of all rational individuals. Therefore the first maxim states that a moral decision must always be put to the so-called "universalization test": *Act only on that maxim through which you can at the same time will that it should become a universal law.*[6] Because of his belief in the objective nature of reason, Kant was convinced that an immoral decision would show itself as logically untenable if universalized. For example, Kant would argue that universalizing a decision to break one's promises would undermine the entire notion of promise-keeping, and that it is therefore immoral. Note that breaking a promise in a particular case is not judged immoral because of its potential negative effect on those involved, as the utilitarians would have it, but because it cannot be willed as a universal maxim.

The assumption that all rational individuals would agree that the breaking of a promise is immoral under all circumstances, may, however, prove somewhat contentious among those who make their living doing business. Under certain circumstances a business practitioner may, for instance, have made promises to several different stakeholders

[6] Kant, *Groundwork*, p. 31.

in good faith. A situation could arise where such an individual is no longer able to fulfill all these various promises as anticipated. When this happens, he/she would be forced to choose where to direct his/her efforts and resources. In a case where corporate layoffs are deemed necessary, for instance, the promise of a sustainable income made to employees might come into conflict with the promise of profit made to shareholders. Such a situation then creates conflicting categorical duties. In its non-consequentialist orientation, Kantian deontology does not allow one to consider the concrete consequences of rationally constructed, universal moral imperatives in particular situations. As a result, Kant cannot assist us in deciding between two equally "rational" moral directives.

Business ethicists inspired by Kant's deontology have responded to this dilemma with all kinds of deft discursive maneuvers. Norman Bowie has argued, for instance, that large-scale layoffs may be acceptable within Kant's Ideal Kingdom of Ends, as long as there is no deception or coercion in the employment relationship. Jones, Parker and ten Bos have criticized Bowie's argument in this regard. Though Bowie's argument may be in line with Kant's insistence on the freedom and autonomy of all individuals, it reflects a far greater confidence in the possibilities of rational and autonomous behavior than that expressed by Kant himself.[7] Within an employment system where layoffs can be unilaterally announced, it is clear that not everyone is in a position to make free and autonomous decisions. In fact, a decision that subjects some individuals to the potential hardships of unemployment for the sake of other individuals' financial interests might be highly questionable from the perspective of Kant's theory. This becomes particularly clear in the second formulation of Kant's categorical imperative.

Kant's second maxim is formulated as follows: *Act in such a way that you always treat humanity, whether in your own person or in the person of any other, never simply as a means to an end, but always at the same time as an end.*[8] This second formulation of the categorical imperative betrays the worldview on which Kantian deontology is based. Kant's world is one that is governed by immutable laws. The self-imposed laws of Kant's "Kingdom of Ends" give human morality

---

[7] Jones *et al.*, *For Business Ethics*, p. 46.
[8] Kant, *Groundwork*, p. 38.

structure and order in the same way that causal relationships do in the "Kingdom of Nature." Just as scientific enquiry can reveal the basic structure and dynamics of nature, so human reason can discover the moral order that makes human life possible. As such, it is our very humanity that demands the rational formulation of universal moral laws. For Kant, human beings, as autonomous law-givers, enjoy a status that should not be compromised. However, this deontological worldview, with its anthropocentric orientation, may not always translate easily into a world where business organizations are treated as though they were moral agents.

It is nevertheless clear that rationality lies at the heart of the Kantian test of universality. Business ethicists like Norman Bowie, who draw on the work of Kant, have made this the basis of their approach to ethics. In fact Bowie regards the ability to be rational as essential to moral agency.[9] He stresses the importance of rational beings' ability to "see future consequences" and to "reason abstractly." He sees this capacity for abstract reason as the quality that constitutes our humanity.[10] From Bowie's perspective, it would be permissible to consider the moral appropriateness of a particular act in relation to specific relationships and situations only for the purpose of formulating hypothetical imperatives. Such hypothetical imperatives are, however, always trumped by categorical imperatives.[11] In this interpretation of Kantian theory, it is assumed that the mature moral agent has the ability to rationally retreat from his/her immersion in particular role-responsibilities and employ the universalization test, in order to judge the categorical validity of various possible courses of action. It is by no means clear, however, that this kind of decision maker actually exists. Is it really possible to claim, for instance, that the actions of those who participate in the complex and competitive world of the contemporary capitalist economy are ever devoid of considerations of self-interest? Can the erratic convulsions and feverish expansions of the stock market really be attributed to the considered actions of rational, self-possessed and independent agents?

The deontological approach has also been accused of being internally inconsistent. Some critics of Kant have even argued that there is a certain kind of "pretzel logic" to using the universalizability test to

[9] Norman Bowie, *Kantian Business Ethics* (Malden: Blackwell, 1999), p. 45.
[10] *Ibid.*, p. 62. [11] *Ibid.*, p. 64.

judge the morality of an action while claiming to ignore, at the same
time, the potential consequences of one's choice. As van der Ven points
out, an injunction against something like false promises has to do with
the calculation of the multitude of advantages and especially – in this
case – disadvantages that would ensue in the intra-personal, interpersonal and societal domain if this principle were to be adopted as a
universal maxim.[12] In other words, the universalizability test does not
really avoid the consideration of consequences in judging the morality
of an act; it simply translates it into more abstract terms. Instead of
considering the anticipated consequences of a particular action on a
specific constituency, it asks us to reflect on the potential implications of
a particular *kind* of act for an ideal *kind* of world. This interpretation
may be derived from another oversimplification of Kant's theory that
often takes place within business ethics. Jones, Parker and ten Bos
criticize Norman Bowie's Kantian business ethics for depicting Kant as
the arch-enemy of utilitarianism. It is certainly true that, for Kant, it is
the moral intent, and not its consequences, that makes an act good.
This does not mean that Kant is entirely uninterested in ends. Kant's
interest in ends, however, lies with the logical implications, rather than
the utilitarian consequences of particular kinds of actions. It is up to
autonomous, rational individuals to consider the logical implications of
particular kinds of actions and to formulate moral maxims that can
withstand logical scrutiny. It is only when people lose sight of the fact
that Kant is concerned with the logical implications of actions that his
theory begins to appear internally inconsistent.

Critics of Kant have argued that there is a certain instrumental
principle at work in his proposals. In deontological moral reasoning,
particular kinds of actions are sanctioned only if, and because, they
serve to secure that kind of world that the decision maker considers a
desirable end. Korsgaard unpacks this instrumental principle in Kant's
work and comes to the conclusion that it cannot stand alone.[13] She
explains that if the instrumental principle is to act as a rationale for
action, one must be prepared to accept that one's willing it alone
renders a particular "end" worthy of pursuit. One must effectively

---

[12] Johannes van der Ven, *Formation of the Moral Self* (Michigan: William B.
Eerdmans, 1998), p. 145.
[13] Christine Korsgaard, "The Normativity of Instrumental Reason" in G. Cullity
and B. Gaut (eds.), *Ethics and Practical Reason* (Oxford: Clarendon Press,
1997), p. 245.

take the act of one's own will to be normative, at least as far as one's own actions are concerned. The instrumental principle can only be normative if we consider ourselves capable of laying down laws for ourselves or, as Kant might have put it, if we take our own will to be legislative. According to Korsgaard this way of thinking is based on the belief that the moral maxims that rational individuals formulate could never infringe on their status as ends-in-themselves.[14] However, if an agent wills something through an act of rational self-legislation, his/her decision does not automatically achieve normative status. Unless normative status is somehow bestowed upon his/her "ends," there can be no requirement to employ the "means" necessary to realize them. This creates all sorts of practical problems. Who, for instance, is to decide which rationally willed "ends" should prevail as a point of normative orientation in business life? Some business practitioners have clearly made profit maximization their "end." From a deontological perspective they may argue that this is a worthy "end" because the maximization of profit is perfectly reconcilable with humans' status as ends in themselves. Others would, of course, dispute this claim. They may argue that in the single-minded pursuit of profit, human beings are often treated as if they were no more than "means" for achieving profit "ends." Whether they are exploited as labor within the production process, or co-opted as consumers in the consumption process, there is no question in the minds of some that human beings are anything but "ends" in themselves when profit maximization becomes the ultimate end of business. The fact that some rational agents find such a state of affairs morally defensible, says something about the ideal end-state that they have in mind for the world. This ideal end-state represents normative judgments that cannot be justified *a priori* and are certainly not self-evident.

Do rational agents always act out of concern for morality, or do they formulate moral maxims/laws to create a world that serves their own purposes? It is important to note that Kant himself was well aware of how human beings can delude themselves. It is precisely for this reason that he stressed the importance of considering the intentions that inform moral imperatives. If an individual formulates a moral maxim in accordance with his/her own interest or inclinations, he/she is not acting out of duty, and hence, such a maxim could not be

---

[14] *Ibid.*, p. 249.

truly moral, from Kant's point of view. For Kant, "looking into the depths of one's own heart" to gauge the nature and role of one's own motives is an ongoing struggle. The careful and complex analysis that Kant would have us undertake in the formulation of moral maxims serves as a reminder that his theory should never be watered down to rule-driven morality.

Kant was well aware of the fact that his theory, if interpreted as rule-obedience or blind duty, could be used to justify a rationalized and technocratic form of morality. The problem with this kind of morality is that it entrenches rules to such an extent that individuals no longer conform to them out of concern for morality, but merely because they have been inculcated with an inclination to do so. For Kant, there is no moral merit in this. Kant cautions that making moral decisions often requires one to resist one's habituated inclinations. The uncritical acceptance of rules and the internalization of duties are therefore contrary to Kant's understanding of morality. However, business ethicists often interpret Kantian morality as a rationale for the imposition of codes, policies and procedures or managerial systems that condition employees to the point of mechanical compliance. This is a fundamental misconstrual of Kant's intentions. For Kant there can be no hiding behind the broad shoulders of the law. For him, this would amount to an abandonment of the autonomy with which he so closely identified our humanity.

There are two main problems with the way in which business ethicists interpret and employ Kantian deontology. The first has to do with the fact that few business ethicists take sufficient cognizance of the complexities of Kant's moral theory. Whereas Kant himself was not entirely confident about our ability to act freely and autonomously, Kantian business ethicists don't always approach deontology with the same caution. Kantian business ethics theories create the impression that the formulation and application of moral maxims is simply a case of utilizing our rational faculties. There is little acknowledgement of the struggle and uncertainty that Kant himself associated with it.

The second problem relates to the fact that many business ethicists interpret Kant's proposals with respect to the formulation of *a priori* maxims, as a rationale for the institutionalization of immutable universal laws. This creates the impression that business ethics, from a Kantian perspective, has to do with following rules and acting out of duty. In the process, the moral autonomy that Kant considered so central to our humanity, is undermined.

There are, however, problems with employing Kantian theory in business ethics that go well beyond the misinterpretation of his thought. These primarily have to do with Kant's postulation of a rational, independent moral agent, capable of distancing him/herself from personal prejudices and contextual biases for the sake of objective moral deliberation. As my analysis of moral agency in Chapter 3 will demonstrate, there is ample reason to doubt the existence of such an agent. Moral agency is arguably a far more subtle and complex affair than Kant's enlightened rational agent suggests.

Rawls' justice as fairness

John Rawls' work was very influential in the formulation of normative parameters in the liberal democratic state and free market system.[15] This makes his ideas particularly relevant in the consideration of business morality. Rawls tried to find a normative dispensation that could both accommodate extensive liberties and address social inequalities. Rawls shared Kant's belief that the moral agent had to be impartial and objective in his/her judgment. He realized, however, that their social position, power interests, and concern for negative consequences always influence the way that human beings look at things. Rawls wanted to find a way to eliminate, or at least neutralize, the effect of these influences on moral judgment. To guarantee that society would be organized in a way that is fair to all, he proposed that the formulation of its organizing principles should take place behind a hypothetical "veil of ignorance." The idea is that in order to judge what would constitute a fair organization of inequalities in society, the decision makers must be unaware of the position that they themselves will occupy within that society. In this way, they could not organize society in a way that benefited them to the detriment of others. Rawls knew, of course, that such a situation would never exist. He proposed the notion of the veil of ignorance as a thought experiment that would allow people to rationally consider the principles of a fair society in an "objective" manner.

[15] John Rawls, *Justice as Fairness* (Irvington, 1958).

Proceeding from the hypothetical "objective" position of the veil of ignorance, Rawls formulates the basic principles of a fair society. He believed that, under the conditions of the veil of ignorance, any rational individual would come to the same conclusions. Rawls' first principle, also called the "liberty principle," proposes that each member of a society should have an equal right to the most extensive basic liberty. In other words, any liberty could be extended to an individual, as long as it was judged to be compatible with a similar liberty for others.

In formulating his second principle Rawls argues that, though one may wish to base justice on the principle of equality, most societies are characterized by social inequalities. It was therefore essential, in his estimation, to deal fairly with social inequality. His second principle, also called the "difference principle" states: *Social and economic inequalities are to be arranged so that they are both (a) reasonably expected to be to everyone's advantage, and (b) attached to positions and offices open to all.* Rawls also believed that social and economic inequalities should be arranged in such a way that it would still be to the greatest possible benefit of the least privileged members of society.

The limitations of Rawls' approach quickly become apparent when one considers it within the context of the business world. One would expect most business practitioners to agree readily enough with Rawls' first principle. It allows them the freedom that they need to do business, to compete with one another and take profit. The only condition is that they do so in a way that does not impede the freedom of others to do the same. However, one anticipates that Rawls' second principle may be received with somewhat less enthusiasm among the ranks of business practitioners. Inequalities in business are certainly not arranged in such a way as to be to everyone's advantage, nor can it be claimed that positions of power and influence within the business world are open to all. As a result of free-market capitalism, the gap between rich and poor is widening in many places, and the economic system is certainly not set up to arrange inequalities in a way that serves the interests of the poor. In practice, the most influential positions and offices in business cannot be truly open to all, since competitive hiring, performance-based pay and promotion are set up to expose inequalities. To be appointed to a top job in the corporate world, one often needs to be not only gifted but also well educated. Having an appropriate sort of education, however, requires substantial financial means, which puts it beyond the reach of many. America may be the land of entrepreneurship and opportunity, but in order to make use of these freedoms one requires some sort of start-up capital and know-how. In a very real sense, making money requires money. It seems then that there are a lot of things in the business world that are set up in a way that tends to keep the poor in a position of disadvantage. Interventions like affirmative action, which is designed to bring about a more fair distribution of opportunities, are yet to be proved to work.

There are a number of business ethicists who have employed Rawls' theory. One of the main proponents of Rawlsian business ethics is Edwin Hartman, who argues that Rawls' procedure is as helpful in establishing organizational justice as it is in establishing political justice.[16] Hartman explains that Rawls' procedure differs from traditional contract theory in that it does not "conjure up a just state from ignorant self-interest in a moral vacuum."[17] Instead, it describes a procedure by means of which reasonable people who value freedom and equality can formulate the basis of a fair institutional dispensation. It accepts the possibility of a plurality of morally acceptable theories. This means that principles can be tailored to suit specific institutions, as long as they remain effective at what they have to do. The Rawlsian veil of ignorance guarantees that those involved will be impartial by eliminating their ability deliberately to secure their own self-interest to the detriment of others. Behind the veil of ignorance, participants will know only that they are to be stakeholders of a particular organization, but they are not to know which stakeholder position they will occupy.

---

[16] Hartman was criticized for the fact that he employed ideas developed in political philosophy and transferred them to an organizational context, especially since Rawls himself made it clear that the original position is a heuristic device suited to the political context, and not to organizations. Organizations are considered voluntary forms of association, whereas states aren't. Hartman disputes the claim that organizations always represent "voluntary" associations, in the strict sense of the word. His response to these objections is to argue for a more intimate relationship between general moral theories and organizational life. He argues that because he is a moral realist, he does not subscribe to a strict is-ought distinction. Nor does he attempt to apply universally applicable abstract principles to business situations. See Edwin M. Hartman, "Moral Philosophy, Political Philosophy and Organizational Ethics: a Response to Phillips and Margolis," *Business Ethics Quarterly*, 11(4) (2001), 673–685.

[17] Edwin Hartman, *Organizational Ethics and the Good Life* (Oxford University Press, 1996), p. 108.

The problem with establishing principles for fair business institutions from behind a veil of ignorance is that they are likely to be too general and vague to account for all the context- and relationship-specific variables that continually inform dynamic stakeholder relationships. It is also not easy to identify all those who are likely to be affected by an organization's operations from the outset. In the complex and dynamic network of relationships that characterize the contemporary business environment, not all stakeholders are likely to be closely associated with an organization, and new stakeholder groups may emerge as relationships evolve. Phillips distinguishes between stakeholders to whom the organization has a moral obligation, i.e. normative stakeholders, and derivative stakeholders, whose actions and claims must be considered by managers because of their potential effects upon the organization and its normative stakeholders.[18] There is an implicit acknowledgement, in this distinction, of the way in which the boundaries of stakeholder relations may shift as a result of power dynamics and the complex interactions between an organization and various stakeholder groups. The "balancing" of stakeholder interests is not informed by the principles of equality,[19] but depends instead on the purpose of particular stakeholder interactions. Obligations exist between discrete entities, rather than as diffuse, all-encompassing imperatives.[20] The question that therefore arises is what role these shifting stakeholder relationships should play in the determination of principles of fairness behind the veil of ignorance. The truth is that these shifting stakeholder relationships leave Rawlsian theory in somewhat of a conundrum. This is because Rawls' theory does not allow the consideration of particular relationships to be brought into the equation behind the veil of ignorance. Without such consideration,

---

[18] Robert Phillips, "Stakeholder Legitimacy," *Business Ethics Quarterly*, 13(1) (2003), 30.

[19] In this respect, what is being proposed here differs from what Bowie proposed in his analysis of "the firm as a moral community" (see Bowie, *Kantian Business Ethics* p. 89). He argues that in a business firm organized as a moral community, the interest of every member is equal to the interests of every other member. Because of the shifting power relationships within a network, relationships are never equal. However, inequality does not undermine moral responsiveness. I also dispute the viability of Bowie's insistence that there be consensus with respect to categorical imperatives, between all the members of an organization.

[20] R. Phillips, R. E. Freeman and A. C. Wicks, "What Stakeholder Theory is not," *Business Ethics Quarterly*, 13(4) (2003), 493.

however, the principles that are formulated to govern and regulate stakeholder relationships are meaningless.

A similar problem plagues the use of Rawls' ideas in corporate governance. Freeman and Evan's proposals are an example of the way in which the veil of ignorance has been employed as a heuristic device in the realm of corporate governance. Freeman and Evan argue that rational stakeholders would be able to agree upon principles for fair contracts if they were to apply Rawls' veil of ignorance to their deliberations.[21] In their estimation, rational stakeholders would agree upon the moral necessity of stakeholder-oriented management and board representation for non-shareholding stakeholders. A number of objections have been brought in against Freeman and Evan's use of Rawlsian theory. The most serious of these probably has to do with the fact that the kinds of principles that Freeman and Evan believe would ensure fair contracts could only have been formulated if there were some understanding of the various positions that all those involved would occupy. Child and Marcoux point out, for instance, that it is essential to understand something like "opportunity cost" in the design of a reasonable moral order in a corporate context.[22] The "veil" therefore has to be somewhat transparent if Freeman and Evan's principles are to make any sense. The application of Rawlsian theory to corporate governance is another example of how problematic it is to try and sustain the theoretical ideal of independent and impartial moral judgment.

Iris Young offers a more general philosophical critique of Rawls' theory.[23] She is particularly disturbed by its modernist appeals to impartiality. She argues that impartiality, as the hallmark of the moral reasoning of the transcendental subject, undermines the acknowledgement of difference in at least three ways. First, it denies the particularity of situations, since the reasoning subject, emptied of all

---

[21] These principles include: the principle of entry and exit, the principle of governance, the principle of externalities, the principle of contracting costs, the agency principle, and the principle of limited immortality. See Edward R. Freeman and William M. Evan, "Corporate Governance: a Stakeholder Interpretation," *Journal of Behavioral Economics*, 19(4) (1990), 337–359.

[22] James W. Child and Alexei M. Marcoux, "Freeman and Evan: Stakeholder Theory in the Original Position," *Business Ethics Quarterly*, 9(2) (1999), 207–223.

[23] Iris Young, *Justice and the Politics of Difference* (Princeton University Press, 1990), p. 100.

particularity, treats all situations according to the same moral rules. The more rules can be reduced to a single rule or moral principle, the more impartial and universal they supposedly become. Secondly, impartiality requires that a subject approaches a problem dispassionately. The goal is to eliminate heterogeneity by eliminating subjective emotions. The subject is required to rationally dissociate him/herself from his/her bodily being, with all its various needs and inclinations. Through such an exercise in abstraction, the subject supposedly gains some sort of objective distance from feelings that attach to the experience of the particularity of things and events. Young points out that even though Rawls insists on the plurality of selves as a necessary starting point for a conception of justice, the reasoning of his original position is nevertheless monological.[24] The veil of ignorance removes any differentiating characteristics among individuals, and seeks to ensure that all will reason from identical assumptions and the same universal point of view. This universal category requires expelling those differences that do not fit into it. Like other instances of the logic of identity, the desire to create an impartial sort of moral discourse results not in unity, but in the construction of a dichotomy between reason and feeling. However, theoretical distinctions cannot contain the meaning or significance of real-life experiences. Young explains: "Feelings, desires, and commitments do not cease to exist and motivate just because they have been excluded from the definition of moral reason. They lurk as inarticulate shadows, belying the claim to comprehensiveness of universalist reason."[25]

Rawlsian justice theories also assume a certain instrumental relationship between individuals within communities. For Ricoeur, the main problem with Rawls' approach is the clear individualism at work in his contractualism.[26] The position from which Rawls would have us start in our consideration of the principles of social justice is that of individuals. There is a question, though, as to whether a social contract between individuals constitutes a community. It is also not clear that such a community would be an ideal context to live in. It seems as though, ultimately, procedural justice alone may not provide an adequate basis for social justice. Substantive ideas may be necessary to define social priorities. As van der Ven explains: "Substance transcends procedure;

---

[24] *Ibid.*, p. 101.   [25] *Ibid.*, p. 103.
[26] Paul Ricoeur, *Oneself as Another* (University of Chicago Press, 1992), p. 208.

procedure does not correspond to the fullness of substance."[27] Ultimately, procedure is negative; it can indicate only what should not be done, not what should be done. Rawls rejects utilitarianism because of its teleological orientation, but there is an implicit utilitarianism in his insistence that a balance be struck between inequality and that which benefits all. He proposes that we formulate our response to social inequality with an eye to that which secures the greatest possible benefit for all. In this, he is asking us, in effect, to use a utilitarian principle in the way we balance the interests of various members of society.

Rawlsian appeals to impartiality suffer from the same deficiencies as Kantian deontology. Both theories sacrifice particularity for the sake of universality. Rawls and Kant believed that reason is objective and universal and they therefore expected all rational individuals to reason in the same way. Because of this, they were unable to acknowledge or address the role that different worldviews and personal interests plays in moral judgments. As much as they try to hide their substantive normative commitments, both Kantian deontology and Rawlsian justice have ideal worlds in mind. In their inability to recognize this lies the most important limitation of non-consequentialist approaches. If tacit normative commitments are not recognized and articulated, ethics cannot really be approached as practice. Ethics as practice relies on an awareness of the particularity of individual experience and perception, as well as contextual variables and contingencies, in moral judgment.

This makes ethics as practice very difficult to reconcile with non-consequentialism. Over the last several years, however, a number of prominent business ethicists have begun to develop so-called "contractarian" theories to try to respond to the lack of substantive content in non-consequentialist approaches. It is to an examination of their efforts that I now turn.

Contractarian theories in business ethics

For Tom Donaldson and Tom Dunfee the problem with deontological and utilitarian approaches to business ethics is their inability to deal with the nature of the business world and the specific challenges that it poses to decision making. Their contractarian model was born out of their analysis of a variety of different business ethics models. In their

---

[27] Van der Ven, *Formation of the Moral Self*, p. 169.

analysis, they looked at the attempts of business ethicists like Bowie and Evan and Freeman to utilize Kantian and Rawlsian thinking in business ethics. They also studied rights-based approaches informed by deontological theories or theories of social justice, such as the work of Werhane on human resource management. Lastly, they examined attempts that were made to utilize utilitarian thinking in business ethics.

Donaldson and Dunfee's analysis eventually lead them to conclude that these approaches cannot adequately accommodate the realities of the contemporary business world. They argue that in the business world we deal with "bounded rationality."[28] Their concept of "bounded rationality" draws attention to the fact that human cognition is always framed by physical and psychological variables. Because of this, systematic errors are common in the way individuals reason. Decisions are often made on the basis of insufficient information and under significant time constraints. Donaldson and Dunfee also remind us that the business world is institutionally "thick." Business organizations are human creations, designed for the pursuit of particular goals. In this sort of environment, they argue, the formulation of normative guidelines requires a unique approach.

To this end Dunfee and Donaldson developed an approach called "Integrative Social Contracts Theory" (ISCT).[29] It essentially combines a variety of different philosophical approaches in a contractarian model. In Dunfee and Donaldson's approach, the normative standards that guide stakeholder management are context-specific. As such, their contractarian model combines procedural guidelines with substantive, normative content. In ISCT, normative content is provided by so-called "hypernorms," which have to be validated at various levels of consent. Robertson and Ross explain that there are two such levels of consent in Donaldson and Dunfee's ISCT model.[30] In the first place, consent is based on a theoretical "macro" social contract between all rational actors. Secondly, members of different localized communities consent to the terms of specific, real "micro" social contracts. Donaldson and

[28] Tom Donaldson and Tom Dunfee, *Ties that Bind: a Social Contracts Approach to Business Ethics* (Boston: Harvard Business School Press, 1999), p. 29.
[29] *Ibid.*, p. 181.
[30] D. C. Robertson and W. T. Ross, "Decision-making Processes on Ethical Issues: the Impact of a Social Contract Perspective," *Business Ethics Quarterly*, 5 (1995), special issue on Social Contracts and Business Ethics, 213–240.

Dunfee[31] emphasize the hypothetical character of the "macro" contract as opposed to the non-hypothetical, actual agreements in the contracts within and among communities. Macro contracts, in short, fill in what micro contracts leave out, and vice versa.

There are two concepts that are crucial in Donaldson and Dunfee's ISCT. The one is the idea of "hypernorms" and the other is the notion of "moral free space." Hypernorms represent universal limits to what the members of a community can consent to in micro-social contracts. If it was possible for all the members of a society to come together to decide what parameters to impose on individual moral free space, hypernorms represent the agreements that they might reasonably be expected to consent to. Hypernorms are principles so fundamental to society that they shape and inform all those "second-order" norms that are formulated to guide specific kinds of social behavior. Donaldson and Dunfee distinguish three distinct types of hypernorms, namely procedural, structural, and substantive hypernorms.[32] They claim that their efforts are not directed at articulating a universally valid moral code or a kind of global ethics Esperanto. They are not foundationalists in the traditional sense. What they do have in mind is a form of moral minimalism. It is based on the idea that there are a number of basic normative principles that are common to all human societies, even though they may be articulated in various ways at different times and in different places. They readily acknowledge that the various idioms that are used to express these principles in different contexts reflect different histories and understandings of the world. Nonetheless, they offer us a list of philosophical assumptions and collective agreements that they

---

[31] Donaldson and Dunfee, *Ties that Bind*, p. 19.

[32] Procedural hypernorms specify the rights of exit and voice essential to support micro-social contractual consent. The right of voice, for instance, encompasses and extends beyond Habermas's recognition of the substantive rules of argumentation. The right of exit prohibits coercive restrictions on egress from micro-social communities. Secondly, structural hypernorms exist that are necessary for political and social organization, for example, the right to property is supported by an economic hypernorm that obliges members of society to honor institutions that promote justice and economic welfare – within, of course, the bounds of other hypernorms. Finally, substantive hypernorms specify fundamental conceptions of the right and the good. Whereas the sources of procedural and structural hypernorms are specified or implicit in the macro- or micro-social contract, Donaldson and Dunfee argue that the sources of substantive hypernorms are exogenous (*Ibid.*, pp. 51–59).

believe are indicative of the basic normative commitments of all human societies.[33]

Donaldson and Dunfee deliberately avoid taking a position on whether hypernorms have a purely rational basis, as Kant argues, or a partially empirical and historical basis, as Hegel argues. Despite this, their list shows a clear preference for commitments and priorities based on rational, hypothetical thought over ones that come into being in response to historical and empirical contingencies. Their hypernorms are in fact abstract principles that transcend the contingent specificity of particular contextual commitments and agreements. As such, their proposals suffer from the same sort of deficiencies as those of Kant and Rawls. Both Kant and Rawls claimed that their approach guaranteed impartiality, but in the end these claims only served to obscure the power-interests, cultural biases and institutional parameters that inevitably color and inform the way in which an individual or community rationalizes his/her/its moral commitments and normative agreements.

Donaldson and Dunfee insist, of course, that ISCT *does* allow contextual contingencies and individual biases to come into play in the formulation of micro-contracts at the individual and community level. ISCT recognizes the existence of a *moral free space*, which allows an individual or community to self-define significant aspects of their moral commitments.[34] Donaldson and Dunfee understand that ethical rules develop both formally, through explicit contracts, and informally,

---

[33] Philosophically, Donaldson and Dunfee point to the work of Hans Küng, John Kline, Richard De George, John Rawls, Amartya Sen, Immanuel Kant, John Locke, and Confucius. Collective agreements that they point to include the Universal Declaration of Human Rights (1948), the Council for a Parliament of the World's Religions (Towards a Global Ethic, 1993), Global 2000 Report from Millennium Institute (1993) and the Caux Round Table (1994). They do not claim to have found a final list, expressible in a particular moral language and valid for all moral situations, since that would constitute a form of moral absolutism (*Ibid.*, p. 54).

[34] Donaldson and Dunfee (*Ibid.*, p. 39) describe the "community" as a self-defined, self-circumscribed group of people who interact in the context of shared tasks, values and goals and who are capable of establishing norms of ethical behavior for themselves. Individuals may belong to multiple communities whose norms may function in any given situation. In order for a community to exist, it must pass the "self-awareness test" by which the members of a community recognize their association with the group and view it as a source of obligatory ethical norms (*Ibid.*, p. 83).

through implicit agreements. Because of this, they consider it essential that norms be articulated in a way that is meaningful to those who will be subject to them. In fact, they provide at least four reasons why they think it important to allow a certain amount of moral "free space" in the formulation of micro contracts.[35] The first has to do with the fact that the application of general ethical rules to a specific business context is often problematic. Secondly, because of the enormous variety of moral priorities among individuals and communities, business firms often develop their own distinct organizational values and traditions. Thirdly, business organizations frequently reflect the religious or cultural attitudes of their employees. Finally, they point out that, if business organizations are to accomplish their goals efficiently, they need to be able to generate new ethical norms and modify existing ones from time to time. Donaldson and Dunfee consider as "authentic" only those norms that represent an actual community consensus and are recognized as genuine priorities by its members. Such norms are influenced by the ethical climate in an organization. Variables such as the quality of an organization's leadership, the way in which it is structured, its policies, its incentive systems, its formal and informal decision-making systems, and the legal parameters (such as the US Corporate Federal Sentencing Guidelines) to which it is subject, all play a role in the formulation of "authentic" micro agreements among its employees.

Donaldson and Dunfee are adamant that their ISCT model is built around the notion of tolerance. Tolerance, as they see it, is an extension of the principle of consent and choice. If one were to draw up a continuum to plot the relative degree of freedom that a moral agent is given in various ethical approaches, extreme relativism would occupy one end, with cultural relativism, pluralism and modified universalism following in succession as one approached the other end, where extreme universalism (absolutism) would be situated. On such a continuum ISCT would fall roughly in the middle where pluralism is located. ISCT allows for the fact that communities and cultures may have their own unique perspectives on ethical matters. It also acknowledges that, inasmuch as they are informed by different cultural perspectives, opposing ethical perspectives may be equally valid. ISCT is also pluralistic in its capacity to accommodate different kinds of moral theories. However, it also

---

[35] *Ibid.*, pp. 84–85.

leaves open the possibility that the views of a particular culture may be judged invalid because they fall outside of the boundaries of a universally binding moral precept, or because priority is given to the view of another culture or community.

Of course, there are also priorities in the capitalist economy that function very much like hypernorms. For instance, in many cases the overriding and universal concern of those who participate in the market is with the maximization of profit, and this shapes and informs the various micro agreements that are entered into. This overriding priority often trumps other, less universally recognized, considerations. Although rules and procedures are adopted to ensure that everyone has a fair opportunity to pursue profit, people are left largely unprotected in circumstances where their interests are in conflict with the market's hypernorm. A universal value, or hypernorm, has no content in and of itself. It is the things that society strives for that give it content.

The downside of ISCT lies in the level of generalization that is required for a moral priority to rise to the status of hypernorm. Hypernorms have to be both general enough to allow universal application, and concise enough to guide particular decisions. As a consequence a hypernorm is often either too vague to have real effect, or too restrictive in its specifications. There is no denying that hypernorms are designed to allow the normative beliefs of communities and individuals to be disregarded, when and where it is deemed necessary. As such, they are instruments of power that may be used in both good and bad ways. Carol Gilligan points out that to disregard the interests of a particular group of people in order to be able to claim the moral high-ground or sustain one's commitment to an abstract principle, could, in some cases, amount to cruelty.[36] In fact, the attitude of detached impartiality that is required to apply universal principles objectively often undermines the kind of responsiveness and care that is the true hallmark of morality. To avoid this, a moral theory needs to be attuned to the relationality of human existence. This happens to be one of the hallmarks of communitarianism, to which we now turn.

---

[36] Carol Gilligan, *In a Different Voice: Psychological Theory and Women's Development* (Cambridge, MA: Harvard University Press, 1982).

Communitarianism

Communitarianism is a teleological approach that tries to come to terms with the way in which normative priorities are communally defined. It derives its name from the word "community" and sees morality as something that is defined in and through individuals' participation in a community. As such, communitarians are particularly interested in how conceptions of good (i.e. values) are formed, transmitted, justified and enforced.[37] All communitarians are committed to the importance of the social realm in informing moral commitments, but they differ as to how individual rights are protected within communities. For example, Amitai Etzioni, a communitarian who has written on business ethics, stresses the balance between individual rights and freedoms, on the one hand, and the pursuit of social goods on the other. He also emphasizes the importance of using persuasion rather than coercion in securing the members of a community's commitment to, and compliance with communally defined values and norms.[38] Etzioni's communitarian reading of stakeholder theory suggests that all those individuals and organizations who stand in some sort of relation to a particular organization may be seen as part of one community. Etzioni argues that though these individuals and organizations may have many different interests and values, their shared goals and relational ties draw them together in a meaningful form of association.[39]

In general, communitarians believe that each community has a *telos*, an aim or end-state to which all of its members aspire and which acts as a shared source of moral orientation. Communitarianism is heavily indebted to the virtue-ethics of Aristotle. For Aristotle the ultimate aim (*telos*) of human life is a happy life (*eudaimonia*). Such a happy life cannot, however, be attained in isolation from the social life of a community or polis (*politicon zoon*). Aristotle believes that it is the quality of a life that makes it a happy one. More specifically it is the cultivation of good ways of living (*euzoia*) and good ways of doing

---

[37] Amitai Etzioni, "A Communitarian Approach: a Study of the Legal, Ethical and Policy Implications Raised by DNA Tests and Databases," *Journal of Law, Medicine and Ethics* (Summer, 2006), 214.

[38] *Ibid.*, 215.

[39] Amitai Etzioni, "A Communitarian Note on Stakeholder Theory," *Business Ethics Quarterly*, 8(4) (1998), 679–691.

things (*eupraxia*) that lends quality to a life. In this way of living, happiness is not identical with pleasure, but pleasure is the outcome of living virtuously and acting excellently. To achieve a state of true happiness, therefore, one must cultivate habits that have an edifying effect on the community. This is done through practice. If you are a worker, for instance, you could achieve happiness by training yourself to always approach your work diligently. Should you choose instead to be a soldier, it is your characteristic bravery that would make your life virtuous and admirable and allow you to live a happy life within your community.

Communitarians like Alasdair MacIntyre found inspiration in these Aristotelian ideas.[40] MacIntyre was especially interested in the role that community life played in Aristotelian ethics. Taking this as his point of departure, he proposed that individual behavior be guided by practices and principles that are developed within the context of community life. As such, communitarianism can be described as an approach to ethics that takes community membership as its primary point of departure.[41] For MacIntyre a community is a collection of individuals who participate in each others' lives and who have a number of significant beliefs, values, and norms in common. These beliefs, norms and values are articulated in stories. The metaphors, symbols and ideas that are employed in such foundational narratives act as points of common orientation and allow the community to express and continually reaffirm its moral priorities and commitments.

According to another communitarian, Charles Taylor, shared "horizons of significance" determine what individuals value.[42] The moral significance of decisions and actions is established in and through the social interaction of members of a community. Through our interaction with others in our community we come to recognize, for instance, that it is morally significant when people discriminate against one another on the basis of race. In the same way, we also come to accept that something like a preference for blonds, rather than

---

[40] Alasdair MacIntyre, *After Virtue: a Study in Moral Theory*, 2nd edition (University of Notre Dame Press, 1984), p. 2; Alisdair MacIntyre, "Social Structures and their Threats to Moral Agency," *Philosophy*, 74 (1999), 311–329.

[41] Van der Ven, *Formation of the Moral Self*, p. 22.

[42] Charles Taylor, *The Ethics of Authenticity* (Cambridge: Harvard University Press, 1993).

brunettes, is not necessarily morally significant. As a community we come to a sort of understanding that racism is immoral, while discriminating taste is not.

One of the main philosophical objections to communitarianism is that it defines membership in a community in terms that don't really allow for the possibility of dissent. Within the business environment, decision makers are often subjected to an institutional and bureaucratic straightjacket that undermines individual discretion and responsiveness. Critics like van der Ven argue that moral decision makers should always have the freedom to break with tradition because social habits, customs and rites can limit the freedom that is necessary for morality.[43] Van der Ven insists that an individual's autonomy should never become less of a priority than the coherence of the community. There is a dangerous imbalance in an organization's priorities when its organizational dynamics are such that it does not allow individual employees to challenge its business practices from the perspective of their own consciences.

Apart from the organizational community in which they participate, individuals may also belong to other communities. Because of this individuals often develop unique configurations of moral priorities. When these unique sensibilities are suppressed, it becomes all but impossible for such individuals to exercise their moral discretion and imagination. Communitarianism therefore sacrifices the individual for the sake of the community. It consistently gives preference to the general over the specific. This foundational priority sometimes makes communitarianism difficult to reconcile with the notion of ethics as practice.

Communitarianism's reliance on moral consensus is also problematic in this regard. Because the communitarian community needs a central *telos* or "goal" to serve as a shared point of moral orientation, communitarians seek to define moral priorities in unambiguous terms. The moral priorities of the community are also secured through its institutionalization. One example is the adoption of universal "codes of conduct" within the business environment. Even though these codes are well intentioned and play a role in creating normative parameters for business practitioners, they often risk either over or under defining moral guidelines. Codes that attempt to provide exhaustive and very concise rules to regulate business behavior often border on a form of moral absolutism. Because of the emphasis in such codes on consistency and conformity,

---

[43] Van der Ven, *Formation of the Moral Self*, p. 27.

they are ultimately incapable of adequately appreciating the role that different organizational cultures and contexts play in shaping business morality. For example, the values of democracy and respect for individual human rights advocated by many communitarians are not common to all groups. These values are of a Western, modernist origin and as such they may not have the same meaning and significance for business practitioners who work in other cultural and ideological contexts. On the other hand, codes that seek to provide only very general, minimalist guidelines lack specificity and practical force. So-called "core values" are general and vague and deliberately try to avoid being too specific in their proscriptions. Because of this, they are often of little value in mediating between different moral sensibilities or reconciling opposing views on a specific moral dilemma. In either case it is clear that when communitarians seek to provide content to their *telos*, they are forced to rely on modernist assumptions, which do not allow them to accommodate moral plurality adequately. The communitarian *telos* is either postulated in unambiguous, unitary terms, to the exclusion of other possible priorities, or in terms so general, that potentially significant differences among the members of a community are glossed over.

Philosophers who seek to employ communitarian thought in business also have to contend with a lot of criticism. Most objections relate to the fact that the business world does not resemble the kind of community that communitarians have in mind. The communitarian community has its roots in the ancient Greek city-state. As such, its goals seem ill-suited to the realities of the contemporary business world, where multinational corporations operate simultaneously in many different kinds of communities. Some business ethicists like Robert Solomon have nevertheless argued that important similarities exist between communities and business organizations.[44] Etzioni agrees with Solomon on this point. He argues that since "property" is a social construct, organizations belong to all those who invest in them. There may be a variety of stakeholders who make major investments of scarce goods in an organization. Employees who work in an organization for a long time invest their time and energy to ensure its prosperity and secure its future. Communities may also make significant investments in an organization by building

---

[44] Robert C. Solomon, *Ethics and Excellence: Cooperation and Integrity in Business* (New York: Oxford University Press, 1992). I discuss Solomon's position in more depth in Chapter 4.

special access roads to accommodate its operations or by granting it special loans to grow or perpetuate its business. Etzioni's argument is that these investments give them at least as much of a right to be members of the organizational "community" as any of its shareholders have.[45] In fact, for Etzioni, those individuals and communities that invest, not only a part of their financial means, but a part of themselves, to secure the prosperity and perpetuation of an organization are, in a sense, its real "owners." It is a view that has significant implications for corporate governance. Creditors, clients, and many others invest in an organization and should therefore have a say in how it is governed. Etzioni acknowledges that this makes it difficult to determine how much of a say each of the participants and investors in an organization should have in its governance. In the end, it might simply be too complicated and contentious an affair to try to design a governance model that could accommodate such a complex variety of stakeholders' claims.

Some communitarians envisage an even greater community than that which they associate with an organization's system of relations. They argue that the world is becoming a "global village" with common goals and shared virtues.[46] Etzioni is in favor of a global normative synthesis. He believes that a shared moral understanding could be developed that would inform common policy frameworks. Though commendable in its intentions and inspiring in its vision, Etzioni's proposals seem hopelessly idealistic in a world in which political and cultural conflicts dominate the news.[47] Etzioni stresses the importance of culture in moving towards moral consensus, but he seems to underestimate exactly how diffuse

---

[45] Etzioni, "A Communitarian Note on Stakeholder Theory."

[46] For example, Etzioni has argued that individual rights can only function properly from a communitarian perspective. Etzioni substantiates his belief that a global society is possible by describing what he regards as three conditions for sustaining a society: the means to control violence that exceeds that of its subunits, the capacity to reallocate economic goods, and the ability to command loyalty in key, relevant matters. He admits that a "global society" may not be immediately realizable in these terms, but points out that transnational non-state actors, such as non-governmental organizations, may be able to provide "governance without government" in certain areas. He also draws attention to what he sees as the rise of global norms, shared values, and world public opinion. This, he believes, may eventually lead to the development of global laws.

[47] Colin S. Gray, "Sandcastle of Theory: a Critique of Amitai Etzioni's Communitarianism," *American Behavioral Scientist*, 48(12) (2005), 1607–1625.

cultures are and how they function. Cultures are less cohesive and homogeneous than Etzioni believes. In fact, cultures can be described as hybrids, as complex webs of narratives within which identities are formed and reformed.[48]

Etzioni also seems to believe that neoclassical economics can be synthesized with duty-based morality. He develops his proposals in the form of a socio-economic theory that takes the social, normative and emotive factors of human behavior into account. Individual behavior is always informed by the social system within which the individual functions. The shared value and power dynamics within the social system is the context for moral commitments and economic factors that "co-determine" individual behavior. Etzioni argues that individuals are always likely to experience tension between their individual interest and that of the community in which they participate, and between their sense of moral duty and their desire for pleasure. He believes that the sense of moral duty with which individuals are inculcated through their participation in social structures will almost always trump their hedonistic impulses and concerns for their own self-interest. Diane Swanson's main criticism of Etzioni's theory is that his confidence in the motivational force of moral duties is not sufficiently underpinned by a grounded theory of value.[49] Though Etzioni's theory is based on the belief that individuals' sense of moral duty is derived from their participation in a community, he does not provide a sufficient rationale for how values come into existence. Instead there seems to be a naïve belief in the existence of some yet-to-be-defined general consensus around values operative within his account.

Despite its various shortcomings, communitarianism is not without value. As will be made clear in Chapter 4, there are aspects of communitarianism that could aid in the restoration of the relationship between ethics and practice. On the whole, however, communitarianism's insistence on moral consensus within communities remains a major limitation. It underestimates the importance of dissent, as well as the subtle but significant differences in perspective and values that often exist among those who participate in a social system

[48] Seyla Benhabib, *The Claims of Culture: Equality and Diversity in a Global Era* (Princeton University Press, 2002).

[49] Diane Swanson, "A Critical Evaluation of Etzioni's Socioeconomic Theory: Implications for the Field of Business Ethics," *Journal of Business Ethics*, 11(7) (1992), 545–553.

of relations. As a result, it tends to discount the fact that the beliefs and expectations that inform behavior within an organizational system are neither static nor uniform. Communitarians' attempts to identify and define values that are common to all the members of a community betray a certain foundationalist tendency in their thinking. Foundationalism is the belief that moral directives should articulate and be based on indisputable, universal truths. Foundationalist beliefs can easily degenerate into moral absolutism. In this respect, communitarianism suffers from the same deficiencies as some of the other theories already discussed.

Some responses to the problematic features of many approaches to ethics

There are problematic tendencies that are common to all of the theoretical approaches that typically inform business ethicists' views of, and approach to, organizational ethics. The first has to do with the fact that many of these moral theories either privilege substance and content over process and procedure in moral reasoning, or place so much emphasis on procedure that little attention is paid to the meaning of the good that these procedures embody. A second problem is the tendency to either universalize, and thereby over-generalize, or to individualize and particularize to the point of fragmentation. A third problem, closely related to the second, pertains to the relationship between individuals and groups, as well as the way in which moral beliefs and priorities are believed to be constituted within organizations.

A common feature of the moral theories that often inform business ethicists' treatment of organizational ethics is the claims of rational superiority that are attached to their principles and procedures. Substantive claims must be irrefutable and procedures immutable. Rosenthal and Buchholz argue that one of the main limitations of current approaches to moral decision making lies in the attempts that are made to provide rational legitimacy for moral claims.[50] Morality is described as the rational application of objective principles to practical problems. It is this view of morality that is primarily

---

[50] Rogene A. Buchholz and Sandra B. Rosenthal, *Business Ethics: the Pragmatic Path beyond Principles to Process* (Prentice Hall, 1998), p. 38.

responsible for the theory versus practice distinction that plagues the field of business ethics. Different moral theories emphasize different "rational" principles, but none make adequate provision for the consideration of contingent contextual parameters and conflicting claims. In both their substantive and procedural claims, most of the theories that typically inform business ethicists' thinking about morality purport to offer a comprehensive account of how moral decisions should be made. They have the character of grand schemes that offer a secure framework for moral certitude. In this respect, they function as "grand narratives," in which reality is subjected to a comprehensive set of substantive categories. Not only do they determine moral priorities in categorical terms, they also prescribe procedures that allow these priorities to be translated into specific directives. What makes moral theories that function as grand narratives dangerous is the way in which their priorities and procedures invariably take precedence over every other concern and consideration. This leaves them open to exploitation by those who seek to foreclose other views of how things are and how things ought to be. If a moral theory's "narrative," or conception of morality, cannot be challenged by other narratives, it can easily become a vehicle for the legitimization of existing power configurations. As such, it can provide a moral justification for discriminating against those who do not benefit from prevailing value priorities.

"Grand narratives" also have the effect of masking the significant relationship between a moral theory's procedural approach and its normative priorities. Privileging the one over the other, or misreading the way in which they influence one another limits our ability to critically interrogate the validity of these approaches. This has led some business ethicists to combine procedural and substantive considerations in a more integrated approach. Edwin Hartman,[51] for example, has tried to combine Rawlsian justice-principles with an Aristotelian understanding of the good community. His proposals include both procedural guidelines *and* substantive, community-based normative imperatives. Procedurally, he insists on the importance of the right of exit and voice. These procedural proposals are complemented by the substantive value priorities that he stresses. These include loyalty and

---

[51] Edwin M. Hartman, "The Commons and Moral Organization," *Business Ethics Quarterly*, 4(3) (1994), 253–269.

appropriate second-order desires. Unfortunately, this does not seem to be a happy marriage in all respects. For instance, Hartman readily acknowledges the influence that expectations, perceptions and beliefs within an organizational system can have on individuals' moral reasoning, but does not fully appreciate the way in which it problematizes the deliberate exercise of their right to exit and voice. Nor can he fully account for how it impacts loyalty and the development of personal virtue. The problem of developing an integrated perspective on both procedural and substantive aspects of moral reasoning remains.

Buchholz and Rosenthal have attempted to devise an approach to moral reasoning in business that is procedural in nature, but nevertheless capable of accommodating the variety of concrete situations within which moral reasoning takes place. They call theirs a "process approach" to ethical theory. It is informed by the philosophical perspective of American pragmatism and attempts to steer clear of both moral absolutism and moral relativism. They argue that moral precepts are formulated neither entirely subjectively nor solely on the basis of rational inference and analysis. In their view, morality is something that is discovered through ongoing experimentation in concrete situations. They are critical of the reified moral schemes and conflicting demands that they associate with utilitarian, deontological and communitarian theories. From a pragmatist perspective, it is important to appreciate the complexity of concrete moral dilemmas and not to oversimplify them. It is also necessary to be aware of the value-ladenness of each situation and to remain continually responsive in the course of its development. Pragmatists argue that moral growth is achieved if one can deal with problematic situations and conflicting values in a way that enriches the moral fabric of both individual and community. The goal of this ongoing process of experimental engagement is to make it possible for people to have rich and meaningful lives. The experiences that pragmatists aim for can arise only in specific, concrete contexts, which is why it is so important to pay attention to the particularity of experience. The incapacity to consider the particularity of experience is a significant limitation of many of the other approaches that typically inform business ethicists' understanding of morality.

The fact that most ethical theories attempt to provide an immutable rational basis for moral precepts has implications in terms of their ability to accommodate specificity and difference. Most theories are irrevocably invested in a quest for generalizable moral truths that transcend differences on all levels. At the root of this preoccupation lies a technological, scientific and empirical orientation. The prospect of identifying objective moral "facts" has become so compelling that the value-ladenness of all moral concepts is often overlooked. Pragmatists like Buchholz and Rosenthal have exposed the fallacy of the fact–value distinction. They insist that "values are just as real as all other qualities in nature."[52] They also point out that what we consider valuable influences what we perceive as facts as well as how we interpret those facts. It is therefore important to attend to the specific way in which facts and values are intertwined in each specific case. Appealing to a set of immutable universal moral principles makes this impossible. Buchholz and Rosenthal argue that moral reasoning should not be determined by the imposition of one's own reflective perspective or abstract principles on the differences and conflicts that characterize a moral dilemma. They suggest instead that the understanding required to deal with a moral dilemma comes from "a more fundamental level of human rapport."[53] One gains access to it, in their account, by "penetrating through" conflicting principles. Like most pragmatists, Rosenthal and Buchholz are optimistic that some form of consensus, or "consummatory" experience can be summoned in most cases. In this, they may inadvertently be slipping into a new form of fundamentalism. Though they allow for the emergence of normative insights through the process of experimentation, they do seem to believe that a universal normative orientation underpins all experiments.

There are other business ethicists who have tried to combine a concern for general principles with an attentiveness to the specifics of particular cases. Robert Solomon has suggested, for instance, that an interaction between justice and care may be possible in the business world.[54] He points, in this regard, to the central importance of care and compassion in the context of the central managerial virtue of justice. Justice as fairness holds institutions together and it is the virtue of fairness that above all marks a good manager. Fairness does not consist of the application of abstract and impersonal principles, although administrative equity is important. It cannot be equated with respect for employees' or other stakeholders' rights either. According to

---

[52] Buchholz and Rosenthal, *The Pragmatic Path*, p. 90.
[53] *Ibid.*, p. 59.   [54] Solomon, *Ethics and Excellence*, p. 155.

Solomon, "rights" normally only enter the picture when the harmony of a community has broken down. They determine legitimate demands rather than cooperative or mutually formulated decisions. Solomon therefore associates justice, first and foremost, with an attitude of caring, a sense of compassion for those in a less advantageous position and relationships. For him, its association with rights, equality or merit is only of secondary importance. Solomon's acknowledgement that the specificity of caring relationships has to inform any principled account of justice is certainly a step in the right direction. The only question that remains pertains to how relationships within communities can be open-ended enough to avoid becoming a deterministic straightjacket. The relationship between individual and community therefore has to be interrogated.

Many moral theories seem incapable of simultaneously accommo-dating both the role of the individual moral agent and that of the community in which he/she participates, and the institutions with which he/she associates. The locus of control in morality is almost invariably exclusively associated with either the one or the other. Though individuals may not be impervious to the influence of others in the way that they perceive morality, neither are they passive receptacles in which the prejudices and priorities of a community or institution may be freely deposited. The fact is that communities and institutions do inform people's perceptions and views of what is morally acceptable and commendable. As such, their influence cannot be denied when considering people's moral beliefs and behavior. The relationship between narrative, community and ethics, that is so central to com-munitarians' view of morality should therefore be taken seriously, but not at the expense of an individual's freedom to associate and to co-define and redefine the terms of his/her association.

To avoid the exclusive association of morality's locus of control with either the individual or his/her environment (social, cultural, insti-tutional), van der Ven proposes what he calls an "interactionalist" approach.[55] Van der Ven's interactionalist approach to morality rejects both personal and environmental determinism. It is an attempt to synthesize the paradigms of individualism, communitarianism, and institutionalism by emphasizing reciprocal interactions between indi-vidual, community, and society. Personal determinism is the view that

[55] Van Der Ven, *Formation of the Moral Self*, p. 29.

morality can be entirely attributed to individual cognition, emotions, motives, intentions and choices. The influence of environmental factors is thus either neglected or denied. Environmental determinism is the proposition that the social forces to which individuals are exposed in their environment control all moral thinking, feeling, striving and behaving. From an interactionalist perspective, the individual is not only counteractive but also proactive. The environment influences the individual, but the individual also orchestrates, conducts, and even creates the environment. Interactionalism has both a structural and a process dimension. Structurally, it is characterized by the interdependence of personal and environmental factors. Its process dimension has to do with the gradual conditioning that takes place as individuals continually interact over time. Every interaction influences all future interactions between those involved. This gives interactionalism a dynamic aspect over time.

Solomon envisions a business organization in which the reciprocal influence between individual and institution is recognized and welcomed.[56] The nature of the relationship that comes into being between an individual and an organization is influenced by how people think about organizations. Corporations are sometimes described as a legal fiction or as an artificial person whose only reason for existence is to make money and protect its owners and stockholders. Views such as these can encourage irresponsible corporate behavior and condone social unresponsiveness. Military metaphors, such as the idea of a hierarchical chain of command also often inform people's perceptions of business corporations. These metaphors betray a militarist conception of business organizations, in which their primary purpose is to defeat their competition. This militarist conception of organizations can contribute to ruthlessness, hostility, and mutual destructiveness. Solomon proposes instead that a corporation be seen as a community, a group of people working together for similar goals and with some sense of a shared culture. What distinguishes this view is that a corporation is understood, first and foremost, as a group of people who stand with each other in a variety of personal and professional relationships.

From this perspective, individuals are defined, to a large extent, by the role they play within an organization, i.e. in terms of "the

---

[56] Solomon, *Ethics and Excellence*, p. 150.

individual-in-the-organization." This does not mean, however, that people's individuality is denied. Each individual is treated with respect and dignity, and not as mere means to an end. People engage with one another at work in order to pursue various goals and priorities. As such, these goals and priorities provide the context for collegial interaction. Individuals have the capacity, however, to determine the nature and extent of their investment in such interactions. However, their participation in collegial interactions in turn shapes and informs their beliefs and behavior. The individual is thus at the same time subject and object in his/her interaction with the organizational system in which he/she participates. The influence that the group has over individuals cannot be denied, yet the ability of individual subjects to determine their own course of action and beliefs has to be maintained. Subsuming individuals under their professional roles fails to allow them the freedom to dissent, or to introduce elements from the other groups that they associate with and from the variety of significant episodes that inform their lives. As such, it blunts the critical abilities and oversimplifies the complex relational realities that are crucial in establishing ethics as practice.

Towards new perspectives

Business ethics models that use utilitarian, communitarian, deontological, rights-based and contractarian suppositions and principles as their starting point may ultimately do the cause of ethics in organizations more harm than good. Though conceived as vehicles for creating authoritative normative frameworks in business life, these approaches often facilitate the abdication of moral discretion and responsibility. It is in this respect that the notion of ethics as practice is so crucial for business ethics. To approach ethics as practice requires that normative priorities and commitments be integrated with the context of their application. As such, it is an understanding of morality that is antithetical to the theory–practice divide on which most modernist approaches to ethics are based. When ethics is understood as practice, it can no longer be something that is practiced at arm's length. Moral agents are required to remain fully engaged with the concrete contingencies and dynamics of the world. Instead of an abstract cognitive exercise, ethics as practice is all about participation, relationships and responsiveness.

The apparent inability of modernist moral philosophies to consider and respond adequately to specific contextual and personal variables in moral judgment may be attributable to the instrumental nature of the logic that they typically employ. Post-Enlightenment critiques of ethics are unanimous in their rejection of the instrumentalism underlying consequentialist, non-consequentialist and contractarian approaches to ethics. Many of them challenge the priority that is given to universal or general moral rules, as well as the concomitant disregard of personal variables, context and specificity. They also question the assumption from which many of these approaches proceed that moral judgment should be based on the impartial reasoning of an autonomous agent.

Pragmatists like John Dewey were critical of the way in which modern philosophy had organized the world in terms of binary oppositions, such as public versus private, fact versus value, and reason versus emotion.[57] In modernist thought, the first term in each of these binaries is typically given greater legitimacy and weight than the second. In its instrumental orientation, that which is considered private, value-driven or emotional is often not considered worthy of debate, discussion or consideration. Because of this, many of the considerations that would be central to moral judgment, if ethics were approached as practice, are simply disregarded. In their concern with finding an indisputable, objective basis for morality, modernist moral philosophers often neglect to consider fully what it means to take care of others and build relations of trust, not in general terms, but simply within the context of the singular contingencies of individual lives. Such considerations are judged too subjective, too vague, and often too contentious to be dealt with "objectively." Should ethics be understood more in terms of practice, however, these kinds of contingencies would be exactly the sort of considerations that would be central to people's moral judgments.

We have seen that business ethicists who employ pragmatism seek a more meaningful integration between procedure and substance, and that their theories can accommodate particularity. They are also more inclined to acknowledge the interaction between the individual and

---

[57] John Dewey, *The Essential Dewey: Volumes 1 and 2,* edited by Larry Hickman and Thomas Alexander (Indiana University Press, 1998).

community in the emergence of people's moral sensibilities. As such, they realize that people's perceptions about what is morally acceptable and commendable are shaped in an ongoing process of experimental engagement and interaction with others, which makes it impossible to articulate moral imperatives meaningfully in general terms. This insight is crucial in re-establishing ethics as practice, and we will continue to draw on this aspect of pragmatist thought in Chapter 4.

Pragmatists' insights are valuable in balancing procedural and substantive considerations, as well as individual and communal interest. However, pragmatism also has serious limitations. The belief that conflicts of value can be resolved through the spontaneous emergence of a "consummatory" consensus represents a serious underestimation of the complexity of business life. The contentious messiness of relational life within a complex organizational system belies pragmatists' account of the emergence of consensual values. Pragmatism seems unable to offer a convincing account of normativity in complex organizational environments where conflicts are not easily resolved. Rosenthal and Buchholz claim that: "This understanding [of common morality] can emerge because human beings are fundamentally the same and confront a common reality in an ongoing process of change." This appeal to commonality not only betrays signs of a problematic foundationalist orientation but is also overly optimistic.

Pragmatists also put great faith in a process of deliberate rational engagement to identify worthy ends and resolve problematic situations. Pragmatists underestimate the extent to which human subjectivity is informed and formed through people's participation in practices. It discounts the fact that people are often unaware of the dynamics that shape their existence.

Pragmatism is also inadequately attuned to the subtleties of the language in and through which people express their perceptions and understanding of events, as well as their moral beliefs and priorities. It pays little attention to the way in which moral language reflects traditions, power dynamics and ideologies. As such, it is incapable of questioning the terms within which questions of value are addressed. It is this oversight that allows pragmatists to assume that people who appear to be expressing different moral views are in fact conveying similar convictions. In their discussion of leadership in business,

Buchholz and Rosenthal place great emphasis on the importance of perspectival pluralism. They argue that diverse groups or individuals bring different perspectives into an organization. Through a process of communicative interaction individuals can take one another's perspectives and use them to develop a "common content" for a "community of meaning."[58] Buchholz and Rosenthal's confidence in people's ability to find common moral ground discounts the fact that there may be significantly different perceptions, expectations and beliefs, not only among people, but also within the same individual. It is as if, beneath pragmatists' insistence on ongoing experimentation in the search for moral truth, there remains a kernel of foundationalism. There may be a significant relationship between this foundationalist tendency and the instrumentalism that is at work in pragmatist theory. Because their primary commitment is to the optimum solution in every situation, pragmatists tend to brush over the complexities that pertain to particular individuals and contexts. This "whatever works best" attitude does not always serve pragmatists well. It allows only limited scope for critique, interrogation, dissent and discontinuity. As such, it may perpetuate morally dubious situations or condone less than satisfactory compromises.

The continental tradition

The significant limitations of pragmatism's account of normativity in organizations make it necessary to draw in other critical perspectives. It is in this regard that we will draw inspiration from the perspectives offered by particular exponents of the continental tradition in philosophy.[59] Continental philosophy places great emphasis on the history of Western thought. Its primary interest is in providing a critical account of how we came to believe what we do about ourselves and about the world. The goal of its critical analyses is to effect transformation(s) of our ways of thinking about our own existence, and emancipation from the constraints that particular ways of thinking

---

[58] Buchholz and Rosenthal, *Pragmatic Path*, p. 418.
[59] I will specifically focus on the reinterpretation of Western thought that emanated from Nietzsche's critique of Western metaphysics, and its influence on twentieth-century continental thought. As such, it will involve revisiting certain aspects of classical Greek thought.

impose on us. As such, it involves the critical scrutiny of a specific praxis, i.e. the way that things are conceived of and done.[60]

By drawing on the thoughts of particular continental philosophers, I will seek to understand the way in which human subjectivity is shaped and informed in and by the confluence of historical, societal and cultural variables in the lives of individuals. From this perspective, there is no objective, independent vantage point available to an individual subject. Instead, in this tradition there is a general acknowledgement and appreciation of the role that people's emotions, bodies, relationships, histories and contexts play in shaping their sense of self and any perceptions and beliefs that they may have. This makes it possible to develop a more realistic appreciation of the constraints and possibilities that pertain to ethics as practice. I will draw on the work of those continental thinkers who challenge individuals to be responsive to what is required of them from moment to moment within the context of particular engagements with others. Since the moral responses of individuals are seen as being, in a sense, called forth by appeals that emanate from a particular set of situational, contextual and relational contingencies, the continental philosophical tradition rejects the idea that they can be prescribed or proscribed in the form of immutable principles, codes or laws. It requires instead that individuals remain constantly attuned to the nature of their involvement and participation in particular situations and relationships, as well as to what is required of them therein. I will align myself with the twentieth-century continental philosophical tradition that closely associates morality with thoughtfulness and care in the midst of everyday challenges and contingencies.

Continental philosophers also provide valuable perspectives on the notion of moral truth. There are various strands of continental thought that reject the idea of "objective," *a priori* truth. For example, in its analysis of language and subjectivity, poststructuralist thought undermines the idea that the way in which we name, categorize and relate to the world by means of language creates accurate and objective "pictures" of reality. Instead, it is argued that individuals can never fully transcend the various biases and value priorities that

---

[60] For a concise, insightful introduction to the concerns of continental philosophy, see Simon Crichley, *Continental Philosophy: a Very Short Introduction* (Oxford University Press, 2001).

are embedded in the languages that they use to conceptualize, speak and write. From this perspective, it is important to use moral language with care, circumspection and a constant awareness of its inherent limitations. The willingness to reinterpret, rephrase, and translate moral intuitions and insights into different terms is an integral part of moral responsiveness.

From the perspective of the continental philosophical tradition, the dissociation of ethics with practice is not simply taken as a given, but is interpreted instead within the context of the long developmental history of moral thought in the Western tradition. In the continental understanding of this history, Aristotle is a valuable and important point of reference. There are valuable aspects of Greek moral thought that were lost or neglected in the Western philosophical tradition as it became preoccupied with rational certainty. These perspectives have an important bearing on the way in which the relationship between ethics and practice is conceived and are therefore worth revisiting.

There are also a number of nineteenth- and twentieth-century philosophical critiques of metaphysics that are significant for moral thought in the continental philosophical tradition because of the light that they shed on the dissociation of ethics from practice. The focus of many of these critiques is the way in which Enlightenment thinkers conceived of moral truth. They generally object to the instrumentality of modernist thought and question its disavowal of power interests and other subjective influences for the sake of moral objectivity. These philosophical critiques of modernist prejudices and presuppositions are of central importance in reconstituting the relationship between ethics and practice in less oppositional terms. As such, they will inform important points of reference in the discussions that are to follow.

The goal of the analysis and proposals that are presented here is not to replace the rigorously systematic accounts of moral reasoning that currently inform business ethicists' approach to morality with a theoretical model that promises even more certainty and security. In fact, I believe that a comprehensive *descriptive* or *prescriptive* account of the multiple personal and contextual variables and complex relational dynamics that inform, or *should* inform, individuals' perceptions of what is morally appropriate in particular situations is ultimately impossible. What I do propose is that we question our most basic beliefs about moral agency and moral epistemology. In Chapter 3, I therefore consider how the complex relationships between an individual and his/her context influence moral agency. The goal of this discussion is to facilitate a thorough re-examination of how we make moral decisions. In Chapter 4, we turn our attention to the nature of moral values. What I will attempt to show in my analysis is that substance and process are so intricately intertwined in normativity that it is futile to try to separate them. These chapters will provide a critical challenge to the way in which many business ethicists understand moral agency and epistemology.

Contemporary continental thought is often accused of dismantling philosophical certainties without offering alternative proposals. The various critical analyses that are associated with this tradition have been criticized for being obscurantist, relativist, and even irresponsible. It is certainly true that to develop a comprehensive ethical theory, or a systematic moral methodology, would be contrary to the intentions of this tradition of critical philosophical engagement. To do so would be tantamount to the endorsement of an epistemology of certainty, which blunts the critical capacities that are so prized in the continental tradition, and that ultimately sustain moral responsiveness.

The importance of constantly questioning one's own suppositions and perspectives is a theme that is often reiterated by those who are associated with this tradition. For continental thinkers, a moral theory that purports to be comprehensive in the scope of its analysis and proposals would therefore elicit unacceptable associations of finality. This does not mean, however, that continental philosophers are not interested in practice. Quite the opposite is true. Continental thinkers are very concerned with the social, political and economic realities in which we live every day. They see it as their task to facilitate meaningful change by critically interrogating the assumptions that support and secure the way in which such systems of interrelation are structurally configured. The continental tradition of moral thought presents us, not with a theory, but with a practice. It challenges us to remove the conceptual and procedural restraints with which we have tried to secure morality, and continually allow ourselves to be challenged by the various contextual and relational realities that fill our everyday lives. If business ethicists and practitioners were to take up this challenge, ethics would once more become a practice, instead of something that needs to be "managed."

3 | *Moral agency reconsidered*

It is not uncommon for business ethics practitioners to encounter skepticism when they make proposals aimed at improving the commitment of an organization's employees to ethical behavior. In my experience as corporate consultant, I have come across some corporate executives who argue that ethics is a case of "motherhood and apple pie" and that there is really very little that can be done to influence people's ethical behavior at work. They insist that those individuals who act unethically represent no more than a few "rotten apples" who need to be removed. From their perspective, enforcing company rules and dismissing those who transgress the law, is the best strategy for managing ethical risks in the workplace.

However, events at the beginning of the twenty-first century have made this sort of attitude seem untenable and irresponsible. In the post-Enron world, there is a great deal of concern about the way in which corporate agents fulfill, or fail to fulfill, their fiduciary duties. The checks and balances that professionals and governance structures were supposed to provide have proved unreliable and have eroded the public's trust. Discipline and legal penalties no longer seem to provide sufficient safeguards against those who would behave unethically. Firing, fining or imprisoning transgressors provides little consolation to those who have been affected. Under these conditions, the argument that ethics is a case of "motherhood and apple pie" seems little more than a convenient ruse to allow business organizations to shirk their responsibility for the unethical behavior of their agents.

There seems to be a growing consensus, both from within corporations and without, that something more should be done to prevent unethical business behavior. What is required, it seems, is some kind of proactive intervention to ensure that business practitioners stay committed to ethical business practices. This shift towards proactive measures is reflected in recent changes to the US Federal Sentencing Guidelines. Where the emphasis used to be almost purely on compliance, the new Guidelines encourage business organizations to promote "ethics" and engender a *culture* of compliance among their employees. Because of these changes, business organizations can no longer hide behind the claim that the ethics of individuals is not the concern of the employer. The new Federal Sentencing Guidelines seem to suggest that the environment that is created within an organization can somehow help to ensure that employees remain committed to ethical behavior. It is the responsibility of the organization as a whole then to ensure that steps are taken to engender a culture of responsible behavior and ethical compliance.

It is not always clear exactly what the new Federal Sentencing Guidelines require organizations to do in practice. Its recommendations seem to be based on the assumption that an organization can identify and address the cause or origin of employees' unethical decisions and behavior. If business organizations are to respond in an appropriate way to the recommendations of the new Guidelines, this assumption needs to be carefully considered. What is ultimately at stake here is the locus of moral agency in the relationship between an individual employee and the organizational environment in which he/she works.

Much research has been devoted to questions about the nature of an organization's moral agency. In building their case that an organization can act as a moral agent, some legal and moral theorists routinely draw parallels between the way in which individuals and organizations, as collective entities, make decisions.[1] Those who oppose this view question the validity of such comparisons. What neither side adequately considers, though, is whether the understanding of individual moral agency on which they base their arguments is truly accurate. This is an important oversight, because it seems more than likely that this debate may ultimately hinge on the outcome of exactly such an enquiry.

Ethical decision making in the workplace is typically conceived in deceptively simple terms – people and organizations think through ethical dilemmas, make decisions, and act on them. If this is an

---

[1] For instance, see the agency theory of Peter French, *Corporate Ethics* (Trinity University Press, 1995). He argues that since corporations have the capacity to make decisions that have effects, they should be held accountable for those effects, much in the same way as we would hold individuals accountable for the effects of their actions.

accurate description of how people and organizations come to do the things that they do, then holding them to account for their actions seem a simple and reasonable enough affair. It becomes a mere question of how to reward them fairly for the positive outcomes of their actions or hold them liable for the harmful ones. However, a closer, more rigorous consideration of the *thought* and *decisions* to which the actions of individuals and organizations are so easily attributed may reveal a far more complex set of dynamics at work in shaping moral behavior. There are good reasons to revisit this matter.

As we saw in Chapter 2, many business ethicists and practitioners, for example, continue to rely on deontological principles in their approach to ethics. This significantly informs their understanding of how individual employees and organizations come to do the things they do. The cogency of deontology relies, as we have seen, on the ability of human beings to make decisions in a dispassionate and unbiased way, which assumes a certain rational aloofness in moral deliberation. This assumption has, however, been challenged by a number of influential twentieth-century philosophers. Their objections were based on their analyses of language and the role that cultural biases, contextual contingencies and power dynamics plays in the way people perceive and make sense of things. They came to realize that the "isolated decision maker" may in fact not be so isolated, and that the rational duties and rights that direct these individuals are in fact not so universally self-evident. In their analyses, these theorists claim that an individual is not swayed or directed by deliberate rational argumentation alone. In many cases, individuals do not consciously refer to clearly defined universal duties and rights for their normative orientation. Furthermore, even when the notions of universal duties and rights are employed, they are always interpreted by individuals from the perspective of their own beliefs and experiences. Naturally, observations such as these have significant implications for how we construe the locus of moral agency in the relationship between individual employees and their organizational work environments. As such, they are worth considering in more detail.

In what follows then, I will draw on the work of a number of philosophers to develop an account of how and why moral agents come to think and do the things they do. I will begin by situating my analysis within the context of a number of important philosophical considerations. First, I will look at philosophical objections to the idea that moral agents can reason in an entirely unbiased, "rational" way.

Secondly, I will consider the role of the body in the way people perceive and make sense of situations and ideas. Finally, I will reflect on the relationship between embodied decision makers and their social contexts.

Rethinking our understanding of how individuals make sense of things

Moral behavior is, at least in part, a response to the way in which an individual perceives and makes sense of a situation and the moral directives to which he/she is expected to subscribe. Many business ethicists continue to work on the assumption that an individual can gain a completely objective, rational understanding of what is morally required of him/her in a particular situation. A look at the approaches some prominent business ethicists suggest clearly illustrates their emphasis on deliberate rational analysis and emotional detachment. Bowie describes being *rational* as essential to moral agency.[2] He explains that rationality entails the utilization of the Kantian test of universality, i.e. that valid moral maxims will be accepted unanimously in an ideal Kingdom of Ends. He also explains that the ability to "see future consequences" and to "reason abstractly" characterizes humanity.

Donaldson and Dunfee's social contract theory approach suffers from the same kind of appeal to abstract rationality. Many business ethicists employ similar approaches to ethical decision making. Dreilinger puts forward a systematic problem-solving model that starts with identifying the desired outcomes of a decision and carefully avoids subjectivity and personal perceptions that can create barriers to objectivity.[3] He stresses that emotions get in the way of logic and suggests that one should avoid words like "fairness" or "doing right" since they carry an emotional content that might introduce bias. These business ethicists expect responsible moral agents to be able to "transcend" whatever contextual pressures may be brought to bear on them, as well as the way in which they have been socialized to think and respond. They are also supposed to be able to detach themselves from their private biases and emotions to ensure that their assessment

---

[2] Norman Bowie, *Business Ethics: a Kantian Perspective* (Malden: Blackwell, 1999), p. 45.

[3] Craig Dreilinger, "Ethical Decision Making in Business" in Hoffman, Frederic and Schwartz, *Business Ethics: Readings and Cases in Corporate Morality* (Boston: McGrawHill, 2001), pp. 95–96.

of moral propriety remains completely objective. Thus conceived, the individual moral agent is often referred to, in philosophical discourse, as the "transcendental subject." Given the fact that the first cracks in the armor of the "transcendental subject" began to appear soon after its heyday in the Enlightenment, it is somewhat surprising that it has survived for so long. Perhaps even more surprising, though, is the fact that so many business ethicists continue to think about moral agency in this way.

It was the German philosopher Friedrich Nietzsche who leveled one of the first criticisms at post-Enlightenment moral philosophy. Nietzsche supported the Enlightenment philosophers' insistence on the necessity of thinking autonomously about moral norms and values. He is also vigilant in his rejection of moral imperatives based on religious beliefs. Nonetheless, some of the ideas that would later serve to undermine Enlightenment thought were already present in Nietzsche's writing. Most importantly, Nietzsche insists on an understanding of the psychological and anthropological dimensions of any truth claims. He expressed doubts about the ability of human beings to transcend the limitations that time, space and embodiment impose on moral judgment. In fact, he argues that our moral values are a direct product of the human relations that we are immersed in. Nietzsche describes moral truth as metaphors and anthropomorphisms that human beings employ in the struggle for self-preservation.[4]

One of the most comprehensive attacks against Enlightenment thought, however, came from another German philosopher, namely Martin Heidegger. Heidegger challenged the notion of the "transcendental subject" in various ways. He believed that Western philosophy had completely misconstrued the nature of morality and the moral agent. In his essay "Letter on Humanism," Heidegger bemoans the fact that philosophers have abandoned their post as defenders of some of the essential elements of our humanity in their efforts to formulate universally valid moral imperatives.[5] Heidegger argued that philosophers' desire to have their discipline accepted as a legitimate science led them to adopt certain subject–object dichotomies. He

---

[4] Friedrich Nietzsche, "On Truth and Lie in the Extramoral Sense" in W. Kaufman, *The Portable Nietzsche* (New York: Penguin Books, 1954).
[5] Martin Heidegger, "Letter on Humanism" in David F. Krell (ed.), *Basic Writings* (New York: Harper & Row, 1977).

pointed out that when human beings begin to think of themselves as "subjects," the entire world is objectified and forced to become useful. When an individual assumes the right for him/herself to "rationally" dictate the terms of existence, people and things can only be meaningful or significant inasmuch as they have an identifiable use or purpose from that individual's perspective. Heidegger argues that in this process, man loses his respect and appreciation for the non-instrumental meaning and significance of individual lives.

Heidegger uses the German word *Dasein* (literally: there-being) to refer to an individual's existence, in all its singular and concrete specificity. For him, the meaning and significance of an individual's existence is so embedded in a specific set of concrete practices, historical conditions and social relations that it cannot adequately be represented in abstract, general terms. The messy realities in which an individual's existence is always inscribed simply do not lend themselves to the tidy protocols of the transcendental subject's conceptual abstractions. The transcendental subject assumes that its capacity for rational abstraction gives it not only the ability, but also the right to prescribe the meaning and significance of things on behalf of everybody else. It is precisely this that Heidegger contests. He insists that it is neither possible, nor moral, to make sense of things in such generalized, abstract terms. To do so is to fail to recognize the concrete particularity of an individual's existence and to reduce the existence of everything and everybody to its instrumental value.

Furthermore, without the rootedness of human beings in everyday practices, it becomes impossible for truly authentic moral responses to emerge. For Heidegger, there is no elevated position of rational detachment from which humanity, in all its infinite particularity, can be surveyed. The moral agent is someone who recognizes instead that he/she perceives and makes sense of the world from the position of his/her own particular position in it. For Heidegger, the possibility of morality lies, not in the moral agent's ability to "rationally" distance him/herself from those considerations that pertain to the concrete particularities of individual lives, but precisely in his/her readiness to recognize and respond to such realities as they become manifest in the course of everyday life.

The objectification of human beings is a theme that was also taken up by Karl Marx and Herbert Marcuse. Marx observed that human beings were being treated as if they were little more than instruments in capitalist production processes. For him, this represented an unacceptable form of objectification. Marx realized that the source of this objectification lay in the material realities of capitalist production. He rejected Hegel's belief that the development of the Absolute Spirit held the key to the future. In fact, Marx literally wanted to bring us down to earth. What his work suggested, then, was that the way in which we rationally organize the world is deeply rooted in our experience of the material conditions under which we live. The conceptual schemes that we create are designed to justify the distribution of material goods according to particular patterns. As such, they are instruments of power that may be used to secure the interests of some to the detriment of others. Marx claimed that many of the institutions and social controls that served to secure the organization of capitalist society relied on this power for their effect. Marx understood that the persuasive power of these conceptual schemes lay in the association of abstract rationality with a kind of privileged, objective autonomy. For him this was a pernicious myth that suppressed the legitimate aspirations of the disenfranchised.

Marcuse proposed an even more radical critique than Marx. He argued that the individual need not be objectified, since the social controls of modern society have become part of individual identity.[6] The individual no longer has a non-instrumental understanding of the meaning and significance of his/her own life. In his description of "introjection," Marcuse argues that, through a variety of relatively spontaneous processes, the "self" transposes its perception of itself with what lies outside of the self. This leads to the erosion of the individual's private self and his/her immediate identification with those objectifying ideas that secure the material organization of society. Marcuse believed that this identification was being orchestrated through careful organization and sophisticated scientific management. According to Marcuse, the hegemony of consumerism and the hypnotic effect of sound-bites like "the Free World" create a "one-dimensional" man, an individual whose sense of self is completely swallowed up by his/her objectified existence.

A common theme in the work of Heidegger, Marx and Marcuse is their view of the ironic way in which the "transcendental subject" has

[6] Herbert Marcuse, *One-Dimensional Man: Studies in the Ideology of Advanced Industrial Society* (Beacon Press, 1964).

become the victim of its own ingenuity. In a book entitled *The Dia-lectic of the Enlightenment*, Horkheimer and Adorno present an excellent analysis of how the project of the Enlightenment carried in itself the seed of its own destruction.[7] They describe how Enlightenment thinkers initially developed the notion of the "transcendental subject" in an effort to free themselves from oppressive mythologies and gain independent scientific knowledge about the world. However, through its objectifying binary structures the "transcendental subject" was founded on a metaphysics that imprisoned the very individual that it was designed to free.

Together, the work of philosophers like Nietzsche, Heidegger, Marx, Marcuse, Horkheimer and Adorno, as well as a host of others call into question the idea that a moral agent can make sense of things objectively, through an act of rational detachment. They not only dispute the possibility of doing so, but also draw attention to the various negative implications of continuing to believe it. The question that business ethicists hardly ever think about is how the structures, concepts and metaphysical truths that we devise to make sense of our reality may in fact change, or even inhibit our ability to act as moral agents. Many business practitioners are still being trained and encouraged to interpret their everyday experiences and problems from the perspective of general normative imperatives. What does this habit of thinking in the most general of possible terms do to the way in which business practitioners see and experience those moments in their professional lives that call for personal discretion and a truly authentic and imaginative response? Are we asking of employees, in effect, to shape the unique moral problems that they encounter to fit the organization's standard solutions, instead of determining what an authentic response to the specific situation would be? The Federal Sentencing Guidelines expect business organizations to take responsibility for the actions of their agents and employees by creating a work environment that is conducive to ethical behavior. The question is, however, whether a system of authority and oversight based on generalized normative imperatives really is the best way to ensure that employees come into their own as moral agents. In a sense, this strategy may blunt the instrument most crucial to moral responsiveness, and that is the decision maker's own humanity.

[7] Max Horkheimer and Theodor W. Adorno, *Dialectic of Enlightenment*, translated by John Cumming (Herder and Herder, 1972).

Rethinking "rationality" from the perspective of embodied morality

What exactly does it mean to say that we expect of individuals in corporations to make "rational" moral decisions? From the perspective of the Enlightenment's "transcendental subject," it means, as we have seen, that everything that may corrupt the objectivity of abstract, syllogistic rationality should be eliminated. Considerations pertaining to an individual's private feelings, the caring personal relationships in which he/she might be involved, the duties that he/she associates with his/her specific role in a group or community, and the web of power relations in which he/she is embedded are therefore rendered inadmissible. The same is true of elements of thought and perception that emanate from the individual's embodiment. The fact that human beings have gendered, aging bodies; the fact that their physical existence is inscribed within the concrete parameters of institutional settings and social conventions, all of this is seen as a threat to rational thought. The introduction of variables such as these reveals differences in perspective and opinion that disrupt the orderly uniformity of modernist rationality. Modernist ethics relies for its validity on the reconciliation of such differences in universally valid normative principles. However, embodied, emotional agents, who carry within themselves the biases of their own particular life-situations, simply don't see the world in a homogeneous way and therefore pose a threat to the notion of universal truth.

The pursuit of universal truth may, however, have left us with an impoverished conception, not only of "rationality," but also of what actually happens in moral decision making. Bauman describes the modern pursuit of "objectivity" as a process involving the removal of the walls of moral decision making in order to facilitate the examination of the ceiling.[8] By denying that moral agency is intimately related to our embodiment, we undermine our ability to understand what happens when we actually make moral decisions. Merleau-Ponty described the body as the formative milieu through which everything comes into existence.[9] From his perspective, we cannot understand

---

[8] Zygmunt Bauman, *Postmodern Ethics* (London: Blackwell, 1993).
[9] Maurice Merleau-Ponty, "Carnality" in Mark Taylor, *Altarity* (University of Chicago Press, 1987), p. 73.

ourselves as moral agents, nor can we develop any concept of morality as such, if we do not acknowledge the role that our embodiment plays in the way we perceive and make sense of the world.

According to Michael Polanyi, people actually "know" far more than they are able to consciously articulate. He calls the understanding of things that people have, without being aware of it "tacit knowledge." Although this form of knowledge is very personal, it does not render perception random or completely subjective. When an individual perceives an object or considers an issue, he/she integrates thousands of changing particulars into a single constant impression or thought. Inasmuch as this integrated impression is directly related to those particulars that contributed to its formation, it is not random at all. Kant also alluded to such an act of integration in his notion of synthesis.[10]

Polanyi interprets Kant's observations in this regard as an acknowledgement of "unformalizable powers of thought." However, he criticizes Kant for "preferring to let such sleeping monsters lie." In Polanyi's view, the key to understanding this act of integration lies in the body. He sees the body as the instrument of all intellectual and practical knowledge.[11] Polanyi argues that we generalize in certain ways because of the fact that we dwell in human bodies. Both our interaction with the external world and the conceptual structures that make language and science possible are based on our awareness of our bodies. This means that when we talk, analyze or reason, we are unconsciously following a set of tacit rules. However, we do not just passively follow instructions. Even though tacit knowledge is unspecifiable, it has a vectoral quality. In other words, there is intentionality involved in the way we utilize our tacit knowledge of things. When we are confronted with a new situation or problem, we direct our attention towards it and use the tacit knowledge that we have accumulated through experience to generate an integrated impression of it. Despite its vectoral operationalization, tacit knowledge remains largely unconscious and unarticulatable and, as such, inseparable from actual acts of understanding. Polanyi uses

---

[10] I. Kant, *Critique of Pure Reason*, translated by Norman Kemp Smith (Palgrave Macmillan, 1929).

[11] A. F. Sanders, *Michael Polanyi's Post-Critical Epistemology: a Reconstruction of Some Aspects of Tacit Knowledge* (Amsterdam: Rodopi, 1988), p. 10. According to Sanders, Polanyi naturalizes knowledge by placing the quest for knowledge in an evolutionary, cultural and moral perspective.

cycling to explain the way in which tacit knowledge is used. Cycling, he explains, is a skill that is developed through practice. However, once mastered, it requires no conscious mental effort. In fact, such effort may imperil a cyclist more than it benefits him/her. Polanyi argues that tacit knowledge develops as individuals and groups of individuals continually try to make sense of their experiences.[12] Polanyi's observations have intriguing implications for the way in which we understand moral agency in an organizational context. If there are forms of tacit knowledge that develop among the employees of an organization, for instance, how does it shape and inform employees' sense of moral propriety? Furthermore, can this unarticulated understanding of the way in which things are supposed to be done be altered, if deemed necessary? Is it at this level that the Federal Sentencing Guidelines expect organizations to intervene? The work of George Lakoff and Mark Johnson sheds some interesting light on questions like these.

Lakoff and Johnson are interested in how our bodily existence shapes our moral vocabularies and sensibilities.[13] They claim that conceptual structures are directly related to neural structures and sensorimotor experiences. Moral concepts are derived from the way in which the body experiences and deals with physical challenges. Like Polanyi, Lakoff and Johnson believe that the mental categories that we employ to make sense of things are not so much a product of conscious reasoning as a manifestation of the brains and bodies we have. Far from hollowing out moral concepts, Lakoff and Johnson's proposals give the mental structures that we develop to make sense of our experiences an intrinsic sort of meaning and significance. Their meaning and significance lies, however, not in the detached autonomy of the reasoning "mind," but precisely in their connection with the body and embodied experience.

According to Lakoff and Johnson, the human capacity for integrative perception and image formation allow so-called "basic level" concepts to come into being. These concepts give rise to "primary metaphors," which facilitate the conceptualization of abstract concepts such as "justice." This is done on the basis of the same sort of inferential patterns that are used in sensorimotor processes. What this means is

---

[12] *Ibid.*, p. 11.
[13] Georg Lakoff and Mark Johnson, *Philosophy in the Flesh: the Embodied Mind and its Challenge to Western Thought* (New York: Basic Books, 1999), p. 18.

that the development of abstract concepts like "justice" is directly related to corporal experiences. Lakoff and Johnson suggest that concepts such as love, causation and morality are conceptualized via complex combinations of multiple primary metaphors. These primary metaphors are not always consistent with one another.[14] Without them, however, concepts such as "justice" or "morality" are skeletal and have no inferential structure. The complex ways in which these metaphors combine in the formation of moral concepts may explain why people who subscribe to the same principle may interpret its meaning and significance differently under a particular set of circumstances.

It is of course fairly common for people to interpret the same moral concept or normative imperative in different ways. Every business ethicist who has ever worked or advised in a corporate context has experience of this and knows how problematic it can be. In one case, for instance, a senior manager was charged with discriminating against women. This charge was brought about by his refusal to appoint a qualified female candidate to a position in his division because of her gender. Interestingly enough though, this manager happened to pride himself on his fairness. Because of this, he was quite taken aback when asked how he reconciled his actions with his open commitment to fairness. From his point of view, he explained, it would have been quite unfair to expose a woman to the rigors and responsibilities of a managerial position. His view of women was deeply shaped by the religious tradition in which he was raised. From the perspective of this tradition, a woman's primary duties and responsibilities always lay with her family. Because of this, he could not justify the potential impact that managerial duties would have had on the female candidate's family life. He seemed to believe sincerely that it would have been unfair to expect her to take on so much "extra" responsibility.

What this case demonstrates is how an individual's latent understanding of an apparently self-evident moral imperative can differ radically from how others interpret it. It seems that it may simply not be possible to assume that individual employees will assign the same sort of content to the general moral imperatives that are inscribed in codes of conduct. Codes of conduct cannot accommodate or articulate the various complex ways in which primary metaphors may combine through the embodied experiences of employees. The types of generic

[14] *Ibid.*, p. 73.

codes that are often adopted as part of global initiatives may reflect something of our common experience of human embodiment, but they are incapable of doing justice to the more complex metaphoric interrelationships that shape our individual and collective understanding of things. It is impossible[15] to anticipate accurately the meaning and significance that variables such as age, gender, and profession will have in the way in which individuals interpret general moral directives. Perhaps it is because of this that codes so rarely really affect the way in which employees go about their everyday business. Ultimately, it seems, employees may simply develop their own "sense" of what is morally expected of them by their colleagues and clients, irrespective of what is written in their employer's code of conduct.

Verner Petersen refers to the "sense" of right and wrong that develops in the minds of individuals as "the silent patrons of our hearts."[16] These silent patrons of the heart help the moral agent to produce and evaluate multiple fleeting sketches of possible decisions and actions before he/she consciously reasons about what to do. He agrees with Lakoff and Johnson's view that somatic (bodily) markers, developed in the process of biological and social evolution, pre-select responses before the moral agent engages in conscious reasoning. The notion of "somatic markers" may be seen as a more sophisticated explanation of what is more commonly known as a "gut-feeling." They are the result of an individual's many diverse experiences of pleasure, acceptance, punishment and praise. An individual's moral sensibilities therefore begin to develop at the level of visceral reactions in his/her interactions with others. In this process, positive or negative feedback is integrated and combines to produce in the individual a tacit sense of what is appropriate.

In Peterson's view children develop their personal sense of agency through a process that involves negotiating relationships with others and the world.[17] Peterson's observations in this regard provide an interesting perspective on the role of leadership example in the development of a culture of ethical responsibility within an organization. Senior members

---

[15] To be sure, the poststructuralist notion of the possibility of thinking the impossible may be what moral imagination requires.

[16] Verner Petersen, *Thinking with our Hands – the Importance of Tacit, Non-Algorithmic Knowledge*, Working Paper 99–10 (The Aarhus Business School, 1999), p. 40.

[17] Verner Petersen, *Beyond Rules in Business and Society* (Northampton: Edward Elgar, 2002), pp. 309–357.

of business organizations often provide moral guidance unconsciously, through the ways in which they respond to the behavior of new colleagues and subordinates.

Petersen draws attention to the crucial role that observation, imitation and participation play in the process of moral inculcation. Moral agents don't learn through explicit instruction. Instead they experience and interpret patterns of co-variation in their interaction with others. The norms and values that are established in this process often resist articulation and formalization in a readily transmittable form.

Peterson's account of how individuals develop their moral sensibilities has potentially significant implications for how we think about the possibility of inculcating a workforce with a sense of moral responsibility. It suggests that to try and convey to someone the fluid sense of morality that informs the behavior of colleagues within a particular set of professional relationships by formulizing it into a distinct set of static "knowledge-components" is somewhat like giving him/her a dictionary to learn a language. Such a person may end up knowing the vocabulary, but he/she is unlikely to be able to use it in a meaningful way. In order to be able to converse intelligibly he/she would have to possess some understanding of how to put words together appropriately, as well as sensitivity for the role that context plays in shaping the meaning of words. Peterson's observations seem to suggest that these are forms of knowledge and awareness that can ultimately only be gained through the experience of interaction with others who "speak the same language." "Speaking the same language" in terms of an organization's ethics program requires sensitivity to the multiple influences that shape an institution's social grammar.

As we have seen, Polanyi believes that the tacit rules that guide our integrative sense-making are something that develops as individuals and groups continually try to make sense of their experiences. If this is the case, then it could be argued that individuals and groups develop their tacit sense of moral propriety as they continually confront and try and deal with new moral dilemmas. As they do so, they are engaging in what Polanyi describes as "creative problem solving." According to Polanyi, creative problem solving involves the combined operation of the faculties of imagination and intuition. He understands imagination as all those thoughts of things that are not present or not yet present. It is intentionally directed at goals or solutions that are as yet only vaguely anticipated. Intuition, on the other hand, is the faculty that allows an individual to surmise the presence of a hidden coherence in nature. It operates at a subsidiary level and utilizes clues and integrative principles that are not fully identifiable. The joint operation of deliberative imagination and spontaneous, integrative intuition accounts for an inquirer's sense of gradually deepening coherence.

If employees' behavior at work is shaped and informed by how they imaginatively and intuitively make sense of new situations and problems, then it is interesting to consider what role a business organization can play in all of this. Polanyi's observations seem to suggest that, if organizations were interested in influencing their employees' behavior by shaping their moral sensibilities, they would have to address both the imaginative and intuitive aspects of moral decision making.

The more deliberate imaginative aspect of moral decision making is something that business ethicists have grappled with for some time now. Pat Werhane is one of those business ethicists who have contributed to this discourse. Drawing on the work of Adam Smith, Immanuel Kant and Mark Johnson, she has developed an account of how imagination may be employed in making sense of moral dilemmas. It involves three consecutive phases:

1) Becoming aware of social, economic, organizational and personal factors that affect perception of a business problem and understanding how these might conflict;
2) Reframing the problem from various perspectives to understand the potential impact of different solutions; and
3) Developing alternatives to solve the problem that can be morally justified by others outside the firm.[18]

The deliberate unpacking of all relevant considerations and the conscious envisioning of alternatives that Werhane associates with the employment of imagination in moral decision making shows some correspondence with Polanyi's observations. In a sense, both describe the employment of imagination as a process involving a directed, intentional effort to draw on the tacit knowledge resources that are available to the individual. However, there is also a significant difference in how they see this process unfolding. For Polanyi, imagination is co-dependent on intuition. Intuition, as he sees it, is a process of

---

[18] Patricia Werhane, *Moral Imagination and Management Decision Making* (New York: Oxford University Press, 1999).

understanding that is spontaneously initiated as the individual engages with the concrete contingencies of a problem. As such, it is not something that can deliberately be operationalized from a position of disengagement. It is on this point that he and Werhane differ. Werhane acknowledges that "conceptual schemes" influence the way individuals think about moral dilemmas. She also recognizes the role that social dynamics and metaphoric language plays in the way that individuals conceptualize moral dilemmas. Despite this, Werhane insists that: "moral imagination entails the ability to disengage."[19]

It seems much harder for a business organization to take responsibility for the behavior of its workforce when morality is so closely associated with individual employees' intuitive understanding of what is morally appropriate within a particular context and situation. To understand the role that an organization might play in shaping the moral sensibilities of its employees therefore requires a much closer look at how individuals' intuitive responses are influenced by social interactions in their immediate surroundings. What also needs to be considered is whether there is indeed a position of imaginative "detachment" available to the individual employee within the network of social relations that constitute an organizational environment.

Beyond isolation: moral agency in organizations

If employees' behavior at work is based on their tacit understanding of what is morally required of them in particular sets of circumstances, it seems somewhat contradictory to expect them to somehow "detach" themselves from these unconscious and unarticulatable sources of meaning in order to make a moral determination. If a moral agent's sense of moral propriety is always steeped in intuitive impressions and a tacit vocabulary of appropriate responses, it is hard to see how he/she can recognize, let alone make any sense of, a moral dilemma without these resources.

Both Judith Butler and Martha Nussbaum have studied the notion of subjectivity to try to determine whether a detached, self-reflexive position is indeed available to the individual human agent.[20] Although

[19] *Ibid.*, p. 104.
[20] Martha C. Nussbaum, *Love's Knowledge* (New York: Oxford University Press, 1990); Judith Butler, *The Psychic Life of Power: Theories in Subjection* (Stanford University Press, 1997).

they have different reasons, both philosophers come to the conclusion that such a position of detachment is beyond the reach of the human subject. Judith Butler argues that the subject is culturally constructed all the way down. We come to know ourselves as subjects through our various interactions and performances in the world, but this does not mean that we can talk about ourselves as existing independently from these iterations. We in fact depend on them to have any sense of self.[21] Nietzsche understood what this meant in practice. Butler cites his view of the role that morality plays in allowing us to know ourselves as subjects: "Violence founds the subject. Morality performs that violence again and again in cultivating the subject as a reflexive being." Butler argues that individuals only know themselves as subjects because they elicit certain responses in and through their interactions in the world. In the process, structure is given to their sense of self. This means that the decision-making agent or subject will not be able to engage in morally imaginative thought if detached from the very fabric that constitutes the conditions of its subjectivity. This is an important point because it suggests that an organization's internal culture provides its employees with the tacit frames of reference that allow for self-reflexivity to take place, or eliminate such possibility.

In this regard, Bourdieu's notion of *habitus* provides a model for understanding the interaction between the embodied subject and its environment.[22] *Habitus* is the word Bourdieu uses to describe the subjectivity of an individual. It comes into being as a result of the individual's interaction with the world. He describes *habitus* as "systems of durable, transposable dispositions, structured structures predisposed to function as structuring structures."[23] Bourdieu's notion of *habitus* suggests that an individual's subjectivity comes into being as a result of his/her embodiment. For Bourdieu, the embodied existence of an individual is a form of incorporation that acts as a constraint on his/her subjectivity. The individual's body and physical environment has everything to do with the way in which that individual thinks about him or herself, and

---

[21] D. Stern, "The Return of the Subject? Power, Reflexivity and Agency," *Philosophy and Social Criticism*, 2 (2000), 109–122.

[22] Pierre Bourdieu, *The Logic of Practice* (Cambridge: Harvard University Press, 1990).

[23] Pierre Bourdieu, *Outline of a Theory of Practice* (Cambridge University Press, 1977).

the way in which he or she makes sense of the world.[24] It entails the principle of a selective perception that tends to conform to, and reinforce, existing frames of reference, rather than transform them. Bourdieu's notion of *habitus* suggests that the moral sensibilities of individual employees may be strongly shaped by the tacit parameters of unarticulated expectations within their work environment. As they interact with colleagues and clients at work, employees are gradually, and more or less unconsciously, inculcated with a set of tacit expectations until they develop a strong sense of how things are supposed to be done. The notion of *habitus* also suggests that, once an individual has gone through this process of inculcation, new evidence and events, as well as other sources of additional feedback, tend to be interpreted in a way that strengthens, rather than challenges, his/her existing sense of propriety.

Bourdieu situates the inclinations and dispositions of *habitus* within the dynamics of broader forces and parameters. He uses the word *field* to describe the relational space within which *habitus* functions.[25] Bourdieu's *field* can be defined as the totality of relevant actors or institutions that, in aggregate, constitute a recognized area of institutional life. Within the *field* of business, this may include actors such as key suppliers, resource and product consumers, regulatory agencies and even organizations that produce similar products.[26]

Fields are defined not *a priori* but empirically. They are networks of relations that are always in flux. Bourdieu's understanding of *fields* bears some resemblance to the way in which some theorists have recently begun to think about stakeholders. Phillips, Freeman, and Wicks suggest that stakeholders should be defined on a contingent basis in the spirit of pragmatic experimentalism.[27] One of the possible implications of these ideas is that the tacit sense of moral propriety that develops within an organization may be affected by the dynamic relationships and sporadic interactions of its agents with external

[24] T. M. S. Evens, "Bourdieu and the Logic of Practice," *Sociological Theory*, 17 (1999), 11.

[25] C. Lemert, "Bourdieu on American Imperialism," *Theory, Culture and Society*, 17(2000), 101.

[26] L. Oakes, B. Townley and C. Cooper, "Business Planning as Pedagogy: Language and Control in a Changing Institutional Field," *Administrative Science Quarterly*, 43 (1988), 257–292.

[27] R. Phillips, R. E. Freeman and A. C. Wicks, "What Stakeholder Theory is Not," *Business Ethics Quarterly*, 13 (2003), 479–502.

actors and institutions in an expanded network of cooperative and competitive relationships. Individual employees' moral sensibilities may therefore be shaped and informed, not only by tacit expectations that develop among colleagues within an organization, but also by their experiences in, and perception of, contingent relationships with stakeholders and competitors "outside" of the organization's institutional parameters. Bourdieu's notion of the *field* not only adds an extra layer of complexity, but also introduces an additional element of fluidity to the tacit sense of propriety that informs individual behavior.

There are clear parallels between Judith Butler's idea of performative subjectivity and Pierre Bourdieu's notion of *habitus*. Both draw on J. L. Austin's concept of *performativity*.[28] The basic idea inscribed in the notion of *performativity* is that speech acts can effect what is asserted, merely through being uttered.[29] This means that what we say and how we operate throughout our various interactions and assertions, creates certain parameters that shape our reality. Butler concedes that *habitus* is generative rather than determined, in that it suggests potential meaning, yet does not govern it completely. This is important, since it allows one to acknowledge the hold of institutional norms through practice, without compromising the ability of the subject to act as an agent. She also agrees with Bourdieu that the reproduction of social norms is habitual and largely unreflective. Furthermore, both Butler and Bourdieu are opposed to an entirely deterministic orientation and the loss of agency that such a position would imply. However, Butler does charge Bourdieu with narrowing the scope for individual agency. Butler argues that Bourdieu's notion of the *field* reduces the power of words to the power of social institutions. She insists that, in order to sustain the possibility of agency, agents must remain capable of resisting the influence of institutions. She argues that such resistance becomes possible as a result of multi-layered subjectivity. In this respect, the fractured nature of the language we use opens the possibility that we can assign meaning in many different ways, and that we are not necessarily restricted to one set of determined responses. Furthermore, the fact that we are often only tacitly aware of all the things we know and respond to, that we are able to rely on our

---

[28] Performative subjectivity refers to the way in which the subject is formed in and through its interaction or "performances" in the world.

[29] T. Lovell, "Resisting with Authority: Historical Specificity, Agency and the Performative Self," *Theory, Culture and Society*, 20 (2003).

unconscious, is very important to the notion of a more intuitive account of agency.

Butler treads the tightrope between free will and determinism by explaining how the subject is neither fully determined by power nor in control of determining power. In fact, as subjects we are significantly and partially both. The fact that one can acknowledge that subjects are wielding power and are the objects of power at the same time, exceeds the logic of contradiction.[30] Butler's account of the internalization of norms turns the whole idea of "principled" reasoning on its head. If principles are produced and reinforced in the process of a subject's social interactions and practices within institutions, they already exist as those aspects that constitute the decision maker's subjectivity as such. It is therefore nonsensical to think of norms as general principles that are to be "applied" to specific cases. The common practice of teaching employees how to apply the general principles that are inscribed in their organization's code of conduct to specific situations through the use of case study exercises may therefore not be the best way to empower them as moral agents. Moral agency defies this *explicatio–applicatio* logic. Employees cannot find abstract principles in the hypothetical realm of a case analysis. They are more likely to find it embodied within themselves whilst in the thick of things.

Butler's theory of subjection is informative as far as the interaction between subjects and institutions is concerned.[31] She developed this hypothesis as an explanation of the process through which individuals become subjects. Human beings, as subjects, need to have their presence acknowledged by others, develop reputations, and survive within a specific context. According to Butler, regulatory power uses the fact that human beings have these needs, and keeps subjects in subordination by playing up to these needs. However, what you see is not exactly what you get. She argues that though the subject is produced as continuous and visibly located within a specific space, he/she remains haunted by aspects that cannot be fully assimilated within this presence. This "inassimilable remainder" refers to those aspects of agency that open the possibility for unique, imaginative and intuitive responses. The subject always retains an aspect of iterability, in other words, the ability to construe meaning differently, or to open new opportunities for understanding. Its agency lies in its ability to oppose

---

[30] Butler, *The Psychic Life of Power*, p. 17.   [31] *Ibid.*, p. 11.

and transform the social terms by which it was spawned. What Butler clearly wants do with this account of subjectivity is to retain the possibility of some sort of agency for the subject, despite the way in which subjectivity is unconsciously constructed.

Merleau-Ponty was also interested in exploring the relationship between those aspects of subjectivity that seem to be socially determined and the ability of the individual to be creative. He describes the world as "universal flesh," a network of relations within which everything is intertwined or interlaced. The "texture" produced by the "universal flesh" is not completely contingent or chaotic, but gives structure to reality. At the same time, however, it allows the interplay of differences. The embodied consciousness of the individual moral agent receives information from the world yet simultaneously organizes it, which means that everything he/she knows or understands is natural, yet also at the same time created, articulated and socially framed.[32] The fact that much of our moral orientation is structured and informed tacitly does not eliminate the importance of our own responsiveness to, and utilization of our creative sense-making capacities.

From a business ethicist's perspective, it is clearly crucial to reconcile the idea that material or social pressures predispose individuals towards particular kinds of behavior with the notion of free will.[33] On the one hand, the notion of free will makes it possible to hold individuals accountable for their actions. On the other hand, it is only really possible to hold an organization accountable for the actions of its individual employees if one acknowledges that social pressures and expectations in his/her work environment significantly influence an individual's behavior. It is possible to reconcile the two, though, especially when one considers how an individual's sense of moral propriety comes into existence. The individual's moral sensibility is shaped and informed, not only by the tacit expectations that he/she perceives and internalizes in the course of their interaction with others at work, but also by perceptions and dispositions that relate to the contingent life-experiences of the individual. The fact that individual variables co-contribute to the formation of an employee's moral

---

[32] Douglas Low, "Merleau-Ponty on Truth, Language, and Value," *Philosophy Today*, 45 (2001), 69–76.

[33] For more detail on the free will, determinism and compatibalism options see Harry Frankfurt, "Freedom of the Will and the Concept of the Person," *Journal of Philosophy* (1971).

sensibilities does not mean that each individual's perspective is totally subjective. Although embodied truth is not objective truth, the individual's embodiment and other structural and social influences prevent his/her moral sensibilities from being purely subjective or arbitrary. This means, for instance, that an organization can "signal" appropriate behavior through the way in which constraints are set up and through the positive and negative feedback that is given to employees.

It is important to recognize, however, that because a subject's sense of self is so intimately bound up with the tacit, unarticulatable norms that exist in the organizational environment, it is often very difficult for individuals to express dissent. The subjectivity of agents is continually constituted through the social interactions and performative utterances in which they take part. An individual can therefore only really develop a position that differs from the norm in, and through, this process. To change tacit knowledge, new tacit references, or clues, need to be integrated into an individual's sense of self. One has to engage with what Butler calls the "historically sedimented linguistic intentions" that allow for certain performative utterances. Within organizations, this can be described as the way in which organizational practices open up certain possibilities and eliminate certain others. This takes place on a tacit, not explicit level. In a very real sense, what is required is a careful hermeneutic exercise that plots the relationships between the way individuals view themselves within the organization and the value priorities of the organization as they are reflected in its everyday business practice.

The question then remains: if an individual's behavior is significantly influenced, but never entirely determined, by the tacit pressures and expectations that he/she is exposed to in an organizational environment, how is one to think about enhancing moral decision making? To address this question, it is necessary to consider how linguistic practices, historic events, rituals, and personalities contribute to the tacit understanding that develops among colleagues in an organizational context.

Knowing, thinking, deciding in organizational settings

It is interesting to note that the kinds of considerations that I have been discussing here did not impact management or organizational behavior literature until the late 1990s. For most of the twentieth century, business practitioners and executives, within what may be thought of as the "modern" management tradition, implicitly, if not overtly, continued to think of knowledge as something that is gained through deliberate rational analysis and design. This is partially attributable to Taylor's introduction of a scientific paradigm in modern management theory and practice.[34] When Frederick Taylor started to use precise data-gathering techniques to study behavior in the workplace, management began to be perceived as more of a science than an art. Modern management theorists believed that the application of rational analysis and deterministic models could provide optimum solutions to any management problem. Theorists and practitioners consciously or unconsciously expected business life to function according to orderly rules and predictable patterns, in the same way that something like a machines does. As Mark Taylor points out, this mechanistic understanding of how the world functions was based on Newtonian physics.[35] Newton described the physical universe, as well as society and culture, in terms of intrinsically stable, self-enclosed systems. Within such systems, universal laws ostensibly allowed the objective observer to reliably describe and accurately predict strict cause-and-effect relationships between particular actions and events. From this mechanistic perspective, it was possible, and indeed necessary, to distinguish between objective fact and biased opinion, between public commitments and private allegiances, and between "right" and "wrong," when various possible courses of action were weighed up against one another. However, it soon became evident that this understanding of organizational dynamics does not furnish managers with the kind of knowledge they need to be successful within the twenty-first-century business environment.

The paradigm shift between modern management theory and postmodern management theory was precipitated by the combined impact of new information technologies and globalization, which confronted the scientific management paradigm with challenges that it wasn't prepared for. The volume, velocity and turbulence of the new business environment does not afford managers the opportunity for

[34] Catherine K. Kikoski and John F. Kikoski, *The Inquiring Organization. Tacit Knowledge, Conversation, and Knowledge Creation: Skills for 21st Century Organizations* (Westport: Praeger, 2004), p. 24.

[35] Mark Taylor, *The Moment of Complexity: Emerging Network Culture* (University of Chicago Press, 2001).

scientific analysis, and where such analysis is employed, it is usually of little practical use. GE's Jack Welch, for instance, claims that he can no longer run his company in the way that someone like Henry Ford did. Ford's production line logic called for managers to analyze the work that needed to be done and "then devise rules that even an idiot could follow." Knowledge management scholars argue that the modern manager's "book of standardized practices" comes up short in the disruptive, nonlinear information era of "batch production," "multiple options" and "niche" markets.[36] Since standardized procedural approaches cannot deal with fast-paced change and are not really conducive to innovation, they have actually became more of a liability than an asset.

The inability of mechanistic management models to accommodate the dynamics of contemporary business has led to the exploration of alternative explanatory models. Complexity theorists, for instance, have begun to challenge some of the basic assumptions of the scientific paradigm on which modern management theory was based. Scientists have long assumed that phenomena could only be meaningfully described in terms of stable systems of elements governed by predictable cause-and-effect relationships. However, many complexity theorists now claim that the organization of individual and collective human life can be described more appropriately in terms of the dynamics of so-called "complex adaptive systems." Other authors use the name "nonlinear dynamical systems" to refer to such organizations.[37]

"Complex adaptive systems" are open and dynamic. They continually adapt to new developments. Despite the dynamic nature of such systems, a kind of "orderliness" can emerge among the elements that participate in it. However, this "orderliness" does not allow one to describe the system as a whole in terms of the aggregate of cause-and-effect relationships among its elements. Parts within the whole connect in multiple ways, with components interacting both serially and in parallel. Because of this, the actions of elements within the system cannot be connected with their eventual effect in a linear way. The action of an agent may combine with that of other elements within the system to produce an effect to which both had contributed,

---

[36] Kikoski and Kikoski, *The Inquiring Organization*, p. 28.
[37] S. Guastello, *Managing Emergent Phenomena: Nonlinear Dynamics in Work Organizations* (London: Lawrence Erlbaum Associates, 2002).

but which neither could have fully anticipated.[38] This makes it very difficult indeed to predict the effect that the actions of any particular element will have on other elements, or on the system as a whole. There is nothing about the structure or dynamics of such systems that compels its elements to function in predictable ways or to restore patterns that had previously emerged. In other words, there is no necessary, permanent state of equilibrium in the system as a whole to which its elements are continually compelled or encouraged to return.[39]

Organizations have a number of characteristics in common with other "open systems." They are open dynamic systems in the sense that patterns of interaction with the environment are constantly changing; secondly, they are complex systems in which the interactions of groups of agonists have unpredictable outcomes in terms of system effects; and thirdly, organizations as complex adaptive systems are emergent and self-organizing, despite the apparently chaotic pattern of interaction. From the perspective of this more complex explanatory model, the conventions and expectations that organize and guide business behavior come into being and develop on a contingent basis as colleagues, clients and competitors interact with one another and do business. In a sense, the ethos of business life is something that continually develops among people, as they do business, in order to continue to do business. The "orderliness" of business life is a reflection of the fluid logic of business as a system of dynamic functional relationships.

One of the advantages of this more "organic" understanding of business is that it looks for signs of functional organization within the dynamics of business activity itself, instead of trying to force it to conform to some preconceived operational model. It also offers an intriguing model for describing the relationship between the tacit understanding among colleagues in an organization and the unconscious dynamics that are part of an individual's own sense of self. From the perspective of complex adaptive explanatory models, there is a nonlinear relationship between individual employees' own unique sense of moral propriety and the tacit expectations that exist between

---

[38] See in this regard the special issue on Leadership in Complex Adaptive Systems in *The Leadership Quarterly*, 18(4), (2007). In each of the contributions to this issue, the characteristics of organizations that function as complex adaptive systems are explored.

[39] Paul Cilliers, *Complexity and Postmodernism: Understanding Complex Systems* (London: Routledge, 1998).

him/her and his/her colleagues at work. This means that each affects, and is affected by the other. The same is true of the moral sensibilities of individual employees. Colleagues may reciprocally influence one another's moral sensibilities in unexpected ways. The perceived expectations of one colleague might, for instance, combine with the observed inclinations of another to produce an unconscious disposition in a third, which no one could have foreseen. As such, the relationships of influence in a contemporary business organization defy the deterministic logic of mechanistic modern management models. These models are only meaningful and helpful as long as the relationships between agents in an organization conform to a linear, cause-and-effect chain of causality. From the perspective of complex adaptive explanatory models, however, relationships of influence within the organizational system are complex, unpredictable and reciprocal. In this respect they correspond with the ideas of theorists such as Bourdieu, Butler and Merleau-Ponty, who all described the relationship of influence between an individual and his/her social milieu as something that is reciprocal, uneven and dynamic.

Because of the complexity and singularity of the relationships and dynamics that are involved, it is simply not always possible to articulate, in a conventional manner, the tacit understanding that a business organization's employees and agents have of the way in which things work, and are supposed to work. The nature of this kind of tacit organizational knowledge makes it impossible to codify or quantity it like other, more "explicit" forms of knowledge. Tacit knowledge differs from explicit knowledge both in terms of its source and content. Explicit knowledge allows agents to point to something concrete and demonstrable and assert that they know "that." Such knowledge can be articulated, motivated, contested and debated. Tacit knowledge, on the other hand, is not something that an agent can put his/her finger on. The possession of tacit knowledge allows an agent only the more modest claim that they know "how."[40] It is an embodied form of knowing, an understanding that is only revealed when it is used to make a decision or perform a task. Authors in the field of knowledge management recognize that agents are often not aware of much of the tacit knowledge that they rely on to make moral judgments. Tacit knowledge is the kind of intuitive grasp of something

---

[40] Kikoski and Kikoski, *The Inquiring Organization*, p. 65.

that is hard to verbalize. It is intuitive and experiential because it often involves deep-seated mental impressions of emotional and physical experiences. Because of its intuitive and experiential nature, tacit knowledge is very difficult to analyze and even more difficult to "manage."

Tacit knowledge is the "unwritten rules," which everyone in an organization knows, yet no one ever openly discusses. It is what people are referring to when they vaguely talk about "the way we do things around here." Philippe Baumard ascribes the development of tacit knowledge to the irrational, ceremonial and maneuvering nature of organizational life. Employees and agents gain their understanding of the dynamics of the organization in an informal and non-systematic way. He describes organizations as fast, fragmented and multidimensional operational fields with their own ceremonial conformity. Individual agents "know" what is appropriate because of the complex interaction of a company's history, its past successes and failures, its archives, its internal mail, its customs and its rumors.[41] It is this tacit understanding that is of crucial importance in understanding how an organizational culture or ethos can influence individual ethical decision making.

As we have seen, the lines of influence between an organization's culture and its employees' moral sensibilities are not one-directional. They involve a multidirectional flow of verbal, visceral and mental signals about what is valued and expected by the organization's employees and agents. Employees on all levels contribute to the tacit understanding that emerges among them. Because this understanding emerges in the course of multiple interactions between employees, under various different sorts of circumstances, no one individual can control it. To be sure, certain individuals, like senior executives and charismatic leaders, may play a more prominent role than others. However, it is extremely difficult for a single individual to "step out" of the web of unarticulated expectations, obligations and pressures that make an organizational culture what it is, in order to change or challenge it. Even if it were possible for an individual to do so, through some reflexive act of critical self-awareness, his/her agitations would simply be taken up in the multidirectional flow of tacit interpersonal signals within the organization, where they would combine with other, unarticulated expectations

---

[41] Philippe Baumard, *Tacit Knowledge in Organizations* (London: Sage, 2004), p. 12.

to produce any number of unforeseeable effects on the behavior of employees.

In order to illustrate the role that tacit organizational expectations and pressures play in the decisions that individual employees make, I would like to revisit two well-known cases that have become common points of reference in business ethics discourses. The one involves the circumstances around the Challenger disaster and the other has to do with design problems that the Ford motor company experienced with one of its cars, the Pinto. Pat Werhane has analyzed both cases in depth in her discussion of moral imagination and the power of narrative.[42] Werhane came to the conclusion that an individual decision-making agent's "conceptual schemes" play a very important role in how he/she thinks about a particular moral dilemma. The problem that Werhane points out, is that most people retrospectively study these cases through the prism of their own moral commitments. When they do this, they usually find it hard to comprehend how the individuals involved could have justified their decisions. From the perspective of the reader, their behavior appears simply willfully immoral. What is often not adequately considered by readers in this process, however, is that their own moral commitments may not be the same as those within the tacit frame of reference that informed the behavior of the actors in these cases. She points out that the professional backgrounds and focused expertise of the decision makers in the Challenger case influenced their perception of the situation that confronted them. In the Challenger case, for instance, the notion of "acceptable risk" was normalized to such an extent within NASA's organizational discourses that it began to inform all of its employees' decisions.

Werhane presents a similar analysis of the Pinto case.[43] She carefully considers the explanation that Gioia, Ford's recall coordinator, provided for the company's decision not to recall the Pinto, despite indications that its design made it unsafe in certain kinds of collisions. Gioia explained that, even though he knew that there were moral grounds for a recall, he could not warrant it on practical grounds. He argued that, given the reasonable risk that all drivers of cars take, the Ford Pinto was comparably only slightly less safe than other cars in the market. Furthermore, they were unable to pinpoint the relevant

---

[42] Werhane, *Moral Imagination*, p. 55.   [43] *Ibid.*, p. 56.

design flaw, which meant that, strictly speaking, Ford could not have been held liable. Looking back on the situation years later, Gioia attributes the fact that he overlooked the ethical overtones of the Pinto situation to his exposure to Ford's schematized (scripted) knowledge. He claims that it was only in retrospect that he was able to recognize the power of the scripts that were operative in his belief system while he was working at Ford. Gioia's explanation seems to support Werhane's argument about the limits that conceptual schemes can impose on individuals' understanding of moral dilemmas. After studying various accounts of the case, Werhane also concludes that it is possible to make sense of any case in multiple ways.

Though Werhane recognizes the role that an organization's "conceptual schemes" play in the choices of its individual agents, she insists that it is possible for an individual to "step back" from such a limited frame of reference and "reframe" moral problems from other perspectives. Alasdair MacIntyre, in his recent work, seems to argue for a similar form of self-critical reflection. He argues that morality is impossible without the tensions and conflicts between a social order and an individual. For McIntyre the individual is always able to maintain some sort of critical distance from any particular social order because of his/her simultaneous participation in others. One social order provides the individual with critical perspectives on another. Because of the crucial role that "critical distance" plays in McIntyre's conception of morality, he formulates a new moral maxim: *Always ask about your own social and cultural order what it needs you and others not to know.*[44]

Werhane's and MacIntyre's insistence that a position of critical self–reflectivity is always available to an agent suggests that they may not adequately appreciate the extent to which an individual employee's own sense of morality is related to and influenced by the tacit understanding of propriety that informs organizational protocols. When an individual participates in an organizational system, he/she is part of a complex circuit of reciprocal influence, which runs in and out of the individual's moral sensibilities along multiple channels. Although the dispositions and expectations that an individual senses in the actions and attitudes of his/her colleagues are not left unaffected

---

[44] Alasdair MacIntyre, "Social Structures and their Threats to Moral Agency," *Philosophy*, 74 (1999), 311–329.

by their passage through the individual's own network of embodied experiences, these lines of influence cannot be disconnected either, as long as such an individual continues to participate in the organizational system. Despite the significant extent to which an individual's perception of a situation may be infused by the intuitive impressions that he/she continually receives from the organization's system of relations, he/she remains largely unaware of its influence. The individual simply sees the situation as he/she does, without ever really being aware of *how* he/she is looking at it.

To the extent that an organization's "conceptual schemes" operate on the level of "explicit knowledge," it might be conceivable that the individual could gain some critical perspective on it, either through an act of imaginative self-reflexivity, as Werhane suggests, or because of the dissonance that an individual's participation in multiple social orders creates, as McIntyre proposes. However, the lines of influence that connect an individual's moral sensibilities with those of his/her colleagues are largely of a tacit nature. It is hard to see then how an individual can distance him/herself from something in which he/she is unaware of participating. Bourdieu's notion of *habitus* suggests furthermore that new data is often merely integrated into the agent's existing frame of reference. Since individuals are largely unaware of the tacit frame of reference that informs their perspective, it is even more unlikely that it would be challenged or disrupted by their exposure to a new situation or problem.

It is more likely that the terms of an individual's critical reflection about a situation are suggested to him/her by the tacit, unarticulated understanding that he/she shares with his/her colleagues. These terms intuitively lead the individual's assessment of a situation down certain paths, routes that have unconsciously been cleared and paved over time through many different interactions with colleagues.

In the Ford Pinto case, for instance, the critical questions that seem to have framed Gioia's and his team's assessment of the situation were largely based on the unarticulated sense of priorities that informed the Ford organization's ethos at the time. Gioia and his colleagues asked themselves questions like: Is recalling the cars practical? Is the cost justified in terms of how much safer it would make the cars? Does the burden of proof for a design flaw make us legally liable? Is the safety risk much larger than that of other comparable cars in the market? Does safety sell (are customers willing to pay a premium for safety)?

In the 1960s, the answer to all these questions was "No." Tacitly, the "right thing to do" at Ford at that point in time was to be practical, prudent, law-abiding and competitive. These are the terms in which conversations were conducted, praise or blame appropriated, loyalty displayed, and characters forged. Gioia was only really able to reflect about this situation in different terms once he no longer participated in the Ford organization's system of relations. Years later, teaching ethics as a professor, he finally gained the critical distance necessary to "reframe" the Pinto case from the perspective of another kind of social order.[45]

The NASA organization's organizational ethos had a similar effect on the terms in which critical questions were raised in the Challenger case. NASA employees asked themselves questions like: Is this an "acceptable risk" by engineering standards? What are the odds of us failing this time around? In his analysis of the case, Baumard describes the "normalizing" function that tacit knowledge had on the way in which NASA employees thought about the Challenger's mission.[46] The notion of "acceptable risk" was socially constructed within the NASA environment over time through various interactions and in various ways. This notion, combined with the belief among NASA employees that "they could do anything," led them to interpret the situation around the Challenger mission in the way that they did. NASA employees unconsciously subscribed to these beliefs to such an extent that it never even occurred to them to ask a critical question such as: Is it acceptable to risk these astronauts' lives? Instead, NASA employees framed the situation within the broader context of the risk of space travel in general and the long-established reputation for success of NASA's engineers.

There is, of course, another well-known case that has become something of a common point of reference for business ethicists, and on which the present discussion might be brought to bear: the collapse of the Enron corporation. In the past few years, academic analyses, biographies and documentaries have tried to unravel the tacit expectations, pressures and assumptions that were part of Enron's organizational

---

[45] See the recently published video by Penn State of Gioia teaching the Ford Pinto case in class, Dennis A. Gioia, "Pinto Fires and Personal Ethics: a Script Analysis of Missed Opportunities," *Journal of Business Ethics*, 11 (1992), 379–389.
[46] Baumard, *Tacit Knowledge*, p. 41.

culture. The numerous accounts of the company's rise and fall are proof not only of the extent to which Enron shocked the corporate world and the public at large, but also of how the scandal continues to captivate business practitioners and ethicists worldwide. In his book *The Anatomy of Greed: the Unshredded Truth from an Enron Insider* Brian Cruver[47] draws attention to the fact that Enron's organizational culture contained a number of "unwritten rules" that dictated the terms in which success and respect could be earned by employees. Newcomers quickly learned the first, all-important principle of life at Enron, i.e. "perception is everything." In this sense, Enron exemplified the dematerialization of economic reality and the belief that "truth" is what people believe, no more, no less.

Mark Taylor describes this contemporary trend in his book *Confidence Games*.[48] He argues that business practitioners are rejecting representationalist accounts of the economy for a more relational understanding of its dynamics. Wealth creation is no longer understood as the orderly accumulation of capital through the scientific application of objective economic principles, but as something that takes place primarily within the context of a poker-like game of relationship building and reputation management. Within this environment, the tacit assumption that "perception is everything" influences moral agency in unprecedented ways. Instead of compelling moral agents to ask: Is this the truth? it suggests that they ask themselves: Are we telling the story right?

Another important aspect of the tacit understanding that existed among Enron employees was a particular attitude towards rules. Enron executives boasted that with Republicans in the White House, deregulation is the law of the land. For them, this meant that: "there's only one rule and that's that there are no rules." In a documentary film entitled *The Smartest Guys in the Room*, the Enron motto "Ask WHY?" features prominently in former employees' recollections of life at the organization. It is an ironic reminder of how tacit organizational assumptions and attitudes can inform the way in which one employee interprets directives and instructions. In an ethics class a teacher might encourage her students to embrace a motto such as

---

[47] Brian Cruver, *The Anatomy of Greed: the Unshredded Truth from an Enron Insider* (New York: Carroll & Graf, 2002).
[48] Mark C. Taylor, *Confidence Games: Money and Markets in a World Without Redemption* (Chicago University Press, 2004).

"Ask WHY?" in order to facilitate reflection on the purpose and meaning of life or the goals of business. The motto "Ask WHY?" could also be employed as a means of encouraging people to enquire about the moral justification for certain laws or rules. The way in which it was employed at Enron, however, gave it a quite different sort of meaning. Within the Enron environment, it was used to motivate employees to find creative ways of circumventing industry regulations and rules. As such, it became a motto of transgression. "Ask WHY?" was an expression of that which was most valued and rewarded within Enron: the ability to think "creatively" in the pursuit of profit. At Enron, there was no rule that couldn't be reinterpreted to the point of meaninglessness and there was a tacit belief that, in order to be successful, an employee had to ask him/herself why particular rules had to be limiting or binding. At Enron, "Ask WHY?" functioned as a rhetorical question to which the implicit answer usually was: "Why (the hell) not?"

It is interesting to note in this regard that Judith Butler sees the idea of transgression as a very important element of subjection. From this perspective the subject is constituted in and through the existence of norms or rules that can be transgressed.[49] The possibility of crossing a line allows certain individuals to have a certain sense of self. The fact that there are rules to transgress may institutionalize the possibility of rejection, and rejection reanimates certain aspects of that particular individual's identity. In the process, it makes the desire for misconduct or transgression even more present. One can hypothesize that in a very real sense, the Enron executives' sense of self may have been sustained by the very possibility of transgression. It may bring us to consider why "the thrill of the chase" and the excitement of gambling, or risk taking is so appealing to so many of us. Some may find this kind of explanation slightly too risqué, but it may lure us into exploring the Enron culture a little further.

The documentary film *The Smartest Guys in the Room* also touched on another aspect of life at Enron: the development of a very macho organizational culture. Many of the top executives were nerds in their youth and took great pride in the way they had managed to reinvent themselves on their way to the top. Because of the latent need of so many top managers to affirm their masculinity, many of the

[49] Butler, *The Psychic Life of Power*, p. 61.

teambuilding events at Enron revolved around dangerous sporting events. At such events risk taking was encouraged while employees were socialized in an attitude of invincibility and narcissist pride. What this illustrates is the impact of the interaction between the unconscious dynamics of individuals within organizations and the tacit knowledge of that organization. Together, individual and collective tacit knowledge form an intricate web of clues that employees pick up on and that get reinforced through various interactions.

It is easy to misconstrue the practical implications of a more complex understanding of the relationship between an individual employee's moral sensibilities and a company's organizational culture. This certainly is not a business text that pleads for a re-institutionalization of morals in corporate life and for a list of normative questions that the self-reflexive decision maker should employ before making up his/her mind on a moral dilemma. Neither am I making a case for determinism. This book does not offer itself up as a defense for the ostensibly "helpless victims" of evil corporate cultures. It is the interaction between the individual's sense of self and the various dynamics of meaning creation within a corporation that provides us with a perspective that helps us to steer clear of these two extremes.

The question that this chapter set out to address is whether it is in fact the case that corporations influence ethical decision making. This may have been too simplistic a question, but perhaps it was the only one available to us at the outset. Our perspective on the interaction between individuals' embodied moral sense-making and the development of tacit knowledge in organizations may now enable us to rephrase this question in more appropriate terms. The question is not whether or how corporations can influence individual behavior. Instead, we may try to unravel the relationship between individuals and their corporate settings and seek to understand the development and reinforcement of certain tacit beliefs. It entails the careful consideration of these dynamics as they unfold. Once one has a rough map of the various dynamics, interventions may become possible. These interventions will, however, never be solely detached reflexive analyses, but the creation of alternative insights through participatory practices.

The complex network through which intuitive impressions and tacit expectations are constantly being circulated in an organization is not open to control or manipulation by any one corporate officer or group of executives. Because everybody who participates in an organizational system gives shape to its employees' shared sense of propriety by what they say and how they act at work every day, it is simply not possible to intervene in the organization's complex circuits of influence, unless it is through some sort of participatory practice. Once one gains some understanding of what is involved in these exchanges, however, it becomes possible to participate in the dynamics that shape and inform employees' tacit sense of propriety.

For Baumard, doing research on tacit knowledge is "investigating the non-expressed." It involves taking various routes through both invisible and visible manifestations of knowledge. One way of making the tacit visible is to engage decision makers in what Baumard calls "reflexive practice." This involves a process by which a person is encouraged to consciously make sense of his or her own practices, either while the action is taking place or afterwards. Baumard is, however, quick to point out that one cannot always rely on what managers say about their own practices. Often, they really don't know what they tacitly know, or they are just unable to articulate it. In these cases they tend to invent an explanation for their actions.[50] Another way of accessing tacit knowledge in organizations is to tap into certain repositories of knowledge circulation, which stem from communities of practice that bring certain mythologies to bear on others. They have their own language, distinct symbolic universes, and often employ conjectural knowledge to make sense of a situation, all of which confirms the multiple constructed realities within organizations. Often, these hidden repositories of tacit knowledge become visible in people's reaction to the introduction of a new structure, policy, or an event like a merger. To tap into an organization's tacit knowledge, one needs to be sensitive to its visible manifestations. These visible manifestations provide clues about the tacit beliefs on which they are based.

What does this tell us about the way in which moral agency is exercised in organizations? In the first place, it makes us aware of how difficult it is to know exactly what informs moral decision making in an organizational context. Tacit organizational expectations and assumptions are developed through experience. They are intuitive and are only revealed when, and inasmuch as, they inform specific practices. As such, tacit knowledge resists articulation. This makes it very

---

[50] Baumard, *Tacit Knowledge*, p. 102.

difficult to alter deliberately. Baumard points out that tacit repositories of knowledge are more resistant to change than behaviors, attitudes and codified knowledge.[51] The more collective these repositories, the stronger the resistance to their modification. This is something that Bourdieu also observed. For him, *habitus* is extremely resilient in nature. There is a great deal of self-designing going on in organizations based on the tacit understanding that is shared by employees. This is another reason why it is so difficult to change the behavior of employees through deliberate interventions like the introduction of codes, rules, procedures and new organizational structures. In fact, some of these interventions may elicit unpredictable and even counterproductive responses, because of the way in which they are filtered through tacit organizational attitudes and assumptions in the minds of individual employees. Perhaps it is for reasons like these that apparently well-designed ethics management programs do not always succeed in changing the behavior of an organization's employees.

However, just being aware of how tacit knowledge develops and is circulated among employees within an organizational environment may not be enough when one is concerned with the issue of moral agency. Naturally, any business organization has a stake in ensuring that the tacit knowledge that develops among its employees provides them with a sound normative framework. The question that remains, however, is whether it is in fact possible to guarantee this. If tacit organizational knowledge is something that emerges in an unforeseeable way, in the course of many interactions between multiple agents, and if its content is indeed hard to articulate and manage, how can an organization be held accountable for "promoting a culture of ethics compliance" as the Federal Sentencing Guidelines requires it to do? If an organization or its agents cannot determine the normative content of the tacit knowledge that is circulated among employees, how can they be held responsible for it? From the perspective of business organizations it is therefore very important to determine whether it is at all possible to define and promote certain points of normative orientation within a complex adaptive system. It is to these kinds of questions that we turn next.

[51] *Ibid.*, pp. 134–137.

4 | Reconsidering values

My analysis of moral agency in Chapter 3 has direct implications for understanding not only the process of *how* a particular normative orientation comes into being, but also *what* comes to be regarded as moral truth. It precipitates a radical reassessment of how we make statements about "right and wrong." In this chapter I focus on a concept that is central to the idea of moral truth within an organizational context, namely values. In my analysis, I will challenge some of the conventional ways in which business ethicists and practitioners tend to think about and treat values.

In the case of the Federal Sentencing Guidelines' directives on what constitutes a proper ethics management program, organizations are instructed to formalize their ethics and compliance standards and procedures. As Chapter 1 indicated, there has been a lot of discussion about whether formalized codes really make a difference to employees' ethical behavior. Many are skeptical and argue that these documents often amount to little more than a decorative plaque on the wall or a reputation-enhancing marketing device.

A further interrogation of the validity of these charges is not the main purpose of my analysis. Instead, I would like to take a closer look at some of the unarticulated assumptions that often underlie the use of codes in ethics management programs and initiatives. In my experience, the practical value of codification is limited. I believe that this is partly due to a number of significant misconceptions regarding the nature of that which is supposedly reified in the language of codes. What values are, and how they work, is something that is rarely adequately considered and often misunderstood. I therefore start my analysis by revisiting and addressing some of the misconceptions that exist around this important subject.

Common misconceptions

It is not uncommon to encounter skepticism and resistance towards the whole notion of ethics training among executives, MBAs and undergraduates. The argument is typically made that the goals of business and ethics are fundamentally incompatible. If this is the case, then of course the entire business ethics enterprise, whether in the form of an academic discipline, university course, or indeed an executive workshop is hopelessly oxymoronic and ultimately futile. Although more often than not politely raised and, for propriety's sake, dressed up in the garb of a humorous comment, the sheer consistency with which comments of this nature are offered attests to the power and pervasiveness of these views. This is not something that is lost on business ethicists. In fact, it is something that is taken very seriously and many a defense has been mounted to convince business practitioners of the importance of ethics in business. Some of these defenses are constructed around the contention that good ethics is good business.[1] Others have argued that ethics programs effectively serve to limit companies' exposure to legal liabilities and all their associated costs. However, in all this adroit rhetorical maneuvering a much more fundamental question remains largely unexplored. Could it be that the heart of the problem lies in the way in which "business" and "ethics" is defined? The belief that business ethics is oxymoronic is itself based on a number of assumptions about the nature of both business and ethics.[2] It is these assumptions that I would like to explore, not only to argue that business ethics is not oxymoronic, but to elucidate the value-ladenness of business itself. If, as I will argue, both "business" and "ethics" are concerned with values, then they may have far more in common than is often recognized.

The purported impasse between business and ethics is often sustained by the pervasive assumption that business is something that belongs exclusively to the arena of public affairs. This idea goes hand in hand

---

[1] For an assessment of the relationship between ethics and financial performance, see Lynn Sharpe Paine, "Does Ethics Pay?" *Business Ethics Quarterly*, 10 (2000), 319–330; Lynn Sharp Paine, *Why Companies Must Merge Social and Financial Imperatives to Achieve Superior Performance*, 1st edition (McGraw-Hill, 2003); Joshua D. Margolis and James P. Walsh. *People and Profits? The Search for a Link between a Company's Social and Financial Performance* (Mahwah, NJ: Lawrence Erlbaum Associates, 2001); Curtis Verschoor, "Corporate Performance is Closely Linked to a Strong Ethical Commitment," *Business and Society Review*, 104 (1999), 407–415. See also Curtis Verschoor, "Does Superior Governance Still Lead to Better Financial Performance?" *Strategic Finance*, 86 (2004), 13–14; and Curtis Verschoor, "Is There Financial Value in Corporate Values?" *Strategic Finance*, 87 (2005), 17–18.

[2] William C. Frederick, *Values, Nature, Culture and the American Corporation* (Oxford University Press, 1995), p. 243.

with the association of ethics with personal values or preferences, i.e. that messily opaque class of matter, which is properly and conveniently assigned to the strictly circumscribed domain of so-called "private" life. In this view, ethics is a theoretical discipline that concerns itself with *abstract principles*, whereas business is the *practice* of making money. Ethicists apply philosophical theories to practice, while business practitioners deduce their management theories from what works in practice.

One thing is clear: as long as these assumptions continue to hold sway in the way people think about business and ethics, some sort of uncomfortable compromise will always seem necessary to reconcile them. Those in the ethics field will continue to endure the pains of self-censorship as they struggle to transform their discipline into something less philosophical and more practical, something more capable of dealing with the perceived challenges of a hard-nosed "business world." For their part, business practitioners will continue to try to assuage their consciences and the law by clearing just a little more cerebral space for principled considerations amidst the general stampede for money. Though practitioners on both sides may make the occasional necessary "accommodation" on behalf of the other, the discomfort remains and is undeniable. The truth is that all trade-offs, including the kind of compromises that many believe necessary to accomplish the reconciliation of business and ethics, always represent something less than desirable. As long as these unfortunate misapprehensions persist, the reconciliation of business and ethics will remain an involuntary affair, instigated and sustained almost exclusively by political decree and legal sanction. Though there are those who seem to have reconciled themselves with this situation, I believe that the relationship between business and ethics should not be articulated in legal terms. In what follows, therefore, I will examine the work of a number of scholars whose research has some sort of bearing on the nature of this contentious relationship. Along the way, I will begin the process of constructing an alternative values-theory in terms of which the integration of business and ethics may be effected in a different kind of way.

I begin this section with the work of Martin Parker. Parker is known as someone who is skeptical about the viability of the whole business ethics enterprise.[3] He draws on the Lyotardian notion of the *agon*, or a wrestling match, to illustrate the impasse that separates business ethics

---

[3] Martin Parker, "Business Ethics and Social Theory: Postmodernizing the Ethical," *British Journal of Management* (1998), 27–36.

and business practitioners. The impasse is created by the incommensurability of the language games utilized by ethicists and business practitioners. Parker argues that ethical discourses can only be brought to bear on business practices if both are subjected to an unacceptable form of rationalization. More specifically, Parker objects to the reduction of both ethical discourses and business concerns to a common form of life in the course of this rationalization process. For instance, when business ethicists try to rationalize the adoption of ethics management practices in business organizations, their arguments often include an analysis of their potential financial and social benefits. Parker points out that by asking how much "ethics" costs or benefits a company, one accepts that all pleasures, pains, ends and means can accurately be converted into an easily exchangeable form of common social currency. Rational arguments of this kind implicitly suggest that all people value the same things, in the same way, and to the same degree. Such a comprehensive common denominator of value simply does not exist. Parker therefore warns that those who claim that ethics contributes to a better community, better citizenship and better responsibility, only facilitate the re-enchantment of an increasingly rationalized world. The irony then is that in trying to establish a shared sense of value, business ethicists may inadvertently be reinforcing the rationalization of business life. In the process, "Business Ethics" risks destroying the very possibility of problematizing conduct in organizations.

This view of business ethics is based on a certain conception of ethics, one that positions it as the adversary of business. The assumption is that business itself cannot accommodate the notion of struggle, challenge, criticism and dissent. I think that this is a very simplistic understanding of business. Another way to look at it would be to view ethics, and its critical relationship with the way in which business is pursued, as part of business as such. Most business organizations are embedded in complex relationships that are by no means harmonious. However, sustaining these relationships, agonistic as they may be, is an integral part of business life. My argument is that ethics can, and should, inform these relationships. If this is to happen, however, business ethicists will have to give up their preoccupation with identifying abstract principles and direct their efforts at informing, challenging and *advancing* business practices that speak of the normative orientation to which they are committed.[4]

---

[4] It is the advancement of business that Parker is unlikely to support, as he seems to think that ethics should only challenge and undermine business.

Bill Frederick's development of the concept of the "evolutionary firm" represents an important perspective on the relationship between business and ethics.[5] For Frederick, the key to this relationship lies in the way that values function within the so-called "evolutionary firm." The idea of the evolutionary firm is based on the theory of evolution and the assumption that economics and nature are but two sides of the same coin. In Frederick's theory, the dynamics of a business organization are determined by the interplay of forces among three distinct areas of value orientation, or "value clusters." The first of these is referred to as "economizing" values. These have to do with the need for growth and systemic integrity. The second value cluster that Frederick describes is associated with what he calls "power-aggrandizing values." This includes considerations of hierarchical (rank-order) organization, managerial decision-power, power–system equilibrium and power aggrandizement. For Frederick, the priorities and imperatives that he associates with these two value clusters are rooted in the nature of the physical world and in the operation of its natural laws. He sees them as archetypes that make business what it is. They are always present within business organizations and play a vital and indispensable role in the continuation of business life. But Frederick also includes a third value cluster in his model. The value considerations that he allocates to this cluster have to do with what he calls "ecologizing values." Included are priorities such as linkage, diversity, homeostatic succession and community. If economizing and power aggrandizing values together constitute the very core of business as enterprise in Frederick's conception, then ecologizing values are responsible for sustaining moral action in communities.

Frederick believes that the business-oriented priorities and imperatives that he associates with the economizing and power-aggrandizing value clusters are in tension with ecologizing value considerations. "[T]he moral traits, features and habits of the evolutionary firm," he writes, "are the product of contradictions embedded in diverse neural algorisms." For Frederick, then, ethical ideals are destined to remain in a state of perpetual tension with economizing forces within the firm. That conflicts, paradoxes and tensions exist within every business organization cannot be denied. The question is whether Frederick is

[5] William C. Frederick, *Values, Nature, Culture and the American Corporation* (Oxford University Press, 1995).

right in concluding that: "The evolutionary firm is not only its own worst enemy, but cannot avoid moral condemnation by others both inside and outside the firm." In my view this is an overly pessimistic view based on the assumption that ethics and business goals are fundamentally antithetical.

There is much to commend in Frederick's approach. Frederick has always been intent on making pragmatic sense of those paradoxes in the business world and has been quick to point out how pragmatism is employed even by those who remain loyal to Rawlsian justice principles.[6] In his development of the notion of the evolutionary firm, Frederick seems to draw primarily on evolution theory. However, Frederick's interests are not limited to evolutionary theory. Elsewhere in his oeuvre, he also explores the insights and implications of complexity theory.[7] From the perspective of complexity theory, it becomes possible to think of business organizations as open, complex adaptive systems. To my mind, Frederick does not adequately acknowledge the far-reaching implications of looking at business organizations from this perspective. If he had, he might have reached a significantly different conclusion with respect to the relationship between business priorities and ethical considerations within a business organization.

In my view, complexity theory reframes business activity in a way that renders the business versus ethics dualism void. It also sheds new

---

[6] Frederick shows how many business ethicists have to resort to pragmatism to explain how moral valuation within organizations takes place. See Frederick, *Values, Nature, Culture and the American Corporation*, p. 274.

[7] In his analysis of how the evolutionary firm (EF) makes choices, Frederick comes to the conclusion that the logic of evolutionary effect will consistently select *economizing* algorisms and that this remains the dominant motivating force behind the evolutionary firm's actions. He qualifies this position by recognizing that the moralizer/valuator function of the firm comes into play. He also acknowledges the fact that each individual represents a unique and diverse moral configuration that can be a rich source of independence, creativity and moral imagination. In addition, some creativity and imaginative intelligence is allowed for as part of the firm's innovator/generator and enabler/stabilizer functions. He further acknowledges that mutualisms abound in all systems, and that a firm's values can act as strange attractors that orientate the EF in an ever-shifting fitness landscape. Having said this, we are still led to the somewhat fatalistic conclusion that economizing considerations ultimately trump all others. For another account of Frederick's adoption of certain aspects of complexity theory, see William C. Frederick, "Creatures, Corporations, Communities, Chaos, Complexity," *Business and Society*, 37 (1998), 358–389.

light on how decisions are made and the way in which a sense of normative orientation comes into being within a complex adaptive organizational system. From the perspective that complexity theory affords us, we may develop an understanding of how decision makers operate in an ever-evolving, self-organizing complex system. Far from denying the existence of contradictory or paradoxical impulses within a business organization, a model based on the proposals of complexity theory acknowledges that different forms of normative orientation are at play within all of the system's complex dynamics. It makes it impossible to categorize the various values that circulate within a complex system as being either "business" priorities or "ethical" considerations. Complexity theory seems to suggest that business prudence and people's sense of normative propriety may not be of a distinctly different order at all.

Robert Solomon is another author who has made an important contribution to the debate about the relationship between business and ethics. In his book *Ethics and Excellence: Cooperation and Integrity in Business*,[8] Solomon examines the claim that attempts to reconcile "business" and "ethics" amount to trade-offs between incompatible goods. Solomon is convinced that the source of many of the misconceptions that exist around business ethics are to be found in what he sees as the schism between business and the rest of life. Solomon develops his case along Aristotelian lines. He suggests that we should think of ourselves as members of a larger community, or *polis* (the Greek word for city-state), who strive to excel. Solomon is, of course, well aware of Aristotle's negative assessment of profit-oriented business activity, but he nevertheless uses Aristotle's account of the relationship between the activities of individuals and their community to argue that the reconciliation of business and ethics need not involve uncomfortable trade-offs.

Aristotle argued that by bringing out what is best in ourselves, we also bring about the greater public good.[9] Aristotle's ideas in this regard should, of course, not be confused with the capitalist mantra that encourages individuals to pursue their self-interest and rely on the effect of market forces (the so-called "hidden hand") to bring about

---

[8] Robert C. Solomon, *Ethics and Excellence: Cooperation and Integrity in Business* (New York: Oxford University Press, 1992).

[9] Robert C. Solomon., "Corporate Roles, Personal Virtues: an Aristotelian Approach to Business Ethics," *Business Ethics Quarterly*, 2 (1992), 320.

and sustain a social dispensation beneficial to all. Within the Aristotelian conception, self-interest is defined, constituted and nurtured within a good community. The public good is not some side-product of the activities of individuals. It is part of how individuals define themselves. By emphasizing that individuality is socially constituted and situated, Aristotle effectively abolishes any strict distinction between private and public values. Aristotelian ethics also avoids rationalistic principled morality in favor of the more practical skills of *phronesis*, or "good judgment." From this Aristotelian perspective, moral decision making does not require compromising the practical in order to accommodate some high-brow moral maxim. Solomon's reinterpretation of these elements of Aristotelian thought does much to problematize the perceived need for trade-offs in the reconciliation of business and ethics.

However, Solomon's account is not without its problems. He has, for instance, been taken to task for his claim that corporations are real communities, neither ideal nor idealized.[10] Solomon believes that, since some sense of shared purpose (or *telos*, in Aristotelian terms) exists within every business organization, companies can and should offer care to their employees, and contribute to the cultivation of virtues among their workforces. Jones, Parker and ten Bos object to Solomon's unproblematic equation of the Aristotelian community with contemporary business corporations.[11] They argue that the *koinonia* or "partnership" of business relationships should not be confused with the idea of a political community or state as Aristotle envisaged it. They point out that the mere existence of relationships of trade or physical proximity does not, in and of itself, constitute a community in the Aristotelian sense. Solomon's critics further charge that Aristotelian communities are not, as he seems to suppose, characterized by warm care and concern, but rather by debate and argument.[12] Solomon's analysis is

---

[10] Solomon, "Corporate Roles," 325.

[11] Jones, Parker and ten Bos, *For Business Ethics*, p. 61.

[12] Solomon does seem to accept the fact that corporations are defined by differences and disagreements. In his objections against communitarian interpretations, he makes it clear that he rejects the idealistic conceptions of communal consensus that have recently been proposed by some virtue-ethicists. It is, however, less clear that he would be able to accommodate the fact that corporations are open, complex adaptive systems. Such organizations are in fact very far removed from the idea of a centralized polis (Solomon, "Corporate Roles," 325).

therefore limited by the fact that he fails to give an adequate account of situations where virtues conflict or where people's understanding of virtues differs.[13]

Solomon's attempt to draw parallels between business organizations and Aristotle's *polis* ultimately constitutes an idealized portrayal of contemporary business life. Such an idealization is contrary to Aristotle's own philosophical approach. Aristotle was careful to stress the importance of starting one's analysis in the midst of real life. If Aristotle were to reflect business ethics today he would surely have based his analysis on his observations of real organizations in action. If Solomon had done so, he might have made more allowance in his conceptual scheme for the way in which judgment continually emerges and evolves as a function of contingent situational and relational challenges. Solomon's account of virtue in business life ultimately falls into the trap of over-systematizing ethical judgment. This is, in a sense, a betrayal of his own Aristotelian approach.

Aristotelian virtue ethics is helpful in considering the complex relationship between sites of shared identification and individual behavior. However, a major limitation of an Aristotelian approach to business ethics, as Solomon interprets it, is the fact that shared conceptions of the good tend to be privileged, while the importance of individual choice and creativity remains largely underappreciated. As such, important concerns about biological and social determinism, group-think, bureaucratic straightjackets and a concomitant loss of moral agency are left unaddressed. This represents a serious blind spot in the Aristotelian perspective because it leaves individuals without a basis for challenging oppressively uniform community standards.

This is essentially what, many centuries later, spurred the philosopher Friedrich Nietzsche's radical rejection of the morality of his time. He came to the conclusion that morality was robbing human beings of everything that makes life worthwhile. Nietzsche's theory of values is often thought to be at odds with ethics. However, Nietzsche's observations and proposals actually confront us with the challenge to

---

[13] Solomon does discuss the virtue of "Integrity" as a kind of meta-value that is supposed to represent the integration of an individual's various roles and the responsibilities defined by them. Within contemporary organizational structures, an individual's roles might not be clearly defined, however, and the various responsibilities that are associated with these roles may not be commensurable (*Ibid.*, 328).

embark on a fundamental reconsideration of values. Many of his most virulent diatribes against the mores of his day were aimed at provoking his readers to think afresh about that which they uncritically accepted as "true" and "right." Nietzsche's critique of morality challenges us to realize that there is more to human life than mere self-preservation, and confronts us with the task of employing our creative capacities in redefining what we consider valuable. When carefully considered, Nietzsche's work also challenges us to reconsider our assumptions about "business" and "ethics." This is because, for Nietzsche, values come into being by aiding self-preservation. Many people would agree that the same is true of business. It could be argued then that if, as Nietzsche's analysis seems to suggest, business and ethics are both implicated in the same struggle for individual survival and dignity, they may have far more in common than is generally recognized. In order to establish this relationship though, it will be necessary to investigate why it is that ethics came to be seen as an abstract, theoretical pursuit.

The problem with morality, in Nietzsche's mind, is that it has gradually blunted all those human capacities that sustain and enhance peoples' lives and give creative shape to individual existence. Nietzsche discovers the origin of this process at a particular juncture in the philosophical history of the West when the natural inclinations, desires and passions of individuals were systematically rendered suspect. He finds evidence of this pernicious development in Plato's rendition of Socrates' conversations with the Athenians. Nietzsche believes that Plato's dialogues were informed by his belief that natural inclinations and beliefs had to be rationally evaluated and justified. Plato's prejudice effectively relegated emotions, passions and creative impulses to a lower order of existence. Nietzsche argues that the decadent effects of morality reach their peak in Christianity.[14] Christian dogma, in Nietzsche's view, convinces people that their desires are debased and advises them to treat their lives as no more than an unpleasant, though necessary, passage to an imagined spiritual afterlife. In the process, morality is debased to the point where it turns into a kind of lifeless "herd mentality." Nietzsche describes this mentality as a self-effacing disposition in terms of which only that which serves to protect the herd is considered legitimate. For

---

[14] "Decadent" in Nietzsche's text refers to the loss of what makes human life pleasurable or meaningful.

him, it is an oppressive mindset that is oriented only towards the average and the mediocre.[15]

In his "Letter on Humanism" Heidegger develops a similar critique of the way in which instrumental rationality impoverishes human life. He argues that when "values" are transcribed into universal principles, those singular experiences in which they had their inception are objectified and devalued.[16] Heidegger bemoans the way in which instrumental language undermines the ability of human beings to live authentic lives. Nietzsche already sensed this problem. He reminded his readers that the words we use to articulate our moral beliefs are not expressions of objective truth but situated metaphors, metonyms and approximations, intended for particular purposes. For the most part, Nietzsche and Heidegger's warnings have fallen on deaf ears as far as the history of moral thought in the West is concerned. Instead of acknowledging the contingent nature of moral commitments, ethics as a discipline has sought to establish moral truth in objective, universal terms. There are, of course, business ethicists who would never think of questioning the progression of ethics along this course. These practitioners remain blissfully unaware of the ancient dispute, in Western thought, between those who consider moral truth universal and those who think it contingent. The quintessential expression of this debate is Aristotle's rejection of Plato's account of ethics. One of Aristotle's main quibbles with his former teacher Plato was the latter's "otherworldliness." Plato believed that the world we live in is but a poor imitation of a perfect world of "forms." Plato therefore found it relatively easy to dismiss contingent differences of opinion about value as trivial. For him, the immanent discursive approximations that were employed in such controversies could never threaten the commensurability and unity of truth as it exists in the ideal world of forms. Rationality, in Plato's mind, allows us to transcend the messy complexities of everyday existence and gain access to the orderly realm of rational truths. Aristotle rejected this dualistic worldview. He proposed instead that our moral convictions develop in and through our experiences of everyday life.

---

[15] Friedrich Nietzsche, *Beyond Good and Evil*, translated by R. J. Hollindale (Penguin, 1977), p. 104.

[16] Martin Heidegger, "Letter on Humanism" in David F. Krell (ed.), *Martin Heidegger: Basic Writings* (New York: Harper & Row, 1977), pp. 193–242.

The debate between Aristotle and Plato was rejoined on many occasions in the history of Western thought. However, the accidents of history have unfortunately given wider circulation and more sustained impetus to the Platonic, Stoic and Christian trajectory in Western thought. From this moral tradition we have inherited the pervasive view that "values" are abstract principles, universal in validity and unequivocal in intent. With the clinical realm of rational thought now firmly established as the proper provenance of value determinations, participants in this tradition meticulously guard against the rude intrusion of messy emotions in the process of moral deliberation.

We will briefly revisit the problematic nature of this rationalistic approach to ethics. As was argued in Chapter 2, the rational protocols employed in utilitarian choice models are typical of the ways in which those who subscribe to this tradition seek to guarantee the objectivity and universal validity of their moral determinations. Martha Nussbaum has suggested that the rationality employed in utilitarian models is based on questionable principles of commensurability, aggregation, and maximization.[17] The principle of commensurability holds that all valuable things are measurable on a single scale. The notion of aggregation refers to the social result obtained by pooling data about individual lives. Maximization, of course, has to do with the effort to obtain an optimum outcome in the rational balancing of conflicting interests. To make "rational" moral decisions, one therefore has to assume that what is important to different stakeholders can be accurately quantified and accounted for on a single scale of comparative value. Furthermore, one has to suppose that stakeholders will be willing to estimate and compare the value of what they stand to gain from different courses of action, using the rational quantifications of such a scale as their unit of measure. In other words, it is assumed that people will voluntarily allow rational quantifications and calculations of this nature to take precedence over whatever personal or contextual factors may otherwise inform their experience of value. There are, of course, things like fairness, care, honesty and privacy that are important to most people. However, it is in the nature of moral dilemmas in the workplace to pit various things we consider morally valuable against other things we consider equally important. In such situations, it is impossible to proclaim unequivocally, for instance, that fairness is more important than

---

[17] Martha Nussbaum, *Poetic Justice* (Beacon Press, 1995), p. 14.

caring, or honesty more important than privacy. It is simply not always possible to offset a loss of privacy for the sake of honesty in a way that is uniformly acceptable. This raises one of the main problems with stakeholder theory. Stakeholder theory is based on the assumption that what is considered "good" by various stakeholders can be measured on a common comparative scale of value, in order to determine the trade-offs necessary for balancing stakeholder interests.[18]

Another problem with the assumed commensurability of values is the fact that a group of people may make a common pledge to uphold a particular shared value, but have very different ideas about what is practically required to do so. A body of workers' sense of fairness, for instance, may not correspond with that of their employers within the context of a wage dispute.

The problem with assumptions of commensurability and aggregation is that they do not allow ethical decisions to be made on the basis of particular, non-repeatable, contingent and concrete value considerations. As such, they entrench the theory–practice distinction. They compel us to look at the world through general frames of reference that obscure and debase the specificity of individual experience.

The insistent demand that objective principles be rationally applied to all situations also has the effect of discouraging people in the practical exercise of their personal discretion. There are various reasons why this is problematic for business ethicists. As long as a strict separation is maintained between theory and practice, the latter will always take precedence over the former. Amidst the breathless dynamics of a complex global economy, where unprecedented moral dilemmas arise at a pace that simply confounds our ability to formulate new rules, discretion is of the utmost importance.

I therefore want to propose that we revisit both Aristotle's and Nietzsche's insights and reconsider the definition of values as it has been established within the Western tradition. Aristotle did not believe that all valuable things are commensurable and argued instead for the priority of particular judgments over universal judgments. He also insisted on the validity and value of allowing emotions and the imagination to inform moral decisions.[19] Aristotle's insight into the

---

[18] Nachoem Wijnberg, "Normative Stakeholder Theory and Aristotle: the Link Between Ethics and Politics," *Journal of Business Ethics*, 25 (2000), 333.
[19] Martha Nussbaum, *Love's Knowledge* (Oxford University Press, 1990), p. 55.

metaphorical and emotional aspects that infuse our moral language is echoed by Nietzsche, who called morality the "sign-language of the emotions or affects."[20] His is a more critical account of the dangers of a morality that forgets its naturalistic roots and moves to the sphere of absolute truth statements. But it is also possible to discover, within Nietzsche's critique, the seeds of a morality conceived in radically different terms. Though separated by centuries, both these philosophers have important things to say about the nature of values. In what follows, I will harness these insights to develop a view of values in which business and ethics may finally be reconciled.

Redefining "values"

Values as life-enhancing

Nietzsche describes the "highest values" as psychological appeals for the preservation of a certain kind of life. As such, they are a condition of life's "being alive." Simon May quotes a somewhat cumbersome yet illuminating description of how Nietzsche himself thought about values:

> The standpoint of "value" is the standpoint of conditions of preservation and enhancement for complex forms of relative life-duration within the flux of becoming.[21]

This citation draws our attention to the fact that values reflect particular ways of engaging with the challenges that the world presents to us. Practices gradually emerge that perpetuate or enhance particular perspectives on the world. What is therefore suggested here is that specific frames of reference play an important role in value formation, but that an active cultivation of behaviors is also necessary to protect and nurture a particular experience of life.

In her interpretation of the way in which Aristotle saw the relationship between individual conceptions of value and the nature of specific lives, Martha Nussbaum sheds new light on this issue. To explain her position, Nussbaum proposes that we imagine the existence of a specific individual, which she refers to as "O." She proposes

---

[20] Nietzsche, *Beyond Good and Evil*, Section 187, p. 92.
[21] Simon May, *Nietzsche's Ethics and His War on "Morality"* (Oxford University Press, 1999), p. 9.

that if we were to try and get a sense of what might constitute a good life for someone like "O," we would have to start by taking account of the ingredients of an "O-ish" life and "O-ish" activity, i.e. those features without which a life simply wouldn't be "O-ish." Nussbaum's proposals in this regard are important, because they suggest that the search for values in business life should start with an account of what it is that allows particular activities to be identified as business practices. Her account suggests that to do so we would have to look for a quality or characteristic, in the absence of which an activity could not possibly be identified as a "business" practice.

One can see how Nietzsche's and Aristotle's insights might allow us to think differently about both ethics and business. Certain values emerge in the process of advancing business's most basic goals. Values are those priorities that enable business to enhance life. They are not abstract principles that try to make of business something that it is not. From this perspective, Milton Friedman's categorical claim that "the business of business is business" seems far less amoral. It is in fact a statement about a certain kind of morality, i.e. one that has come to place the highest value on profit making. Nietzsche's work helps us to understand that the lack of concern for certain moral goods that is associated with capitalist values may be ascribable to a particular conception of the role that business activities play in life enhancement. Nietzsche would also have us believe that it is possible to reject these existing values, to redefine our lives and reinvent our values. In fact, this is one of the main tasks of business ethics. Ethics allows us to question what we value and why it is valued.

Questions such as these penetrate to the very heart of who and what we are as human beings and how we want to live. Considering how much time and effort people spend working in organizations, these are questions of the highest order of significance. The litmus test, as far as any form of business activity goes, should be whether it serves to enhance the lives of those who participate in it or are affected by it. If a business enterprise or initiative fails to enhance people's lives, it is effectively a failure, irrespective of the financial returns that it delivers.

If the success of business enterprises is to be assessed in these terms, it is necessary to fundamentally reassess organizations' operational goals. First, however, it is necessary to consider what it means to "enhance" people's lives. This involves people's various perceptions of what a good or happy life is like. The value priorities that shape relational life within an organizational system are informed by how its members perceive the good life. When there is sufficient congruency in the way that individual employees see the good life, it begins to function as a tacit "frame of reference," which allows a sense of normative propriety to develop within an organizational system. This in turn facilitates the practical, day-to-day realization of the organizational system's tacit understanding of the good life.

To really understand the significance and meaning of the tacit normative parameters that people implicitly impose on one another's behavior within an organizational system, it is necessary to consider what it is that they are aimed at.[22] As such, it confronts us with the truths we have adopted in the process of reaching our human goals.

Nietzsche argues that truth is essentially an estimation of value linked to very practical concerns. "Truth" is the result of human attempts to create a stable point of reference from which to advance particular agendas. Though "truth" is a useful construction, it becomes a lie when people begin to see it as something permanent and unchangeable. Truth can therefore never be fixed, because to do so would be to deny life's vitality.[23] Unlike many of his contemporaries, Nietzsche did not subscribe to the Darwinian view that the essence of life lay solely in "self-preservation." Instead Nietzsche emphasizes self-transcending enhancement. In Nietzsche's conception, the enhancement of our lives begins with the projection of higher possibilities for our selves. This helps direct our efforts towards that which we are yet to attain in our lives. Valuation as such is how we bring the essence of our life to fruition.[24] In Heidegger's reading of Nietzsche, values are part of the process by which we schematize chaos just as much as they are required to move us in the direction of self-transcending enhancement.[25] For Nietzsche, the construction of values is part of the creative process that keeps us alive, both physically and

---

[22] This should not, however, be confused with a utilitarian perspective, which is about outcomes. All forms of utilitarianism are teleological, i.e. goal-directed, but not all goals are utilitarian, i.e. derived from a cost–benefit analysis of goods on a single scale.

[23] Martin Heidegger, *Nietzsche Volumes III & IV The Will to Power as Knowledge and as Metaphysics and Nihilism*, edited by David F. Krell (San Francisco: Harper Collins), p. 66.

[24] *Ibid.*, p. 61.   [25] *Ibid.*, p. 80.

mentally. Such creativity is certainly important within the context of business.[26]

If the process of value formation is a creative one in Nietzsche's thought, he is, as we shall see, also fully cognizant of the limits of our creative capacities. In his reading of Nietzsche, Heidegger points out that the Greek word *khaos* literally means "the gaping."[27] This is significant, because it betrays something about the way in which Nietzsche understood the concept of chaos. For most of us, chaos is synonymous with confusion or the absence of order. But this was not the case for Nietzsche. For him chaos denotes a peculiar preliminary projection of the world and the forces that govern its dynamics. This schematizing takes place in and through our embodied existence. As such, life for Nietzsche is "bodying writ large." Nietzsche became convinced that our experience as embodied beings determines, not only *what* and *how* we see, but also what we imagine. He believed that it is from the particularity of our embodied experience that we begin to discover the relative value of that which we encounter in the world. The process of value creation is therefore, in Nietzsche's view, not wholly without constraint. The particularity of our experience of the world as embodied beings not only facilitates but also limits what we see and imagine. It is therefore not completely relative or open to chance. For Nietzsche, the rich variety and sheer dynamism of the world that we encounter as embodied beings can never be adequately reified as truth or knowledge. He therefore suggests that we turn to art to make sense of our experience. For him, art allows us to reveal the order of the world as a body writ large in symbols, images and approximations. In art, that which is fixed and stable in our understanding and appreciation of the world is opened to new possibilities. The "gaping" is the process by which new possibilities are opened.

Nietzsche is by no means alone in his appreciation of art's potential. For Nietzsche, Heidegger, and a whole succession of twentieth-century philosophers after them, it is not rational principles and protocols, but art, poetry and narrative imagination, that hold the key to a richer understanding and appreciation of what we experience in the world. Art reminds us of forms of valuation that are excluded when

---

[26] Philip Evans and Thomas S. Wurster, *Blown to Bits: How the New Economics of Information Transforms Strategy* (Harvard, 1999).
[27] Heidegger, *Nietzsche Volumes III &IV*, p. 76.

values are "rationally" conceived as epistemic principles. It allows us to explore the role that tacit beliefs and unexpressed desires play in the formation of our moral priorities.

Values as emotional

One of Nietzsche's most succinct articulations of the relationship between emotions and moral convictions is his claim that morality is the "sign-language of the emotions."[28] Though Nietzsche argued that our moral values are directly linked to what we desire, he did not see values as completely random, momentary preferences. Nietzsche insisted that affect is not arbitrary. For him, it tells the story of who a person is. Nietzsche believed that individuals are shaped by a specific combination of nature, nurture and life circumstances. This also provides clues about the kind of life that a person is suited to.[29] According to Simon May, Nietzsche is an ethical naturalist who correlates ethical values, motivations, and practices to pre-ethical facts about the human beings who espouse them. Valuing, for Nietzsche, is also directly related to one's seeking and attainment of power. Nietzsche challenges his readers to acknowledge the nature of values and to choose values that give creative form to the lives they desire. Values, in his estimation, will always be derived from someone's particular desires and emotions. He therefore urges us not to allow other people's goals and priorities to determine our own values.

One would expect Bill Frederick to be the one business ethicist who might be open to this more Nietzschean account of values. Frederick recognizes the embodied character of values on various levels of an organization. He argues, for instance, that a manager's values are embodied in his or her perceptions, attitudes, and behavior, which in turn express the forces – natural and cultural – involved in the formation and operationalization of values.[30] Value commitments express symbolic human meanings that are used to bring order and significance into human transactions. Frederick also allows for difference and creative form-giving within an organization. Because of

---

[28] Nietzsche, *Beyond Good and Evil*, Section 187, p. 92.
[29] May, *Nietzsche's Ethics*, p. 10.
[30] William C. Frederick, *Values, Nature, Culture and the American corporation*, p. 110.

the inclusive nature of people's value commitments, their individual life histories play a role in their decisions and actions and cause X-factor values, which cannot always be accurately assessed or predicted.[31] X-factor values refer to the variation that exists between individuals in spite of the sameness imposed on the managerial scene by personal, organizational, and societal filters.[32] Frederick therefore seems to leave room for some creative form-giving in valuation. This would, at least theoretically, allow individual employees to dissent from the values that are present within their work environment. However, Frederick seems less optimistic that this creative form-giving can have an impact on broader business imperatives.

Nietzsche believed that to raise the desires of a few individuals to the level of absolute truth creates a herd mentality. His discussion of the role of emotion in values therefore always contains the warning that we should not confuse these tentative forms of sense-making with moral truth. Nietzsche's warnings against fixed moral truths are often mistaken for a categorical rejection of ethics as such. This is not the case. Nietzsche was just very skeptical of any attempts to formulate collective values. He wanted to challenge us, to dare us to reformulate and reinterpret what is valuable in our own terms. In business ethics, this confronts us with a challenge. We cannot extrapolate, from Nietzsche's work, a positive account of how creative form-giving of values can take place on an organizational level. Yet we have to take seriously the fact that individuals function within organizations and that the interaction between the individual and his/her context is important. Therefore, we may have to retrace our steps in the history of thought. What does community life provide in terms of our own individual sense of value? And how can we draw on this sense, without relinquishing our own creative impetus and critical inclinations?

Aristotle's view of the role of emotions in ethical decision making provides a starting point from which we can begin to construct an alternative account of the interaction between individual and collective values. Aristotle encouraged people to recognize and value their feelings because he considered them indispensable to virtuous agency.[33] According to Martha Nussbaum, Aristotle restores emotions to the central

---

[31] *Ibid.*, p. 100.   [32] *Ibid.*, p. 121.
[33] Martha Nussbaum, *Therapy of Desire: Theory and Practice in Hellenistic Ethics* (Princeton University Press, 1994), p. 78.

place in morality from which Plato had banished them. In Aristotle's conception, emotions function as modes of vision and forms of recognition. He believes that a person's emotional response, rather than detached thinking, guides appropriate decisions and behavior.[34] Emotions have a rich cognitive structure and reflect particular beliefs.[35] As agents, we ascribe value to things that we do not necessarily control. Consequently, we desire things and experience strong emotions as we seek and pursue the things we value. Our interactions with other people shape our sensibilities. They provide us with a strong sense of what is socially appropriate and appreciated in our behavior. In this way, socialization continually conditions us to respond in an emotionally appropriate way.

Within the context of a business organization, employees learn what is appreciated and appropriate through both deliberate instruction and tacit socialization. For instance, if risk taking is valued within an organization, employees may be encouraged to take risks through the introduction of rewards programs, or other forms of recognition. Over time, risk taking becomes associated with such rewards and employees begin to lose their fear. In another organization where due care, consultation and risk-averseness are valued, fear, or at least circumspection, may gradually become reinforced as an appropriate emotional response to risk. Emotions are therefore not "irrational." They are based on beliefs about the worth of particular things. Although such beliefs may be so appropriate in one context that they begin to be seen as part of the natural order of things, they may seem completely nonsensical to those who function under another set of circumstances.[36] What this suggests is that the material, institutional and relational life that is cultivated within an organizational system informs the moral responsiveness of those who participate in it. As such Aristotle poses a political and social challenge. His ideas suggest that we should remain conscious and vigilant about the signals that we send out to others, for such subtle cues may play an important role in shaping people's emotional responses and perception of value.

This challenge has been partly taken up by a number of business ethicists. These theorists argue that the key to ethical behavior lies in the individual's cultivation of appropriate second-order desires. These second-order desires could then serve to control first-order desires.

---

[34] Nussbaum, *Love's Knowledge*, p. 79.
[35] Nussbaum, *Therapy of Desire*, p. 88.   [36] *Ibid.*, p. 93.

Using Frankfurt's model, Hartman explains the difference between
first- and second-order desires: in this model, something like the desire
to smoke would be considered a first-order desire. The desire not to
smoke, however, would be considered a second-order desire, i.e. a
desire about a desire.[37] A good *polis*, or an organization with the right
sort of culture, in Hartman's view, will encourage its members to
cultivate the right kind of second-order desires. At first glance this
approach seems to correlate rather well with the suggestion that a
particular kind of institutional and political life, one that operates
according to rational principles, would regulate emotional responses.
However, there is an important difference. Hartman himself senses
this difference. He acknowledges that Aristotle would never have
pitted reason against emotion. Instead Aristotle associated virtue with
appropriate emotional responses and a disposition to act accord-
ingly.[38] Despite these admissions, Hartman proceeds to utilize Elster's
conception of the wise person. According to this model, a wise person
is someone who exercises rational self-mastery. This allows him/her to
consistently give priority to second-order desires and to act on first-
order desires only under a circumscribed set of conditions. The
problem with this proposal is that it expects individuals consistently to
give priority to second-order desires over first-order desires through an
exercise in rational "self-mastery."[39] Considering the many tacit ways
in which employees influence one another's beliefs and desires through
their interaction at work, the feasibility of such a form of "control"
seems highly questionable.[40] Just how problematic this kind of deliberate rational control really is will become clear in the next section as
I consider the way in which human beings make sense of values.

Values as tropical (trope-like) and rhetorical

In one of the most often cited passages in his essay "On Truth and Lie
in the Extramoral Sense," Nietzsche proclaims:

---

[37] Edwin Hartman, "The Commons and the Moral Organization," *Business
Ethics Quarterly*, 4 (1994), 258.
[38] Edwin Hartman, *Organizational Ethics and the Good Life* (Oxford University
Press, 1996), p. 135.
[39] *Ibid.*, p. 137.
[40] The fact that Hartman reverts to a Rawlsian model betrays his belief in the
ability of human beings to reason about justice as fairness from a
transcendental position of procedural impartiality and independence.

What then is truth? A mobile army of metaphors, metonyms, and anthropomorphisms – in short, a sum of human relations, which have been enhanced, transposed, and embellished poetically and rhetorically, and which after long use seem firm, canonical and obligatory to people: truth are fictions about which has been forgotten that this is what they are: metaphors which are worn and without sensuous power; coins which have lost their pictures and now only matter as metal, no longer as coins.[41]

Nietzsche drew on the insights of the writers of his time to conclude that every language is a dictionary of faded metaphors.[42] He believed that figures of speech and rhetoric preceded all conceptualization. In this respect, his definition of tropes, or "figures of speech" is unique. He did not believe that tropes stood in contrast to literal uses of language, because all language relies on indirect designations. In his view tropes should therefore be considered the fundamental linguistic paradigm and not a deviation. Nietzsche argues that all language displays certain anthropologically necessary constructions that help us to organize our environment and make sense of experience.[43]

Since his account of language and his view of the body are closely related, Nietzsche's tropical account of language is grounded in both rhetoric and physiology. Our awareness of our bodies and our desire to interact with others prompts us to use words as "uncertain allusions to things." In the process, we relate our awareness of objects and experiences to other objects and experiences. Because each designation draws on a broad network of references, it is capable of drawing together a variety of symbols, images, and allusions in a dense network of meaning.

This has bearing on the way in which values are interpreted in an organizational context. For instance, when employees consider the meaning of the word "fairness," they draw on mental images and associations that go well beyond the procedural and political connotations that we typically attach to the word. Each concept develops along its own unique historical course. Etymologically, the notion of

---

[41] Friedrich Nietzsche, "On Truth and Lie in the Extramoral Sense" in
W. Kaufman (ed. and translator), *The Portable Nietzsche* (Penguin Books, 1954), p. 42.
[42] Christian J. Emden, *Nietzsche on Language, Consciousness and the Body* (University of Illinois Press, 2005). See Emden's discussion of how Nietzsche drew on the work of Jean Paul and a host of other writers of his time to develop his metaphoric account of truth.
[43] *Ibid.*, p. 79.

"fairness" can be traced back to the idea of "beauty."[44] As such, the concept "fairness," in its current use as a moral concept, could be taken as a reference to that which is necessary to live a beautiful or complete life. The point is that any description of a "value" has to contend with both the heterogeneity of experience and the difficulty of unequivocally defining rich networks of meaning.

Nietzsche's insight into the trope-like character of language is an important precedent of late-twentieth-century poststructuralist thought. However, before we consider the work that Derrida and others have done on the iterability of meaning, I'd like to revisit Aristotle's views on language and the value of rhetoric. According to Sean Kirkland, the words "rhetoric" and "rhetorical" have come to be associated with the use of words "that fail to address the subject matter in any substantive way."[45] This is the more generous reading of our contemporary use of the word. It could also mean anything from ornamental, insubstantial, to obscuring and insidious. Basically it is used to refer to anything and everything that is regarded as merely subjective, or which is thought to contain some form of untruth. Kirkland points out that Aristotle held a completely different view. In fact, he argues that rhetoric affords us a very special kind of access to truth; that it is in fact an art or a skill with its own special capacities for achieving truth. "Truth" in the Greek sense of the word, refers to something that is revealed.[46] As human beings, we search for what is good. But to be successful in this quest, we need *phronesis*. *Phronesis* is, of course, the Greek word for good judgment or practical wisdom. Kirkland describes Aristotle's take on practical wisdom as "the kind of familiarity one has with one's particular circumstances, which allows one to act appropriately in carrying out one's purposes." To be able to come to ethical decisions, *phronesis* relies on a habituated disposition towards the good that is found within a certain community with a specific ethos. If a person has gone through such a process of habituation, it enables him/her to make specific decisions

---

[44] The German word for justice, *Recht*, also refers to "a right," legal or moral, and can also be translated as "pretty" as in "fairly accurate," or as "completely." In Dutch *recht* can be translated as "justice," but also as "straight" or as "honor or privilege."

[45] Sean D. Kirkland, "The Temporality of Phronesis in the Nicomachean Ethics," *Ancient Philosophy*, 27 (2007).

[46] The Greek description of truth as *aletheuein* is crucial to understanding what Aristotle has in mind here – it literally means "to true," and in the Greek world it referred to "unveiling, uncovering or unconcealing."

about the good. The various points of normative orientation that are the result of habituation are often difficult to articulate deliberately or to draw on explicitly. This is where rhetoric comes in. Rhetorical language allows what is concealed to present itself. In Kirkland's description of it, rhetoric is the art of stepping into a space held open between the speaker and the audience.[47] The use of rhetorical language may allow for this more tacit form of knowledge, and the richly textured metaphorical fabric of moral values, to be revealed.

An articulation of values in the principled language that ethicists often employ can hardly do justice to this rich complexity. It is therefore important constantly to remind ourselves of the possibilities *and* limitations of moral language. Scholars like Jacques Derrida have warned, in this regard, against over-confidently assigning one meaning to a specific term. Derrida employs the neologism *differance* to describe the way in which the final assignment of meaning to words is always *deferred*, or postponed.[48] Derrida's concept of *differance* also expresses his belief that each word contains within itself multiple *different* meanings. The meaning of any moral utterance is significantly determined by the contingencies of the situation and context within which it is made. This gives each moral utterance a certain specificity, which must always be kept in mind.

Within the context of an organizational system, it is therefore important to remember that various moral truth(s) are circulated within each specific situation. Each moral statement or commitment to values contains within itself the possibility of being said and understood differently. Furthermore, any kind of normative propriety must be understood as a relational response to a whole system of codes, generalizations and assumptions. What we assert about ourselves is always already a statement about the other. Any statement about what is just is always already based on how we have categorized certain individuals within certain groups. For example, affirmative action as a mechanism to work towards equality and justice in the workplace assumes that all minorities were treated in an unjust manner and that they are therefore entitled to redress. The fact that there are individuals in minority groups who are socio-economically privileged cannot be accommodated by most

---

[47] I will explore the potential implications of this within the context of speeches and the general use of language within an organization in Chapter 6.

[48] Jacques Derrida, "Differance" in *Margins of Philosophy* (University of Chicago Press, 1982).

affirmative action programs, because the category "minority" forgets the possibility of difference that always lies within it.

Everyday business life is filled with all kinds of images, symbols, rhetoric, and power dynamics. In and through their circulation in an organizational system, moral truth(s) emerge. It is through employees' daily experience of organizational life that they are socialized into particular value orientations and it is here, rather than in formal ethics training sessions, that the key to organizational behavioral lies. Recognizing this challenges us to rethink the way in which we give expression to the latent goals and priorities that inform organizational behavior. For though they may be felt and understood by the employees of an organization, such priorities easily elude the linguistic grasp of conventional value statements and codes of conduct.

Values as relational and responsive

No one philosopher has given us a moral theory that can adequately address all the moral challenges that confront us in business ethics today. Part of the problem, of course, is that moral philosophers do not necessarily anticipate, or specifically make provision for, the application of their ideas in business ethics. This need not deter us, however, from entering into a conversation with these philosophers and taking the questions that they pose seriously. Such a conversation may include many different participants with opposing views. It is precisely these critical relationships that enhance our deliberations within business ethics and allow us the freedom to reconsider our own relational reality.

For instance, it would be irresponsible to argue that all of Nietzsche's insights can be incorporated seamlessly into a neat, coherent theoretical approach to business ethics. As a result of his commitments to radical individualism, Nietzsche's thought will always cast suspicion on organizations, corporate structures, and codes of conduct. Nietzsche would have associated the influence of organizational communities on individual values with a loss of autonomy and the herd mentality that he so detested. According to May, Nietzsche sees "becoming what one is" as a steady process of continual life enhancement. It is a process that demands bold living, strict discipline and the "purification" of values in the light of prolonged experience.[49] Nietzsche's ideal is the creation of a

[49] Simon May, *Nietzsche's Ethics*, p. 116.

sovereign individual who has achieved perfect self-mastery and genuine freedom. His sovereign individual is, in a sense, the epitome of the individualistic sense of authenticity that has become such an important ideal of our modern world.

Charles Taylor blames such individualistic interpretations of authenticity for the subjectivism, narcissism, nihilism and relativism that he detects in contemporary life.[50] Taylor argues that authenticity, in a Nietzschean sense, can only be meaningful within the context of an individual's interaction with others in a specific community. Taylor agrees that authenticity requires original creation, construction and discovery. He is also ready to accommodate the fact that authentic individuals can be in disagreement with the broader social and political consensus that exists within their community. However, he argues that one can only assert one's own autonomy over and against others within a community. In isolation, autonomy loses its meaning. In a similar way, any moral value only makes sense from within a dialogical setting, or a broader "horizon of significance," as Taylor calls it.[51] A value like "privacy" would essentially be meaningless if there were no other people around. Fairness would hardly be required if one lived in a state of supreme isolation. The process of defining one's own values is therefore always relational.

It is important to recognize that as a result of changes in our world and our interactions with one another, the things that we consider "valuable" change. "Privacy" was probably not a value that would have appeared in business organizations' codes of conduct early in the twentieth century. Not only were the relationships between employers and employees structured in a completely different way, but intrusive technologies such as surveillance cameras and computer spyware were not yet available. Identities were not stolen electronically, and personal data could not yet be mined for marketing purposes. If privacy is valued today, it is because of the way in which people relate, and choose to interact with one another in a technologically integrated world. It appears then, that values are relational, rather than individualistic in nature. They are about what is appropriate in our relationship with others and our world.

---

[50] Charles Taylor, *The Ethics of Authenticity* (Harvard University Press, 1991), p. 60.
[51] *Ibid.*, p. 66.

Charles Taylor's critique of individualistic theories like Nietzsche's draws on Aristotelian ethics. Taylor's work is usually associated with communitarian tradition, a distinction that he shares with Alasdair MacIntyre. As indicated in Chapter 2, communitarians emphasize the role that communities play in morality. Though the communitarian belief in the existence of "common values" may be questioned, there is much to be gained from the critical perspectives that some of its proponents provided on modern moral theory. In his book *After Virtue* MacIntyre claims that moral language has lost its relation to the *telos* (goal, end, purpose) of specific communities.[52] For MacIntyre shared goals or purposes of this order are the very basis of a community. Without them, he argues, moral language effectively becomes meaningless.

MacIntyre is convinced that morality has been corrupted through its acceptance of individualistic emotivism, the basic tenets of which remain immanent in the Weberian managerial forms of our culture.[53] If values and morality are as relational in nature as my analysis suggests, communitarians are surely justified in being critical of the excessively individualistic basis upon which ethics is often conceived in contemporary business life. The problem with communitarian ethics, however, is that it cloaks individual morality in a communal straightjacket that curtails dissent and obscures the iterability of moral language.

When it comes to moral truth, we need not only normative congruence but openness and flexibility as well. We need both agreement and the possibility of dissent. A balance therefore needs to be struck between Aristotelian relationalism and Nietzschean individualism. However, when we employ Aristotelian ethics to this end, we need to take special care. Contemporary business organizations cannot simply be equated with the ancient Athenian *polis*, which informed Aristotle's observations about ethics. This is an issue that has already been raised within the context of Solomon's *Aristotelian Business Ethics*. However, we need not be dissuaded from considering the contemporary relevance and implications of Aristotle's proposals by the historical distance that separates us from his world and experience. After all, we need not accept Aristotle's metaphysical biology or his political model to be able to utilize his ideas about ethics. However, if

---

[52] Alasdair MacIntyre, *After Virtue* (Duckworth, 1981).
[53] MacIntyre, *After Virtue*, p. 114.

one takes the full complexity of Aristotelian moral terminology into account, its value for business ethics becomes evident. The Aristotelian notion of "community" accommodates much of the dissent, gossip, conflict and power play that characterize contemporary business organizations. This does not mean that contemporary organizational systems are the "the same" as Aristotle's ancient community. Aristotle's observations do, however, help us to understand how dissent plays out in a social context.

In considering the contemporary employment of Aristotelian ethics by authors such as MacIntyre, it is important to pay attention to the differences between societies, communities and organizations. Martin Parker has offered an interesting analysis in this regard. According to Parker, all organizations *are* cultures. Therefore, he argues, all organizations are communities, albeit only in the very loose sense of the word. The word "organization" is, of course, associated with the verb "organize." "Organization" as a verb also means that we know what others want from us, and that we share some kind of common orientation with them. Parker argues that organizing implies sharing, agreeing on what counts as sameness and difference, or coming to an understanding of what divides and unites people within a particular form of life.

However, this does not mean that communities, organizations and states are all different ways of referring to the same thing. Parker uses the Durkheimian idea of "moral density" to explain the difference between a "society" and a "community." In a society, people identify with a large group of people through weak and generalized affectual ties. A community, on the other hand, is based on individuals' sustained identification with a smaller, more homogeneous group. By definition, neither states nor organizations bear affective ties. They are social or legal constructions that allow individuals to enjoy some rights and benefits on the condition that they agree to certain duties, responsibilities, and restraints. One can live in a particular state, or work at a specific organization, and even engage in some of its practices, without feeling as though one belongs. Organizations are therefore not necessarily communities. However, Parker argues that an individual's work life can have a profound influence on his/her identity. To explain how this happens, he examines the institutional nature of life in an organization. To institutionalize, argues Parker, means to infuse with value beyond the technical requirements of the task at hand.[54] Through techniques such as the elaboration of socially integrating myths, day-to-day behavior is infused with long-term meaning and purpose. Because of this, organizations become places that elicit strong emotional responses and deep attachments. Parker's analysis therefore suggests that organizations can assume the characteristics of communities. The important variable in terms of understanding how values function, is the affective ties that exist within an organization as a community.

In some respects, there is much to be commended in MacIntyre's re-employment of Aristotle. He emphasizes, for instance, the importance of storytelling in moral education.[55] He suggests that individuals orientate themselves by integrating their experience in a narrative structure. The life of an individual thus becomes a story. More importantly, though, from MacIntyre's perspective, is the fact that individual life stories are always set in the context of a particular community. He proposes that the way in which individuals construct their life stories is determined, to a very large extent, by what they see as their specific role within their communities. These role identities are constantly reinforced through the individual's participation in community practices. MacIntyre defines a practice as:

[A]ny coherent and complex form of socially established cooperative human activity through which goods internal to that form of activity are realized in the course of trying to achieve those standards of excellence which are appropriate to, and partially definitive of, that form of activity, with the result that human powers to achieve excellence, and human conceptions of the ends and the goods involved, are systematically extended.[56]

Participation in community-based practices instills appropriate desires in the individual. As such, they contribute to the cultivation of virtues. In MacIntyre's definition, virtues are acquired human qualities that enable people to attain those goods that are internal to practices.[57]

---

[54] Parker draws on Selznick's interpretation of institutional life. See Martin Parker, "Organization, Community and Utopia," *Studies in Cultures, Organisations and Societies*, 4 (1998), 77–91.

[55] MacIntyre, *After Virtue*, p. 121.   [56] *Ibid.*, p. 187.

[57] In MacIntyre's view, it is very important that the good that is to be pursued is internal to the practice itself, and not something external that requires instrumental reasoning to bring about particular consequences. In this sense, it is important to note that MacIntyre's proposals are teleological, but not consequentialist.

By continuously honing the skills that are required to participate in community practices, habits are formed. As these habits are formed, individuals develop desires that support and confirm the practices that they are participating in. Because individuals' desires have already been shaped by their identification with, and participation in, community practices, doing the right thing does not require so much restraint or compromise. Doing the right thing is therefore not seen as a trade-off in terms of one's everyday pursuits within specific practices, but is in fact part of succeeding at the practice itself. MacIntyre's account of the cultivation of virtues within practices is helpful in understanding the nature of moral agency and values. Nietzsche's warnings against a mindless, habitual repetition of community truths and practices must, however, always be kept in mind. It is this tension between belonging and dissenting, which lies at the heart of ethics as practice.

One of the problems that business ethicists have had with MacIntyre's account, though, is that he did not consider business a practice. In MacIntyre's mind, business pursues external goods, such as profit for its owners. As such, it epitomizes the kind of instrumental reasoning that MacIntyre finds most troubling. He is particularly critical of the manager or bureaucratic expert, a central character of modern society that he considers the embodiment of emotivism.[58] Since the sole motivation of bureaucracy is efficiency, moral decision making is reduced to an ad hoc process focused on expediting outcomes. As the priorities associated with short-term goals predominate, normative commitments become eroded. For MacIntyre, this leads to emotive decision making.

It may be argued that this account relies on a number of questionable assumptions. MacIntyre assumes, for instance, that profit is an external good. He considers profit a good desired mainly by the self-interested owners of companies. What MacIntyre fails to recognize, however, is that profit is integral to many business practitioners' understanding of the good life.[59] For many who make their living in business, it has become the very measure of personal and organizational success. As such, it is an integral part of how sustainable businesses and successful

---

[58] MacIntyre, *After Virtue*, p. 73.
[59] We can of course argue about whether this is in fact a legitimate view of the good life, but the fact is, for many business practitioners, it is central to what makes business business. As such, it is an internal and not an external good. The skill involved in running a successful business may be valued and enjoyed in and of itself.

careers are defined. It is also important to note that business priorities do not arise or develop in isolation. They are substantially informed by societal dynamics and respond to its values. The priority that business places on profit cannot therefore be identified with the self-interested behavior of a few wealthy individuals alone. Business's relationship with other stakeholders has a significant influence on the way in which the *telos* of business is conceived. Contemporary stakeholder theory suggests, in this regard, that owners are but one among many stakeholders who have a stake in the success of a corporation. The recent development of "triple bottom-line reporting" belies MacIntyre's assumption that financial profit is the only important good that business organizations pursue. This form of corporate reporting is tantamount to a recognition that business organizations also pursue various social and environmental goals in the course of their activities and operations.

The question one might pose to MacIntyre, is whether an ongoing redefinition of the terms of corporate success within business as practice opens more productive avenues for developing corporate virtue. Defining a business organization in terms of its ability to pursue both profit and social and environmental goals will considerably raise the stakes for business practitioners. Pursuing such a comprehensive agenda will require the kinds of qualities and skills that are usually associated with good chess players. Not surprisingly then, chess is one of MacIntyre's favorite examples of a practice. He uses it to explain what virtue requires. A good chess player is competitive, skillful and thoughtful. The same can be said of a good business executive. Neither business nor chess can function without fairness, rule-abidingness, and ongoing interaction with other players. MacIntyre might say that the difference between a practice, such as chess, and business activities lies in the fact that the business game yields money. But it is by no means clear why this should be so decisive. After all, some games of chess are played for prize money. Are we to believe that whenever money becomes one of the "goods" toward which an organized activity is directed, it can no longer be considered a practice? This kind of reasoning would disqualify most professional sports, as well as professional scientific activities from being recognized as "practices."

For MacIntyre the key lies in what he sees as the difference between practices and institutions. Whereas chess, physics and medicine are considered practices, in MacIntyre's analysis, chess clubs, laboratories, universities and hospitals are classified as institutions. He argues that institutions are primarily concerned with external goods (like money) that are instrumental in sustaining practices.[60] Some scholars who draw on MacIntyre's ideas have adopted this distinction instead of challenging it. Postma, for instance, argues that organizations and practices constitute a duality that should be sustained.[61] Practices, he claims, are self-regulating, but not self-sustaining. Furthermore, practices are in a symbiotic relationship with institutions. This relationship is not harmonious, but is characterized instead by a tension that is directly attributable to the difference between external and internal goods. The point that Postma seems to be making is that institutions are compelled to concern themselves with money and other practicalities, while practices have the luxury of remaining "pure." This is a rather troubling assertion because it suggests that some aspects of institutional life, such as budgets and profit projections, are "dirty," whereas others, like the creation of jobs, protection of the environment, and the delivery of goods are not. It seems that Postma would have us accommodate the "impurity" of business institutions solely for the purpose of supporting practices! This seems like a rather bleak and dismissive assessment of what institutions have to offer. Selznick has observed, for instance, that institutions infuse basic tasks with value and, in doing so, provide people with a sense of meaning and purpose.[62] Insofar as they contribute to something that is valued, institutions function as communities.

In this respect, it is helpful to revisit the insights of the American pragmatists. John Dewey's discussion of the nature of ends goes a long way in dispelling the notion that certain ends, goods or values, are morally superior to others. Dewey approves of Aristotelian thought because it did not advocate a theory of value separate from a theory of nature. However, he did not believe in the notion of fixed ends. Instead, he concurred with Nietzsche's view that values are constructed. Dewey developed the notion of "ends-in-view," which arise out of natural effects. As human beings, he hypothesized, we engage in directed sense-making. By this he means that we tend to work with whatever happens to present itself to us as part of the natural contingencies of our everyday lives. What is at first considered an end becomes the means through which a subsequent end is

---

[60] MacIntyre, *After Virtue*, p. 194.
[61] D. Postma, "ICT Enhanced Communities of Practice: Respecting and Maintaining the Duality between Organisations and Practices," Working paper (University of the Witwatersrand, 2003).
[62] Selznick, "Organisation, Community and Utopia" in Martin Parker (ed.), *Studies in Cultures, Organisations and Societies*, 4 (1998), 77–91.

later pursued. For Dewey, there are no ultimate ends. Ends are endless. We continually stumble upon new ends as new activities occasion new consequences.

From the perspective of American pragmatism, normativity results from our attempts to get out of problematic situations and to facilitate what Dewey calls "consummatory experiences." Such experiences have an aesthetic quality. Dewey believed that premises emerge in and through our thinking, as conclusions become manifest. Conclusions, for their part, emerge as processes of anticipation and accumulation reach completion. Dewey seems to argue for something between the extremes of aimlessness and mechanical efficiency. His analysis of the way in which people draw conclusions about good ends suggests that moral language need not, as MacIntyre feared, fall prey to the bureaucratic managers' goal of optimum mechanical efficiency. Dewey's proposals clearly allow for some creative construction of ends within the parameters of contingent situational, personal, organizational and contextual variables.

Rorty agrees with Dewey that all knowledge, including "moral truth," is constructed to fit social purposes. His discussion of Dewey's insights makes it clear that for pragmatists, the distinction between morality and prudence is not particularly helpful.[63] The distinction between the two is a matter of degree, rather than of kind. By implication, a "good" business decision need not be substantively different from a good "ethical" decision. Pragmatism helps us to appreciate the relational quality of moral values. Rorty advocates a "panrelationalism," in terms of which value is assigned to people and things solely on the basis of their relationships to other people and things.[64] In his mind, moral development within the individual, and within the human species as a whole, is a matter of re-making human selves in a way that increases the variety of relationships that contribute towards the constitution of those selves. It involves increasing people's sensitivity and imaginative power, as well as their responsiveness to the needs of an ever-expanding variety of people and things. Rorty's metaphor for describing moral progress is the sewing together of a very large, elaborate polychrome quilt. It is the very antithesis of moral truth conceived as something deep and foundational.

---

[63] Richard Rorty, "Ethics Without Principles" in Rorty, *Philosophy and Social Hope* (Penguin Books, 1999), p. 76.
[64] Richard Rorty, "A World Without Substances or Essences" *Ibid.*, p. 52.

It is under pragmatism's influence that Bill Frederick came to the conclusion that ethical business behavior has no single meaning. What Frederick proposed instead, is that it is a thoroughly relative phenomenon. It is relative to nature's economizing and ecologizing processes, to varying socio-cultural conventions, to a company's culture and ethical climate, to a firm's commitment to power aggrandizement, to the practitioners' personal values, and to stakeholder participation. However, ethical business behavior does have some substantive moral meaning, in Frederick's conception. This meaning can come from any of the sources that Frederick distinguishes in his analysis of the various value clusters. Nature, culture, society, organizations, individuals, and stakeholders all contribute multiple ethical meanings to what Frederick aptly describes as an "ethics stewpot" within the organization.[65]

It is important to keep in mind that the ethical sensibilities of individual employees are never fully "determined" by whatever organizational "pot" they happen to find themselves in. Nor does the fact that the ethical sensibilities of employees are informed by such a variety of influences mean that there is no basis for distinguishing an appropriate course of action from an inappropriate one. If this were the case, ethics as practice would not be possible. Some form of normative orientation is essential. Since foundational principles are of limited use in navigating the perils of daily business life, employees rely mostly on their interaction with one another for a sense of normative propriety. Values are the result of relationships, and as such, depend on how these relationships are sustained over time.

However, a relational conception of values is not without problems. It confronts us with the question of how individual autonomy is maintained within a network of relationships. In this regard, the work of Michel Foucault provides some important insights. Foucault's approach to "ethics as care of the self and the practice of freedom" is often misinterpreted as a form of Nietzschean individualism. There is no doubt that, for Foucault, there can be no ethics without freedom. In fact, he describes freedom as the ontological condition of ethics, and ethics as the considered form that this freedom takes.[66] On closer analysis, however, it becomes clear that Foucault has his own

---

[65] Frederick, *Values, Nature, Culture*, p. 275.
[66] Michel Foucault, *Ethics: the Essential Works* (London: The Penguin Press, 1994), p. 284.

particular definition of freedom. It is not a freedom that allows one to rise above one's context and attain a vantage point from which it is possible to judge autonomously. Instead, our ability to choose comes from our closeness to events. It is from this position of intimate involvement that we are able to establish the right kind of relationship to the present.[67] Ethics entails navigating, negotiating and manipulating power relationships and knowledge components within oneself and within one's environment. The self is always located at the nexus of a wide array of power relationships and is constituted by various discourses. According to Foucault, one cannot be free if one does not understand the various ways in which these discourses construct the self. Neither can one be free from power relationships or from the desire to influence events and other people. Freedom has to do with how one understands and conducts oneself as one navigates the contingent realities of one's life. Foucault draws on the Greek conception of *ethos* to explain what it means to be ethical. According to Foucault, the ancient Greeks saw *ethos* as a way of being and a form of behavior that is firmly rooted in relationships.[68] It has both an individual and a communal dimension. It requires, first and foremost, that one takes care of oneself and learns to understand oneself. Only then can one conduct oneself appropriately in one's interpersonal relationships and thus occupy one's rightful position in a community.

It is important to note that the kind of organizational identity that is advocated here does not take the shape of a fixed self. This is where the communitarian conception of the relationship between individuals and communities becomes problematic. Individuals' participation in communities does not fix their sense of self in an essentialist sort of way. Furthermore, those characteristics that define a community are never entirely immutable either. Martin Parker has warned, in this regard, against the idea that organizations can function as unitary communities.[69] He argues that, within complex organizations, employees' sense of work identity is divided and hence multiple. The self is constantly negotiated and (re)formed in and through its interactions with the power dynamics and discourses in its environment. Postmodern scholars in cultural theory, such as Wilmott, Smircich, and Calas

[67] See Paul Rabinow's introduction to Foucault, *Ibid.*, p. xviii.
[68] Foucault, *Ethics*, p. 287.
[69] Parker, "Organisation, Community and Utopia," 77–91.

concur.[70] They depict the self as fragmented – influenced by personal, textual, historical and contextual dynamics that often contradict one another.[71]

The existence of these fragmented selves is often ignored in communitarian accounts. A strong communitarian orientation can overlook individual perspectives within a business organization. For instance, when corporate managers make liberal use of the first person plural in their statements, they often do so on the basis of some assumed common denominator. When a manager says something like "we are all in this together," he is, in effect, co-opting those whom he is addressing for his own agenda. For someone like Martin Parker, this borders on a form of totalitarianism.

According to Foucault, moral truth is not a form of knowledge that can be established once and for all. Morality cannot therefore be equated with the application of a fixed body of secure knowledge to a succession of practical problems.[72] Instead, morality requires sustained engagement and continued responsiveness. These Foucaultian insights are based on ancient Greek conceptions regarding the way in which one comes to know moral truth. Ongoing moral responsiveness requires a particular kind of awareness. One needs, for instance, continually to consider one's relationship to other people. In addition, one needs to remain cognizant of the way in which one's reality is informed by things like rules, practices, and the various physical contingencies of one's existence. Foucault would instruct us, in this regard, to keep practicing appropriate skills and continue cultivating a suitable relationship with ourselves and others. Foucault encourages us to consider the way in which the Greeks practiced self-discipline, and exercised their writing skills. He draws attention to the Greeks'

---

[70] H. Willmott, "Breaking the Paradigm Mentality," *Organization Studies*, 14(5) (1993), 681–719; H. Willmott, "Postmodernism and Excellence: the Differentiation of Economy and Culture," *Journal of Organizational Change*, 5 (1) (1992), 58–68; L. Smircich, "Concepts of Culture and Organizational Analysis," *Administrative Science Quarterly*, 28 (1983), 339–358; L. Smircich and M. Calas, "Organizational Culture: a Critical Assessment" in F. Jablin, L. Putnam, K. Roberts and L. Porter (eds.), *Handbook of Organizational Communication* (Beverly Hills, CA: Sage, 1987), pp. 228–263.

[71] Martin Parker, *Organizational Culture and Identity: Unity and Division at Work* (London: Sage, 2000), p. 76.

[72] Will McNeill, "Care for the Self: Originary Ethics in Heidegger and Foucault," *Philosophy Today*, 42 (1998).

use of *hupomnemata*. *Hupomnemata* could be account books, public registers or many other forms of written records. They could also be individual notebooks, serving as memoranda, which would be used as books of life or guides for conduct.[73] These books constituted a material memory of what people heard, thought, read. As such, they formed the basis for later rereading and meditation. According to Foucault, self-formation takes place as one continually reminds oneself of particular codes of conduct, or as one measures one's own activities against some sort of standard. It is important to note that for the ancient Greeks, this practice of recalling truths did not amount to an interrogation of one's own conscience, or hidden thoughts, as would later be the case in Christian confessions. It was rather a process of putting oneself in conversation with what one is striving towards. In a very real sense, an organization's reports, financial records, newsletters, marketing material, email, etc. all constitute practices of writing that leave a record of how people in the organization thought, of the things they valued and of the lessons they learned. More will be said about this in Chapter 6, but what is important to recognize here, is that everyday practices of writing and recording such as these may give us far more insight into the values and ethos of an organization than could ever be gleaned through an examination of its values statement or code of conduct.

Values as congruence

If values are relational in character, then normative orientation is not to be found in epistemic principles that are defined independent of human relationships and institutions. Instead values emerge in and through the interactions between individuals and in and through, individuals' participation in institutional practices. This does not mean, however, that values emerge ad hoc in accordance with the demands of whatever situation may present itself. Values are not constructed anew every time we make decisions. They have a history. They are part of the vision of the good life that the members of an organization strive for every day. For MacIntyre, people's various daily efforts to realize a particular desired state of affairs are inscribed within a kind of "narrative unity." Individuals see themselves as part

[73] Foucault, *Ethics*, p. 273.

of an unfolding story. For MacIntyre, the individual's life within a community is part of an interlocking set of narratives that act as constraints.[74] Each individual also plays various parts in the narratives of others. Whether consciously or not, individuals are constantly checking to make sure that their actions and decisions are reconcilable with their sense of self and that to which they aspire.

It has been claimed that Aristotle's ethics amounts to an empty situation morality. Nussbaum has given careful consideration to this claim.[75] She concludes that an ethics that is based on a readiness to respond appropriately to the demands of each new situation does not amount to relativism. Nussbaum uses the metaphor of theatrical improvisation to explain the strong sense of normativity that remains present even in the absence of fixed directional guidelines or principles. She describes how keenly attentive actors have to be when responding to the other characters in a play when their roles have not been pre-scripted. In such a situation, the actors must be actively aware and ready to respond appropriately at any moment, whereas in a scripted play, that kind of intense attunement is less critical. For such an improvisational performance, an actor needs to consider, at every moment, the nature of the character that he or she is portraying, the context within which each interaction takes place, and the relationship of his or her character to the other characters in the story. The fact that actors do not have scripts does not give them unfettered freedom to do or say whatever they please. Whatever they say or do has to fit in with, and contribute to, a broader understanding of what is meaningful and appropriate within that particular dramatic context. In the same vein, the employees of an organization whose actions and decisions are not made subject to universal, epistemic principles are unlikely to act in an entirely willful and arbitrary way. In fact, to ensure that they respond appropriately to each new situation and challenge, employees are likely to be doubly careful about what they say and do. Not unlike Nussbaum's improvising actors, they'd constantly consider both the nature of the contingencies that they have to deal with and the appropriateness of their actions against the

[74] D. L. Sullivan and M. S. Martin, "Habit Formation and Story Telling: a Theory for Guiding Ethical Action," *Technical Communication Quarterly*, 10(3), 251–272.
[75] Nussbaum, *Love's Knowledge*, p. 94.

background of their role within an organization. Their judgment would be informed by their sense of what it is that people in the organization care about and strive for. They would take care to ensure that their actions are congruent with the role that they see themselves playing in the organization. They'd be very cognizant of what it is that others in the organization expect of them.

Since individuals are part of many groups, they navigate a complex set of demands that all act as constraints. This informs their compliance with certain group norms, but could also trigger their dissent from those expectations that will cause harm to the broader relational fabric upon which all stakeholder interactions depend. In an improvisational play, other characters and the audience rely on the actor to say or do something that makes sense within the bigger scheme of the plot's progression. To do the "right thing," in an organizational context, is therefore, in a way, to do what "makes sense." If a particular action or statement by an individual employee were treated as though it were a snapshot, and if we were to think of the life of such an individual or organization as a movie, then normative congruence requires that it be possible to insert the snapshot in the movie without disrupting the character development or plot. The plot may even change over time, but the sense of congruence, of people working on themselves and on their life stories, should remain.

Rules and habits can also contribute to a sense of normative congruence within an organization. Organizational histories, practices, rules and rewards can shape and inform employees' sense of ethical propriety without blunting their ability to remain morally responsive. Nussbaum beautifully and succinctly describes how this works:

> Perception, we might say, is a process of loving conversation between rules and concrete responses, general conceptions and unique cases, in which the general articulates the particular and is in turn articulated by it. The particular is constituted out of features both repeatable and nonrepeatable; it is outlined by the structure in general terms, and it also contains unique images of those we love.[76]

It is important to understand the role that rules play in the development of employees' sense of moral orientation. In some cases, rules can

---

[76] Nussbaum, "An Aristotelian conception of rationality," *Love's Knowledge*, p. 5.

be harmful instead of helpful.[77] What has to be avoided is a rule-driven inclination that eliminates discretion, creativity, imagination and responsiveness. Rules that narrowly script individuals' responses blunt their moral perceptivity, dismiss their critical capacities and prohibit them from interacting with others in an authentic way. Foucault has warned, in this regard, that if rules are enforced at the expense of the practice of the care of the self, morality and creativity are suppressed. Because ethical challenges almost always arise at the unanticipated intersection of a set of unique contingencies and singular dynamics, rules are incapable of providing the ethical agent with adequate guidelines.[78]

Foucault is well aware of the fact that the subject is constituted on the basis of context-specific cultural rules, styles, and inventions. What should be kept in mind is that these processes of self-formation or self-stylization can either threaten or foster moral agency. Foucault describes the possibility of ethics as a critical relationship of the self to itself. Codes through which the individual measures him/herself against a certain standard can play a positive role in this process.[79] He is, however, critical of the kind of rule-based morality that succeeds in inscribing the individual in a restricted view of the self and hence causes the individual to lose his/her capacity for self-stylization. When freedom is lost, the capacity for ethical responsiveness disappears.

Foucault is particularly concerned about the functioning of the law as "rules backed by sanctions." He views this functioning of the law as indicative of a negative conception of power, which he describes as "jurico-discursive" power.[80] Power need not function exclusively in a coercive way, but the way in which the law and discipline function undermines an alternative conception of power. Individuals can, for instance, develop an essentialist conception of themselves, which robs them of their freedom to utilize power in a more positive way, and as such makes ethics impossible. Discipline is a most insidious force, in that it seeks to define the very being of the individual. From a disciplinary perspective, it is criminality, as such, that defines a delinquent's

---

[77] *Ibid.*, p. 81.
[78] Neil Levy, "Ethics and Rules: a Political Reading of Foucault's Aesthetics of Existence," *Philosophy Today*, 42 (1998), 79–84.
[79] For a discussion of the dangers of "discipline and order" as a kind of counter-law that predetermines action see *Ibid.*
[80] Alan Hunt and Gary Wickham, *Foucault and Law. Towards a Sociology of Law and Governance.* (Pluto Press, 1994), p. 46.

being. The sexual subject, for instance, is defined, not in terms of his or her acts, but by what is regarded as his or her sexual essence. This essence is construed as the only access to his or her identity.[81] Within an organizational context, this is what happens if an individual comes to see him or herself as a mere cog in a machine, with little or no discretion and decision-making power. The danger lies in defining an employee by an essential role and utilizing this as the single point of access to his or her moral identity. Such an individual will perform the roles and tasks essential to that role, but will show no discretion or moral imagination.

Other forms of self-formation that are not based on the idea that individuals have a fixed essence can have a more positive effect. They can enable individuals to understand practices of truth and negotiate power relations in a way that facilitates ethics as the practice of freedom. The interaction of historical conditions of knowledge, normativity and self-relation with codified or uncodified forces, creates a playing field of dynamic and nonlinear influences that do not have a deterministic effect. This play of true and false, this acceptance or refusal of rules, this relation to oneself and others, is a form of consideration that Foucault describes as a kind of thinking that goes beyond theoretical reflection.[82]

All of this has a significant bearing on the role of rules in organizational life. Clearly, it is important to avoid creating an excessively rule-driven environment within an organization. Individuals should not find themselves inscribed in fixed identities, as this would curtail their ability to give creative form to the normative congruence within an organizational system. When excessively prescriptive regulatory regimes are imposed on the members of an organizational system, they are treated as if they were automatons, capable of performing only a limited number of mechanical tasks in a highly circumscribed manner. But ethics involves far more than the application of a fixed set of rules. What is necessary is to encourage individual employees to cultivate the habits of critical self-reflection so that they may develop a sense of who they are, where they come from, and what they should strive for. They need to be able to reconsider, and critically assess the values and priorities of the organization. Things like rules and policies can, of course, prohibit certain forms of behavior, and this can be a helpful form of orientation. However, on their own, rules do

---

[81] Levy, "Ethics and Rules," 82.
[82] David Webb, "On Friendship: Derrida, Foucault and the Practice of Becoming," *Research in Phenomenology*, 33 (2003), 129.

little to encourage employees to find their own ways of contributing towards that which the organization strives for.

Rules and the capacity to exercise discretion are equally important conditions for ethics as practice. You cannot sustain a game of chess if you ignore its rules. On the other hand, simply knowing and playing by the rules does not make you a good chess player. To be good at chess you need practical skills, such as the ability to "read" the board and identify appropriate moves. But you also have to care about the fairness of the game, as much as you care about winning. Without rules, and without players who are capable of competing skillfully and fairly within the rules, chess just would not be chess any more. Business similarly needs rules and practical skills to function as practice. Legal frameworks and organizational policies and procedures create a space within which business practitioners can fairly compete with one another. It makes business as practice safer and more satisfying. The GAAP rules, for instance, create the kind of congruence that business practitioners need to interpret financial statements. Similarly, the SOX legislation instills confidence in the market by providing crucial checks and balances. However, complying with GAAP rules and SOX requirements does not in itself make you good at business. Business practice is not only about following the rules – more than anything, it is about skillfully and thoughtfully responding to challenges and opportunities as they arise. As such, a successful business requires an ongoing concern, on the part of its individual employees, for the way in which their actions and decisions may either contribute to, or detract from that which they and their colleagues strive for.

The behavior and actions of business practitioners are substantially informed by the organizational environments in which they function. Every organizational system has its own unique values, goals and priorities. The nature and content of these values, goals and priorities are intimately related to the resources that are available within a particular organizational environment, as well as the dynamics that shape its internal life. The key to understanding this relationship lies in the idea of organizational environments as complex adaptive systems.

Values as emergent properties of complex adaptive systems

Attempts to influence organizational cultures have become a key component of many business ethics interventions. This is perhaps partly due to the requirements of the new Federal Sentencing Guidelines. The new Guidelines require that companies make an effort to engender a culture of ethical compliance among their employees. Organizational culture is typically defined as "shared values," and commonly understood as "the way we do things around here." This understanding misinterprets "organizational culture" as a kind of "consensualist commonality" and as such, underestimates the fact that it is an ongoing process of meaning creation. In this way, it thoroughly misreads the differences that exist within organizations. A further problem with this understanding is that it conceives of culture as the object of management control. It is assumed that an organization can significantly influence the values of its employees by means of managerial interventions. In the light of the emotional, relational, tropical, rhetorical and responsive nature of values, this is by no means a simple matter. Clearly, training employees in the rational application of a set of supposedly universal principles does not meaningfully alter anything. Formulating yet another set of rules and codes is also of limited use. Part of the problem with such interventions is that they do not adequately consider the way in which normative congruence emerges within organizations. It is in this that complexity theory's observations about the way in which order emerges within complex adaptive, or nonlinear dynamical systems, is so useful.

Lewin and Regine argue that, from the perspective of complexity science, the relationship between business organizations and natural ecosystems is not simply one of resemblance.[83] Instead, business organizations share fundamental properties with natural ecosystems. Both business organizations and natural ecosystems are complex adaptive systems. Both are characterized by nonlinear processes. According to Lewin and Regine, complex adaptive systems evolve to a critical point where they become poised between chaotic and static states. Here, at the edge of chaos, a business organization is at its most responsive and creative. Lewin and Regine hypothesize that it is in this precarious state of heightened creativity that a business organization is likely to be most successful.

There are a number of concepts and observations from complexity theory that have some bearing on the current discussion and need further explication. The tendency of complex adaptive systems to

---

[83] Roger Lewin and Birute Regine, "On the Edge of the World of Business" in R. Lewin, *Complexity: Life at the Edge of Chaos* (Phoenix, 2001), p. 198.

become unstable can lead to sudden changes in the system's direction, character, or structure. These are called bifurcations. During bifurcations, the system rearranges itself around a new underlying order.[84] During such occurrences, multiple variables pull in contradictory directions. When such bifurcations are represented as maps, they resemble scribbled doughnuts (*tori*) or butterfly wings (joined *tori*). Another important concept is that of attractors. An attractor can be described as a pattern of variation, which exhibits regularities, and thus "governs" the chaotic process, producing "bounded chaos."[85] Murphy describes an attractor as an organizing principle, an inherent shape or state of affairs to which a phenomenon always returns as it evolves, no matter how random individual moments may seem. Though some attractors' patterns can easily be mapped and understood through conventional forms of analysis, chaotic systems present special challenges. This is because they are characterized by what Murphy calls "strange attractors." Because of the effect of these strange attractors, outcomes wander constantly and unpredictably within a bounded range.

The role of strange attractors in complex adaptive systems can serve as an explanatory model for the way in which values function within organizational environments. Murphy proposes, in this regard, that an organizational culture may be regarded as a strange attractor, i.e. a common set of values that inform behavior without being articulated in the language of a corporate mission statement.[86] Guastello's account of the way in which attractors function within nonlinear dynamical systems is also helpful in understanding how values function in business organizations.[87] According to Guastello, an attractor is a piece of space that possesses a special sort of property: objects that get close to it are drawn into it. Guastello's observations about attractors are remarkably reminiscent of what Sean Kirkland has said about rhetoric. According to Kirkland, rhetoric opens up a space between the speaker and audience, within which a certain form of truth manifests itself. If values are rhetorical in nature, then it can be argued that they function like

---

[84] J. Murphy, "Chaos Theory as a Model for Managing Issues and Crises," *Public Relations Review*, 22 (1996).
[85] Jane Collier and R. Esteban, "Governance in the Participative Organisation: Freedom, Creativity and Ethics," *Journal of Business Ethics*, 21 (1999), 179.
[86] Murphy, "Chaos Theory," 98.
[87] S. Guastello, *Managing Emergent Phenomena: Nonlinear Dynamics in Work Organizations* (London: Lawrence Erlbaum Associates, 2002).

Guastello's strange attractors within the organizational system. As "attractors," values have the unique ability to solicit the voluntary support of individual employees. They emerge as a kind of inarticulate pattern or quality in the behavior and expectations of those who participate in an organizational system. They create a certain congruence, both in the actions of an individual over time and under different circumstances, and in the behavior of all those who identify with a particular organization. As such, they draw the employees of an organization together in a meaningful and significant, but non-coercive way. They are "strange" in the sense that they have a discernible effect, but elude deliberate articulation and linguistic reification. Through their emergence, an organization's employees develop a sense of propriety that guides decision making more effectively than the deliberate application of principled thought.

The way in which values emerge within complex adaptive organizational systems has to do with the fact that such systems are self-organizing and self-renewing. In fact, the *emergent self-organization* that takes place in complex adaptive systems has been described as complexity theory's "anchor point phenomenon" and as such, it plays a crucial role in understanding how these systems function. In these systems order emerges from the actions of interdependent agents who continually adapt and react to information that they receive regarding what others in the system are doing and saying.[88] Convergent and divergent thinking within an organizational system facilitates creativity and allows the system to renew and reorganize itself as new situations arise over time. It allows an organization's employees to continually respond and adapt to new opportunities, challenges, and contingencies.

The continual self-renewal and self-organization of complex adaptive organizational systems is facilitated by positive feedback loops within the system. The constant circulation of information, observations and experiences through such feedback loops often contributes to the destabilization of the organizational system, but also lends it some coherence. The organizational system is characterized by what Murphy calls "correspondences," or "couplings," among its various stages.

---

[88] Donde Ashmos Plowman, Stephanie Solansky, Tammy E. Beck, LaKami Baker, Mukta Kulharni and Deandra Villarreal Travis, "The Role of Leadership in Emergent Self-Organization," *The Leadership Quarterly*, 18(4) (2007), 341–356.

Because of these, a change in one area of the organization rapidly communicates itself around the entire system. Consequently, different parts of the organization bear the stamp of the same pattern. Murphy describes systems that function in this way as an unstable combination of randomness and plan, broken by flashpoints of change. A meaningful and coherent sense of normative orientation is therefore sustained within an organizational system, through the creative form that individuals give to shared priorities and goals, as well as continuity within a broader narrative. Some authors refer to the forms of cooperation that can exist in complex adaptive systems as "tagging." Tagging allows agents to distinguish among each other and signal when interactions are possible.[89] In this way, it facilitates the creation of aggregates and indicates patterns of interactions that agents then intuitively follow.

It is important to recognize that a company's differentiating responsiveness to the environment is "bounded" by its organizational purpose. An organization's purpose is therefore constitutive of its values. A sense of normative congruence exists only within an organizational system if the organization's goals correspond with, and reinforce, its values. According to Collier and Esteban, an organization can avoid dispersion in a changing environment through purposefulness. Processes of continual internal realignment allow the employees of a company to confront and respond to new challenges from the environment without losing their sense of orientation. In fact, argue Collier and Esteban, an organization's goals are clarified and reinforced in the course of such processes of internal realignment. Once clarified, the organization's goals are reflected and reinterpreted into the whole system through feedback loops. The integrative pull of organizational collaboration tames chaos through chaos. It is a process in which the emphasis is on purpose. Through it, employees' impulse to respond to the external environment is held in a creative and delicate balance with organizational goals and priorities. Some authors describe the process of developing shared schemas as the creation of "cognitive consensuality" within organizations. Individuals' schemas emerge from social interaction with other individuals in a specific context.

---

[89] Kimberley B. Boal and Patrick L. Schultz, "Storytelling, Time and Evolution: the Role of Strategic Leadership in Complex Adaptive Systems," *The Leadership Quarterly*, 18(4) (2007), 411–428.

It is the connectedness of an organization that ensures its inner coherence in a constantly changing business environment. An effective communications network is therefore very important. Connectedness and communication allow organizational processes to assume the character of "continual conversations." Their participation in such organizational conversations allows employees to "make sense" of changes and interpret their meaning on both a personal and organizational level. "Continual conversations" about the purpose, goals, and character of a company and those who are associated with it, are invaluable in sustaining a meaningful sense of moral orientation in an organizational system. Boal and Schultz argue that engaging in dialogue and participating in storytelling are two ways in which this "cognitive consensuality" may be developed.[90] I tend to think that calling the shared sense of normative propriety that develops in complex adaptive systems a "consensus" may be overstating the case. Since it is an emergent property that is dependent on ongoing interactions, consensualist language may be inappropriate to describe the fluid nature of episodic frameworks.

According to complexity theory, chaotic systems are extremely complex and prone to perturbation. Because of this, one cannot discern their underlying patterns by observing their parts in isolation from one another. To form an impression of the underlying pattern of such a system, one has to study it in its entirety. The only feasible way to do so is to study its evolution *a posteriori* and then conceptualize it as an imaginary map. A fractal describes the relative degree of complexity of an object that enables one to identify correspondences or "couplings" between forms that vary vastly in scale but have similar patterns of complexity, by combining iteration with elements of chance.[91] Whereas Newtonian logic generalizes from the part to the whole, chaos theory requires that we study the whole evolutionary process of a system before we begin to draw conclusions about it. This is as valid for its parts as it is for the process as a whole. General patterns only become discernible once a comprehensive overview of all the interactions and iterations of various individual units over time becomes available.

Organizational culture gradually comes into being over time as individual employees interact with one another and respond to new challenges and contingencies. As the underlying pattern of organizational behavior, it is possible to discern organizational culture only

[90] Boal and Schultz, 417.   [91] Murphy, "Chaos Theory," 100.

retrospectively, i.e. by studying the actions and interactions of individuals over time, and across circumstances. Organizational culture always informs the particular actions of individuals in specific situations. However, it is not possible to articulate or define organizational culture solely on the basis of one or more employees' actions during a particular incident. The meaning and significance of the choices that individuals make in response to particular challenges, and their relation to those that others have made under different circumstances, only starts to become apparent when they are considered within the wider context of organizational behavior over time.

This poses special challenges for understanding leadership in organizations that function as complex adaptive systems. Executives are interested in deliberately managing, or influencing, the organizational culture that exists among their employees, but leadership dynamics in complex adaptive systems are more complicated. Executives and managers will face this challenge on various levels. It will influence what they can and cannot know about the cultural dynamics of their organization, and it will have an impact on how they interact with it.

Naturally, any form of cultural intervention starts with some assessment of the culture that already exists within a particular organization. Many companies use statistical surveys and quantitative analysis to this end. In this type of research, a sample population is usually surveyed. The data that is thus obtained is then statistically interpreted to draw conclusions about the culture of the organization as a whole. In other words, the analysis moves from the part to the whole. This, as we have seen, is simply not a feasible way of studying complex systems such as business organizations. What is more, quantitative statistical surveys are usually conducted on the basis of pre-existing conceptual models. They are basically used to measure patterns of variation, i.e. to either confirm or dispel a series of pre-formulated hypotheses. However, the tacit sense of propriety that informs employees' behavior in an organizational system does not lend itself to articulation in the form of pre-existing conceptual templates. One is therefore led to conclude that, given the complex nature of organizational systems, quantitative statistical studies are unlikely to give the leadership of an organization an accurate or reliable impression of the cultural dynamics that inform relational life within the system. What seems necessary instead, is a meaningful qualitative appreciation of how emergent value dynamics contribute to trends that can be monitored over time and across various levels of analysis. In Chapter 6, I will make a number of proposals as to how such an ongoing critical interrogation of an organization's value dynamics might look and what elements it might include. In order to get there, however, we need to develop an understanding of how leadership dynamics are played out in organizations that function as complex adaptive systems.

5 | Leadership and accountability

"Tone at the top!" "Clean the staircase from the top!" "The fish rots at the head." Popular maxims such as these reflect the widely held belief that it is the leaders of an organization who are responsible for instigating and sustaining a corporate culture which encourages employees to behave ethically. Corporate ethics management initiatives therefore invariably start with an effort to secure the board and executive leadership's commitment to the proposed program.[1] What is implicitly assumed in all of this is that it is primarily those in the top echelons of the corporate hierarchy who have to be convinced of the need for an ethics program. An assessment of the ethical risks that the organization faces is often deemed a sufficient rationale. It is believed that once its captains are aware of the dangerous state of affairs, the corporate ship will retrieve its moral compass. The overhaul of an organizational culture is therefore largely seen as a top-down affair, with leadership setting the tone, implementing ethics management initiatives and leading by example.

That high-level individuals can and do play an important role in articulating priorities and shaping the sensibilities of employees within organizations is not to be disputed. However, if the role of such individuals is not to be denied, it is also not to be overestimated. Our analysis of business organizations as complex adaptive systems suggests that the ineffable sense of normative congruence that develops among those who participate in an organizational system over time may be of a far more complex and relational nature. It is certainly not something that lends itself to abstract design, nor can it be unilaterally imposed or sustained through the exercise of authority. This calls for a fundamental reconsideration of how the habits, beliefs and expectations that inform the cultural dynamics within an organization's

---

[1] Michael Hoffman and Dawn-Marie Driscoll, *Ethics Matters: How to Implement Values-Driven Management* (Bentley College, 1999).

179

culture are shaped and sustained. If the habits and behavior of individual employees are shaped and informed by the corporate culture in which they participate, the definition of "leadership" as such has to be reconsidered. If an organizational culture is not something that formally appointed leaders of an organization can design deliberately, impose unilaterally or sustain willfully, then it stands to reason that the notion of accountability should also be fundamentally reconceived.

In what is to follow, I will explore the idea that the various iterations of organizational cultures are shaped not only by those in positions of authority, but by all who participate in them. I will propose that the tasks of nurturing and encouraging a relationally responsive ethical attitude among the members of an organizational system are shared by all who participate in it. From this perspective accountability is less a question of the leaders of an organization being held accountable _for_ the actions and decisions of employees and more a case of all of the members of an organization being accountable _to_ one another. Furthermore, I will argue that in the dynamic environment of a complex adaptive organizational system where it is impossible to anticipate and legislate for every potential circumstantial contingency, creating and sustaining relationships of trust has to be a systemic capacity of the entire organization. Focusing on the legal duty of executives to comply with regulation will not create the kind of moral responsiveness needed to navigate turbulent corporate environments. This represents a fundamental re-conceptualization of accountability and the way in which it is distributed throughout an organizational system. However, if the sharing of this kind of relational responsiveness to the everyday realities of organizational life is to be properly understood, it is important to consider it in its concrete institutional manifestations. In the last section of this chapter I therefore take a look at how an organization in which accountability is understood in relational terms and is shared by all appears and functions.

Leadership is a prominent area of research in many disciplines. Organizational theorists, management experts, industrial psychologists, business ethicists, educationalists, etc. all contribute to an ever-growing body of literature. In fact, leadership studies has evolved into an academic discipline all of its own. As a result, it is a very broad topic – one that a single chapter of a book could hardly do justice to. Our goal here will therefore be confined to establishing a broad overview of important trends in the leadership literature. In much of leadership literature, the focus remains on the role that appointed leaders play in the workings of corporate culture. The fact that those who are formally appointed in positions of authority within an organization are often held responsible for the conduct of all its members is indicative of the way in which their role is often conceived. This conception is based in its turn on particular beliefs about the nature of leadership.

This chapter will argue that focusing exclusively on individual leaders, i.e. those appointed in positions of authority, will not allow us to gain an understanding of leadership dynamics in organizations that function as complex adaptive systems. The conflation of notions of leaders and leadership that exists in much of the leadership literature may in fact play an important role in the formation of legislators' and stockholders' expectations of corporate leaders. In order therefore to address the proper role and responsibilities of an organization's formally appointed leaders with respect to corporate ethics, and to gain understanding of broader leadership dynamics within complex adaptive systems, it is necessary to familiarize oneself with some of the ideas that currently inform many people's perceptions of leaders and leadership. We will start with the research done on "ethical leadership," and then locate certain trends within the broader leadership literature.

Ethical leadership

In business ethics literature, ethical leadership is usually described from either a normative/philosophical perspective, or in more social scientific terms. The works of those authors who look at ethical leadership from a normative perspective usually revolve around the question: What *ought* an ethical leader to do? Those, on the other hand, who are more inclined to social scientific analysis study perceptions about ethical leadership and the way in which it functions within organizations in order to address the question: What *is* ethical leadership? Much of what has been written on the topic of leadership within the business ethics field focuses on the former, more normative, question. Those who believe that the key to ethical leadership lies in the answer to such questions draw on various philosophical paradigms to develop a definitive normative model of a leader's duties and responsibilities. The normative frameworks that are thus developed are typically based on principles of role-responsibilities or virtues.

The work of Joanne Cuilla may be regarded as emblematic, in many respects, of this normative approach to leadership in business ethics literature. In response to some leadership theories that equate "good" leadership with effective leadership, Cuilla suggests that leaders have to be both ethical and effective.[2] In other words, effective leadership does not automatically translate into ethical leadership. Ethical leadership requires a deliberate and sustained commitment to the highest ethical standards. In its philosophical orientation, Cuilla's proposals in this regard are both deontological and teleological.[3] She argues that a leader's decisions and actions should be informed, at all times, by a sense of duty, and should always be directed at attaining the greatest possible good.

According to Cuilla, many of the concepts that have been developed to describe leadership in its various manifestations can be analyzed in normative terms. For Cuilla, a concept such as "servant leadership," for instance, possesses a strong normative element. She points out that the leadership theory that has been developed around the concept of servant leadership draws on both ancient Western and Eastern thought. Its main proposition involves a simple, but radical shift from followers serving leaders to leaders serving followers. This reversal is telling, in that it serves as an acknowledgement of multidirectional institutional dynamics.

In Cuilla's view, the notion of "transformative leaders" can likewise be subjected to normative analysis. To this end she makes use of James McGregor Burns' description of transformative leaders. According to Burns, transformative leaders elevate followers and make them leaders. Cuilla argues that, from a normative perspective, this is the most attractive part of Burns' theory. Cuilla's interpretation of the normative essence of transformational leadership manifests a move away from "inspiring leaders" to acknowledging the importance of *inspired* individuals across the organization.

Transformative leadership is often associated with the idea of "charismatic leadership." In fact, some authors regard charismatic leadership as a necessary ingredient of effective transformational

---

[2] Joanne Cuilla, "Leadership Ethics: Mapping the Territory" in Joanne Cuilla (ed.), *Ethics: the Heart of Leadership*, second edition (Praeger, 2004).

[3] Joanne Cuilla, "Ethics, the Heart of Leadership" in Thomas Maak and Nicola Pless (eds.), *Responsible Leadership* (Routledge, 2006).

leadership. However, because of its ability to exploit those who are moved by it, Cuilla cautiously describes charismatic leadership as potentially both the best and the worst kind of leadership. In Cuilla's view charismatic leadership's potential to do both good and harm demonstrates perfectly why ethics needs to be a central concern in the consideration and evaluation of leadership. A number of authors have attempted normative analyses of charismatic leadership on the basis of virtue ethics. Some of these scholars are skeptical about the role of charisma in leadership. Solomon, for instance, argues that the notion of charisma is no more than a myth. The myth of charisma, as he sees it, draws attention away from what is really important in leadership, namely relationships of trust between leaders and followers.[4]

Most people, however, still associate leadership with an individual's ability to influence others. What is important, though, from a normative point of view, is the question as to how leaders do so. Many ethicists have focused, in this regard, on the emotional dimension of the relationship that develops between charismatic leaders and those who follow them and the potential for exploitation and abuse that accompanies it. In his Aristotelian analysis of leadership, however, Sison draws attention to the importance of persuasion in leadership.[5] Based on his reading of Aristotle, Sison sees the ability of some leaders to persuade their followers as something that relies more on character than charisma. He describes persuasion as something that involves three elements. The first is argumentation (*logos*), the second involves influencing the emotional dispositions of an audience (*pathos*), and the third is about the character that a leader projects (*ethos*). From this Aristotelian perspective, character is associated with the practice of habits that are appropriate within a particular socio-cultural context. There is a close, reciprocal relationship between an individual's actions, habits and character. Sison likens the individual's character to a piece of fabric woven together from various physiological, emotional, psychological and socio-cultural strands. A leader's ability to influence his/her followers is therefore based on his or her ability to embody and articulate, in his/her actions and habits, the values and

---

[4] Robert C. Solomon, "Ethical Leadership, Emotions and Trust: Beyond Charisma" in Cuilla, *Ethics: the Heart of Leadership*, pp. 83–101.
[5] Alejo Jose G. Sison, "Leadership, Character and Virtues from an Aristotelian Point of View" in Maak and Pless, *Responsible Leadership*.

priorities of those that he/she seeks to persuade. From this perspective therefore, effective corporate leadership is inseparable from the possession and habitual display of a particular, contextually defined set of virtues.

Virtue ethics also forms the basis of other forms of normative analyses of leadership. Some virtue ethicists, for instance, focus on the nature of the motives that inform a leader's priorities. They employ the Aristotelian concept of *eudaimonia* (happiness) to account for an individual's perception of meaning and value. From this perspective, an individual's perception of meaning is partly informed by the circumstances within which he/she happens to find him/herself. It is also influenced by experiences and expectations of happiness, and shaped by what is considered meaningful or important within the cultural context of the organization with which he/she is associated. In other words, social influences color perceptions of value, but individual character also plays an important role in shaping a leader's priorities. Virtues that are developed in the process lead to individual characters. Well-formed characters ultimately contribute to a happy society.

Most of these normative analytic models draw on traditional deontological, utilitarian and teleological approaches. Although some of these models associate ethical leadership with a concern for, and willingness to serve, others, most still describe it in fairly individualistic terms. What is often absent from business ethicists' analysis of ethical leadership is an adequate appreciation of the fact that the phenomenon of leadership involves a complex set of relational dynamics and that leaders are therefore not autonomously constituted or self-made.

Thomas Maak and Nicola Pless present an intriguing alternative to individualist models of ethical leadership. In their analysis, Maak and Pless propose a more relational understanding of the concept of leadership.[6] They define responsible leadership as the art of building and sustaining relationships with all relevant stakeholders. This requires socialized not personalized leaders. Relational leaders are described as the weavers and facilitators of trusting stakeholder relations. They are said to be capable of balancing the power dynamics that are always at work in such relations by aligning the different values of the various parties in a way that serves everyone's interests alike. Maak and Pless

---

[6] Thomas Maak and Nicola M. Pless, "Responsible Leadership: a Relational Approach" in Maak and Pless, *Responsible Leadership* (Routledge, 2006).

see such leaders as servants, stewards, coaches, architects, storytellers and change agents. Unlike many other leadership theorists, they are careful to note that the kind of leaders that they have in mind need not be exceptional individuals. Navigating the challenges of a complex and demanding stakeholder environment is a skill that is developed, practiced and sustained over time by remaining contextually aware and relationally responsive. This kind of leadership is developed when there is a real concern for sustaining relationships, protecting and nurturing others, and advancing shared goals.

Because of its focus on what *is*, rather than what *ought* to be, the more social scientific approach that is adopted by some business ethicists may in some respects be better suited to the study of ethical leadership within the context of a situated set of relational dynamics. This is, in a sense, what Brown and Trevino propose in their analysis of leadership.[7] They argue that there is a need for a more systematic and unified social scientific approach to the phenomenon of leadership as it is actually manifested in everyday business practice. Our analysis so far certainly supports this view, suggesting, as it does, that there is a close relationship between an individual employee's sense of normative propriety on the one hand, and the complex system of relations in which he or she participates in the context of an organization on the other. The question as to what leaders ought to be and what they ought to do cannot therefore be asked, or answered without properly considering the role that contextual contingencies and relational dynamics continually play in shaping and informing an individual's sense of moral agency.

A social scientific approach therefore has much to offer to our understanding of leadership and accountability in the context of a complex organizational system. Brown and Trevino draw on social learning theory to give an account of the effect that leaders have on the perceptions and actions of those with whom they interact. Social learning theory suggests that individuals tend to pay attention to, and emulate credible and attractive role models. From this perspective, they define ethical leadership as: "the demonstration of normatively appropriate conduct through personal actions and interpersonal relationships, and the

---

[7] S. E. Brown, and L. K. Trevino, "Ethical Leadership: a Review and Future Directions," *The Leadership Quarterly*, 17(6) (2006), 595–616.

promotion of such conduct to followers through two-way communication, reinforcement, and decision making."

Brown and Trevino performed a comparative analysis of the various approaches to leadership that share a concern for the moral dimension of leadership, namely transformational leadership, spiritual leadership and authentic leadership. All of these approaches emphasize the importance of concern for others (altruism), integrity, role modeling and ethical decision making. The meaningful difference between Brown and Trevino's notion of "ethical leadership" and all three other approaches is the fact that they emphasize the importance of moral management.[8] They see moral management as the process by which leaders deliberately infuse their organizational environment with moral content by means of communication, role modeling, rewards and recognition. Moral management requires the intimate participation of leaders in the organizational system. Brown and Trevino suggest, for instance, that role modeling is a side-by-side phenomenon, i.e. a person is most likely to be influenced by an ethical role model with whom he/she has frequent and close contact. In their estimation, moral management also requires that leaders pay close attention and remain attuned to the climate or culture within an organization.

Brown and Trevino define organizational culture or climate as the extent to which ethical behavior is encouraged or discouraged by organizational conditions, habits, practices, procedures or infrastructure. Trevino was involved in a series of research studies attempting to define organizational culture and its influence on ethical behavior within the organization. Her research has shown that organizational culture is a function of both informal and formal behavioral control systems. It is shaped and informed by factors such as peer behavior, authority structures, codes and policies, as well as reward systems. She argues that leaders can contribute to the emergence of an ethical culture within an organization by consistently and visibly encouraging ethical behavior and discouraging inappropriate behavior, by helping to create organizational conditions that are conducive to ethical conduct, by cultivating and fostering appropriate habits, and by establishing good practices, procedures and infrastructures within an organization.

---

[8] The three other paradigms place their focus on other aspects. Authentic leadership insists on self-awareness, spiritual leadership emphasizes visioning, hope/faith and vocation, and transformational leadership emphasizes the role of vision, values and intellectual stimulus.

Organizational cultures can also be affected by the conduct of leaders in what Brown and Trevino describe as situations of "moral intensity." When the leaders of an organization face a choice with implications that are perceived to be of a serious or grave nature, employees tend to pay especially close attention. Because of this, leaders' conduct in such situations of "moral intensity" can have a great impact on the subsequent conduct of employees.

One of the strengths of Brown and Trevino's social scientific approach to ethical leadership is the amount of attention that they pay to contextual factors that affect ethical leadership. They also touch on individual factors that may influence ethical leadership, such as personality traits, the location of a leader's locus of control, Machiavellianism and moral development.[9] Naturally, there can be no dispute that individual factors such as these influence the behavior of individuals. However, when it comes to the influence of those who occupy formal positions of authority in an organizational system, individual factors like the ones that Brown and Trevino identify are drawn into a wider, more complex interplay of contextual and relational contingencies. The internal dynamics of complex adaptive organizational systems are such that it becomes virtually impossible to construct direct cause-and-effect relationships between individual factors and particular events. This is true not only of the relationship between individual leadership characteristics and their perceived effect on other members of an organizational system, but also of almost every other direct causal relationship that one might attempt to construct in an effort to account for the effect of leadership.

Brown and Trevino attempted, for instance, to identify the nature and extent of the influence of leaders at different levels of the organizational hierarchy. The results seem, perhaps counter-intuitively, to suggest that there are few significant differences between supervisory and executive leadership influence. Executive leaders, by virtue of their position, tend to interact more with external stakeholders and not directly with employees. However, they generally have more say in the way in which institutional structures and procedures are set up. As such their actions and decisions do sometimes influence people's experience and perceptions at work. Brown and Trevino also found that informal, socially communicated information about leaders had a very significant effect on employees' perceptions and beliefs. However, in many respects

---

[9] Agreeableness and conscientiousness was positively related to leadership.

supervisors' direct contact with employees makes them even more likely role models and mentors. It becomes clear that it is not necessarily the most senior people in the organization who exert the most influence. In fact, it is extremely difficult to construct any direct cause-and-effect relationships in the often erratic circulation of perceptions and priorities within a complex organizational system.

In a sense, Brown and Trevino's research demonstrate both the advantages and limitations of a social scientific approach to ethical leadership. While this approach allows ethicists to base their analysis of ethical leadership on real observations of organizational practice, its logic tends to remain too linear in orientation to account adequately for the complex and unpredictable ways in which members at every level of an organizational system shape and inform one another's sensibilities and perceptions.

Brown and Trevino also clearly subscribe to the view that leadership is the function of specific individuals who occupy positions of authority. They also seem to believe that it is these individuals who are capable of "managing" the sense of normative orientation of employees, whether through formal or informal systems. Without denying the important role that these individuals do play within the dynamics that inform the meanings that are circulating within organizational cultures, I will argue that a discussion of their role does not fully address the question of leadership in complex organizational environments. What is needed instead is a model capable of recognizing that influence may be exerted in unexpected ways from any position within a complex organizational system, and not just from formally constituted loci of authority. The nature, role and ethical responsibilities of formally appointed leaders thus needs to be understood as part of a broader interplay of personal, interpersonal and contextual forces that continually shape and inform the sensibilities of all who participate in a particular organizational system. There are indeed signs that such models are in the making as more and more observers begin to grapple with the complex dynamics of contemporary business organizations and the new kinds of leadership that have emerged within them. In what is to follow, we will explore some of the ideas that have appeared in recent leadership literature in an effort to try and ascertain how those roles and responsibilities that have traditionally been associated with the formal leadership of an organization may be reconceived in more systemic terms.

Leaders and leadership from a broader perspective

The focus that the studies on ethical leadership place on individuals is echoed in much of the broader leadership literature. Many, if not most, scholars who study leadership view it as a quality of particular individuals.[10] This view of the nature of leadership is sometimes referred to as the "great man theory" or the "traits" approach. From this perspective, leadership is the privilege and responsibility of a select group of individuals who possess the requisite set of distinguishing traits. The implication of this view of leadership is clear: the impact of a leader on the beliefs and behavior of his or her subordinates is contingent on his or her possession and actualization of these distinguishing leadership traits. Kanji and Moura observe that there are also scholars who identify leadership, not with an inherent set of qualities or traits, but with the adoption of a specific set of observable behaviors.[11] In this view the leaders of an organization are likely to be effective in their efforts to give shape and direction to their subordinates' activities only to the extent that they adopt and internalize this inspiring and persuasive set of habitual protocols. Finally, there are those who believe that a leader's effectiveness depends on how well his or her leadership style fits into a particular business and/or organizational context.[12] Ensuring ethical responsiveness amongst the members of an organization is thus implicitly conceived of as a matter of finding the right kind of individual(s) to lead and inspire a particular organization in an appropriate sort of way.[13]

What these traditional views of leadership have in common is a fixation on the importance of the individual within an organizational system. Influence is seen as something that emanates from the gifted, accomplished or charismatic leader and is dispersed throughout the organizational system by the sheer centrifugal force of his or her

---

[10] G. K. Kanji and P. Moura, "Measuring Leadership Excellence," *Total Quality Management*, 12 (6) (2001), 704.

[11] In Kanji and Moura's analysis this view of leadership is called the "behavioral approach."

[12] Kanji and Moura identify this as the "situational" or "contingency" approach to leadership.

[13] For an overview of the limitations of traditional approaches to leadership, such as the traits-, behavior- and style-approaches, see the special edition on Leadership in Complex Adaptive Systems, in *The Leadership Quarterly* (August 2007), especially Plowman *et al.*

personality and authority. As such, the responsibility for instigating and perpetuating a culture of ethical responsiveness within the organization is consolidated in his or her person and position. The first two approaches suffer from an inability to account for the fact that it is very difficult to identify a complete set of traits or behaviors that would provide a definitive model for leadership success. Furthermore, they cannot take changes of context and organizational specifics into account. Though certainly more contextually responsive, the third approach is also unable to provide a clear account of why certain leadership styles are more effective in certain situations. It also suffers from the same problem as do most situational ethics, i.e. the inability to deal with the charge of relativism. All three approaches have been criticized based on the fact that they can't deal with organizational models that emphasize the need for a balance between quality, flexibility, speed, experimentation, and the maintenance of organizational purpose and direction.

Kanji and Moura identify exchange theory and transformational leadership as alternatives to traditional leadership approaches. These approaches are more attuned to the contextual demands of contemporary organizations. As such, they present valuable perspectives on how the leadership function can be reconceived. Scholars who subscribe to the exchange theory approach to leadership believe that the role of organizational leaders can only be properly understood within the context of teams. Its proponents argue that leaders emerge, not just because of their personal qualities, but equally because of the nature of the tasks and norms that have to be managed and negotiated within a particular organization system.[14] Because of this the distinction between leaders and followers becomes less absolute and more flexible. Theorists of this orientation favor democratic styles of leadership. They point out, in this regard, that different styles of leadership may be required at different stages of a team's development. Exchange theory represents a very flexible approach to organizational leadership. This is perhaps one of its main strengths. However, reservations have been raised about the ability of such an approach to provide an organization with enough direction and continuity in the face of change. The kind of criticism that has been leveled at exchange theorists' proposals has highlighted the need for an approach to organizational leadership that can simultaneously provide both a reliable

---

[14] Kanji and Moura, "Measuring Leadership Excellence," 705.

form of orientation for the members of an organizational system and accommodate change, innovation and adaptation.

A leadership approach that seeks to balance the importance of a strong sense of direction with the ability to respond to changing circumstances is that of transformational leadership.[15] The concept of transformational leadership represents an effort to understand how leaders may initiate, develop and effect significant changes in organizations. Some proponents of the concept of transformational leadership believe that it is the responsibility of the leaders of an organization to inspire all its members by creating a shared vision that gives meaning to the organization's pursuits and clarifies its identity. They argue that transformational leaders provide a focus point for the entire organization with its diverse perspectives, hopes and energies. According to Friedman, transformational leadership creates change and enhances productivity by offering a vision that attracts and inspires followers. Because of this, such leaders are said to be capable of building commitment to an organization's mission and objectives.[16] From this perspective, transformational leaders are described as individuals who appeal to high ideals and moral values and change attitudes and assumptions to bring about changes in an organization's culture. Such individuals supposedly have the ability to balance the "hard" aspects, such as structures, systems and technology, with "soft" issues, such as the vision, mission, values, behaviors and attitudes within an organization.[17] Typically, this kind of transformational leadership is associated with three vital qualities or capacities, namely charisma, consideration and creativity.

---

[15] Most leadership authors insist on a strict distinction between transformational leadership and transactional leadership. Transactional leaders are concerned with the clarification of goals, tasks and standards, and the completion of tasks, as well as compliance-driven incentives and rewards. As such, Friedman argues, transactional leaders are primarily focused on management, rather than leadership. For instance, within the organizational environment of a college or university, a transactional leader might ask: "How can we improve our students' scores on high-stakes tests?" whereas a transformational leader might be more interested in assisting students to acquire the critical insight and skills that they will need to function effectively in an unforgiving and competitive job market.

[16] Audrey A. Friedman, "Beyond Mediocrity: Transformational Leadership within a Transactional Framework," *International Journal of Leadership Education*, 7(3) (2004), 203–224.

[17] Kanji and Moura, "Measuring Leadership Excellence," 705.

However, as was indicated earlier, the ideal of such a "charismatic hero" and the ideology of the "power of one" on which it relies is not universally supported. This is due in part to a growing awareness and acknowledgement among leadership theorists of the role that organization-specific contextual variables may play in determining the nature and extent of a leader's influence. What many theorists are beginning to appreciate is that the inspirational vision and charismatic presence of an individual "transformational leader" is often not the sole determining factor in organizational change.

The alternatives to the traditional leadership approaches are valuable in that they acknowledge the importance of the interaction between leaders and followers in specific contexts. However, they remain committed to the view that leadership is found within particular individuals who occupy positions of authority. Despite the limitations to the notion that leadership is primarily located within particular individuals, it still remains a very prominent aspect of leadership studies. Uhl-Bien, Marion and McKelvey[18] point out that much of leadership theory remains grounded in outdated assumptions regarding bureaucratic systems, which assume that control has to be rationalized. The belief has been that goals are rationally constructed and that managerial practices can be unilaterally employed to achieve them. In their review of recent leadership literature, Plowman *et al.* agree that many still believe that it is leaders who make organization transformation happen by directing change.[19] However, they argue that associating the notion of leadership merely with a few talented individuals cannot meet the challenges posed by a knowledge society in which it has become more appropriate to understand organizations as complex adaptive systems. Plowman *et al.* point out that leaders can no longer be viewed as controllers of organizational trends through their personality traits and leadership style. The "control" model of leadership depends on a view of organizations as mechanistic systems in which predictable forces, basic cause-and-effect relationships,

---

[18] Mary Ul-Bien, Russ Marion and Bill McKelvey, "Complexity Leadership Theory: Shifting Leadership from the Industrial Age to the Knowledge Era," *The Leadership Quarterly*, 18(4) (August 2007), 298–318.

[19] Donde Ashmos Plowman, Stephanie Solansky, Tammy E. Beck, LaKami Baker, Mukta Kulharni and Deandra Villarreal Travis, "The Role of Leadership in Emergent Self-Organization," *The Leadership Quarterly*, 18(4) (2007), 341–356.

hierarchical authority structures and highly prescribed rule-sets are in operation. Organizations can no longer be depicted in this way.

Other theorists, such as Kranz, for instance, concur that the realities of contemporary organizational life make top-down leadership control impossible.[20] He suggests that the emergence of a post-industrial economic order has brought about dramatic changes in the character of authority relations within business organizations. The way in which individuals view their relationship with the organizations that employ them has also shifted significantly in recent years. Because of this, the exercise of influence and control can no longer be treated as if it is the exclusive privilege and responsibility of formally appointed leaders. Kranz explains that to compete globally, contemporary organizations have continually to respond and adapt to the contingencies and peculiarities of a variety of dynamic local markets. The effectiveness of an organization within the contemporary business environment thus increasingly depends on group collaboration and the ability of employees at all levels to exercise informed judgment. Hierarchical, bureaucratic decision-making structures are therefore no longer suitable or productive. As a result, obedience to commands and compliance with obligations have to be replaced with a more personal form of involvement with, and commitment to, the activities and goals of an organization. If leadership has traditionally been associated with the ability to influence and inform the beliefs and activities of those who participate in an organizational system, then Kranz proposes that leadership should be reconceived as a property of the system as a whole. For Kranz, those priorities and imperatives that give shape and direction to the life of an organization are the result of complex interactions amongst important elements of the system.[21]

I agree with these theorists that limiting leadership to the study of individual attributes or behaviors cannot fully account for the multidirectional patterns of influence that characterize contemporary organizations. What my analysis will suggest is that the responsibility for instigating and sustaining a culture of ethical responsiveness cannot be thought of as the responsibility of a number of individuals appointed

---

[20] James Kranz, "Lessons from the Field: an Essay on the Crises of Leadership in Contemporary Organizations," *The Journal of Applied Behavioral Science*, 26 (1) (1990), 49–64.

[21] *Ibid.*, 52.

to positions of authority. In fact, it seems as though the hierarchical, unidirectional channels of influence that once gave shape and purpose to the activities of traditional companies have been replaced with circuits of reciprocal influence that are now distributed throughout the human resources of contemporary business organizations. All who participate in such an organizational system contribute to the ethos that emerges within it over time. As such, the tacit, relationally constituted sense of normative propriety that shapes individuals' beliefs and behavior within an organizational system is everybody's business and everybody's responsibility.

In order to develop a more sophisticated understanding of the leadership dynamics in complex adaptive systems, it is helpful to distinguish between leaders, i.e. those appointed in positions of authority, and leadership as a broader construct. Uhl-Bien describes two perspectives of what she calls "relational leadership."[22] These two perspectives are complementary, but each has distinct implications for the study and practice of leadership. The first is an *entity* perspective that maintains a focus on the identification of individual attributes of leaders as they engage in interpersonal relationships. The second is a *relational* perspective that views leadership as a process of social construction through which particular understandings of leadership come about and gain ontological saliency.

Uhl-Bien points out that even from the *entity* perspective, it is possible to redefine the reality of individual leaders from a more relational point of view. She argues that exchange theory, the study of charisma as a social relationship between leaders and followers, and the notion of collective or relational selves, are all examples of the move towards a more relational conception of leaders. Many leaders define themselves in terms of relationships with others and as such, possess a social self-concept. It is, however, Uhl-Bien's insistence on the *relational* perspective to leadership that allows us to redefine leadership in more systemic terms. It represents a move away from exclusively focusing on leaders as individual persons, to the recognition of leadership as process. From her *relational* perspective, Uhl-Bien defines the broader construct of leadership as a social influence process through which emergent coordination

---

[22] Mary Uhl-Bien, "Relational Leadership Theory: Exploring the Social Processes of Leadership and Organizing," *The Leadership Quarterly*, 17(6) (2006), 654–676.

(such as social order) and change (new approaches, values, attitudes and ideologies) are constructed and produced.[23]

The literature on leadership within complex adaptive systems is helpful in exploring what it would mean to perceive leadership as something that is not restricted to those individuals who are appointed to positions of authority. The recent special edition of *Leadership Quarterly*, focusing on Leadership in Complex Adaptive systems (2007) offers a number of detailed analyses of why the reality of contemporary organizational life demands a radical reconsideration of leadership as such. They point out the fact that within complex adaptive systems, it is impossible to control behavior, pass information to subordinates unilaterally, and reduce complexity.[24] This view of organizations and its concomitant implications for leadership theory are by no means only recent developments. As early as 2000, scholars such as Collier and Esteban described post-industrial organizations as complex adaptive systems, characterized by multiple interconnecting relationships, unpredictability and incessant, fast-paced change.[25] They argued that a different kind of leadership emerges under such conditions. This is because it is impossible for any one individual to possess the kind of comprehensive knowledge, determining influence, or unerring decision-making capacities that are continually required to respond appropriately and effectively to every challenge and opportunity that may present itself in and to an organization. They argue that conventional hierarchical demand-and-control models prove inadequate within the unpredictable and dynamic environment of a complex adaptive organizational system. The kind of priorities and goals that are formulated in boardrooms by individuals at the top of the corporate hierarchy and passed down from on high cannot provide the members of a complex adaptive organizational system with an adequate or meaningful form of orientation. Post-industrial corporate contexts are shaped and moved instead by goals and priorities that emerge from within the organizational system and are thus

---

[23] *Ibid.*, 662.

[24] Other authors point out that interesting complex and adaptive behavior patterns emerge as a result of aggregates of interacting subunits, or agents. See for instance, Boal and Schultz, "Storytelling, Time, and Evolution: the Role of Strategic Leadership in Complex Systems," *The Leadership Quarterly*, 18(4) (August 2007), 411–428.

[25] Jane Collier and Rafael Esteban, "Systemic Leadership: Ethical and Effective," *The Leadership and Organizational Development Journal*, (21)4 (2000), 207–215.

recognized by all who participate in it. From this perspective, the circulation of influence within an organization is not unidirectional or hierarchically centered on one or more pivotal positions of authority. Instead it involves "an ongoing direction-finding process, which is innovative and continually emergent" and which draws in, and on, all the members of an organizational system.[26] Collier and Esteban come to describe leadership as "the systemic capability, distributed and nurtured throughout the organization, of finding organizational direction and generating continual renewal by harnessing creativity and innovation." A balance is continually maintained between the need to remain responsive to the ever-changing challenges and opportunities of the contemporary business environment, and the necessity of maintaining a congruent sense of organizational purpose.

There is considerable corroboration for Collier and Esteban's observations in recent leadership literature. Some of the insights offered by Boal and Schultz strengthen an understanding of leadership as enabling, rather than controlling. According to them, leadership promotes the responsiveness of the entire complex system instead of trying to direct others towards distinct outcomes.[27] Uhl-Bien, Marion and McKelvey argue that leadership can no longer be described exclusively in terms of position and authority, but that it is in fact an emergent, interactive dynamic. This dynamic creates a complex interplay from which the impetus for change is stimulated through the interactions of heterogeneous agents.[28] The insight that the ability to influence and inform the beliefs and behavior of the members of an organizational system is shared by all who participate in it is echoed by Edgeman and Scherer. They describe systemic leadership as the deployment of leadership responsibilities and privileges across an organization's entire human resource.[29] They argue furthermore that when such privileges and responsibilities are shared by all its members, an organization's ability to anticipate and respond to threats and challenges at a local level is enhanced. In a similar vein, Kanji and Moura see the power to influence the life and direction of

---

[26] Collier and Esteban, "Systemic Leadership," 208.
[27] Boal and Schultz, "Storytelling, Time and Evolution," 413.
[28] Ul-Bien, Marion and McKelvey, "Complexity Leadership Theory."
[29] Rick L. Edgeman and Franz Scherer, "Systemic Leadership via Core Value Deployment," *The Leadership and Organization Development Journal*, 20(2) (1999), 94–98.

an organizational system as something which is distributed among all who participate in it.[30]

A large number of researchers have developed an alternative to individualist leadership approaches. Though called by many different names, such as delegated, democratic or dispersed leadership it is most generally referred to as "distributed leadership."[31] In the light of their review of the literature, Bennett *et al.* come to the conclusion that the notion of "distributed leadership" highlights leadership as an emergent property of a group of interacting individuals. They suggest an awareness of the openness and fluidity of the boundaries of leadership within a specific organization. In fact, they even go so far as to argue that leadership may be extended or distributed to the other entities that the organization interacts with. It also takes us beyond associating leadership with certain individual "traits." From the perspective of distributed leadership, varieties of expertise are distributed amongst multiple members of the organization. A prominent exponent of the "distributed leadership" school of thought is the work of Spillane and Gronn. Their observations basically amount to a recognition of the fact that leadership "is stretched over the practice of actors within organizations".[32]

A number of organizational theorists have come to appreciate the value of the insight that an organization's direction is influenced by all who participate in it. It is especially in the areas of organizational learning and change that a more systemic view of leadership capacities becomes invaluable. According to Peter Senge, thinking and acting is not just the task of top managers. It is an ongoing process that must be integrated at all levels. Traditional "great man theories," i.e. the view that leaders are special people and therefore the only ones who are properly equipped to set direction and make important decisions, are rooted in an individualistic and non-systemic perspective that impedes collective learning and change. Senge and Kaufer point out that leaders may play a variety of roles, such as designer, teacher, and steward in the process of organizational learning. These roles are systemic in nature and require skills such as the capacity to build a

---

[30] Kanji and Moura, "Measuring Leadership Excellence," 704.
[31] Nigel Bennett, Christine Wise, Phillip Woods and Janet Harvey, *Distributed Leadership*, Report of the National College for School Leadership (2003).
[32] Friedman, "Beyond Mediocrity," 206.

shared vision, the ability to recognize and acknowledge all the various mental models that may be in operation within an organizational system, and the adeptness to draw on these insights to foster systemic patterns of thinking. Senge and Kaufer also emphasize the crucial role of systemic leadership in facilitating change within an organization. They argue that when it comes to organizational change, it is a case of "communities of leaders, or no leadership at all."[33] Their research into the role of leadership in organizational change has brought these authors to redefine leadership as "a capacity of the human community to sustain significant change." Leadership is viewed as a creative and collective process, distributed among diverse individuals who share the responsibility for creating the organization's future.

The emphasis that is placed on adaptive responsiveness in recent leadership literature can be interpreted as a response to the challenges associated with contemporary organizational systems' perpetual dynamism. Heifetz, for instance, describes the process by which people distinguish what is precious and essential to their organizational culture from that which is incidental and insignificant.[34] He portrays it as a process that requires experimentation. Because of this, Heifetz argues, leadership entails the capacity to balance efficiency with creativity. They have to be able and willing to improvise if they expect to prevail in an environment where a stable point of equilibrium remains elusive. According to Heifetz, the process of adaptation requires the members of an organization to perform an ongoing critical interrogation as to which values will allow them to thrive. In addition, they need to consider the contingencies that may threaten the realization of those values. The deliberate intentionality with which values are created and articulated in Heifetz's view may be questionable, but his observations are nevertheless suggestive of the importance of adaptation in the relational processes of normative re-orientation that play out daily among the members of a complex organizational system.

---

[33] Peter Senge and Katrin H. Kaufer, "Communities of Leaders or No Leadership at All" in Barbara Kellerman and Larraine R. Matusak (eds.), *Cutting Edge: Leadership 2000* (James MacGregor Burns Academy, 2000).

[34] Ronald A. Heifetz, "Anchoring Leadership in the Work of Adaptive Progress" in Frances Hesselbein and Marshall Goldsmith, Leader to Leader Institute (eds.), *The Leader of the Future: Visions, Strategies and the New Era* (Josey Bass, 2006), pp. 78–80.

Does this mean that the idea of individual leaders appointed to positions of authority has become completely discredited? No. Those who have been formally appointed to positions of authority in an organization can help to create institutional conditions capable of recognizing and supporting the complex processes in and through which the congruity between individual members' sense of normative propriety is relationally established. However, these processes are driven, to no lesser degree, by the willingness and ability of all those who participate in the organizational system to make new proposals, to offer a different point of view, and to contest the status quo. Systemic leadership need not amount to an indianless chiefdom. It simply means that whoever is in the best position, with the right kind of "weapons" and experience should lead the fight in the battle that wins the war, which secures the cause. Such a willingness to reorganize, realign and adapt as necessary is ultimately based on an abiding awareness, among the members of an organization, of their interdependency and of the interdependency between an organization and those systems in which it participates.

In order to understand the way in which both individual leaders and broader leadership dynamics operate, it is helpful to draw on the distinction that Uhl-Bien, Marion and McKelvey make between *administrative* leadership, *adaptive* leadership and *enabling* leadership. Administrative leadership refers to the managerial roles and actions of individuals who occupy positions of authority in planning and coordinating organizational activities. Adaptive leadership entails a "collaborative change movement" that allows adaptive outcomes to emerge in a nonlinear fashion as a result of dynamic interactions.[35] Since adaptive leadership refers to a dynamic, rather than to a person's traits or behaviors, it emerges from the interactions of interdependent agents. Enabling leadership is what catalyzes administrative leadership and hence allows for the emergence of adaptive leadership. As such, it deals with the inevitable entanglement between administrative and adaptive leadership. As enabling leadership requires some authority, but is equally reliant on the dynamic between various agents, middle managers are often in an ideal position to take on this role. The combination of their access to resources and their involvement with the everyday boundary situations that an organization's members confront make them ideal enablers. The role that enabling leadership plays can

[35] Uhl-Bien, Marion and McKelvey, "Complexity Leadership Theory," 311.

be described as fostering interaction, supporting and enhancing interdependency and stimulating adaptive tension in order to allow for interactive emergence of new patterns.

It is important to note that Uhl-Bien *et al.* argue that all three types of leadership are operative within one organization. What does this mean for our description of leadership in organizations? At the very least, it means that some new perspectives on leadership, and even on individual leadership characteristics, are in order.

Redefining leadership: contemporary perspectives

Research done by the Center for Creative Leadership suggests that there has been a definite shift in the way in which effective leadership is defined.[36] In a recent survey of practicing managers, 84 percent agreed that perceptions about effective leadership have changed, and would continue to change over the next five years. Many managers believed that so-called "soft skills," such as building relationships, collaboration and change management will become increasingly important. According to researchers at the Center, there is a growing appreciation among corporate leaders of the importance of collaborative and interdependent work.[37] This view is echoed in a lot of contemporary leadership literature. In what is to follow we will trace some of the themes that are commonly raised in this regard. We will see that it has implications for how those individuals who are appointed to positions of authority operate, but also for how the broader leadership dynamics within the organization may be fostered.

Following one's passions

A lot of authors who write about leadership insist that it is important for an individual to care and be passionate about what he/she does. In other words, he/she should find their work meaningful and significant. In their book, *Success Built to Last*, Porras, Emery and Thompson interviewed 200 people who are considered successful individuals, in

---

[36] John Alexander, "The Challenge of Complexity" in Hesselbein and Goldsmith, *The Leader of the Future*, p. 85.
[37] *Ibid.*, p. 90.

most cases, leaders of their organizations. These individuals consistently stressed the importance of doing what they love and investing
their energies in pursuits that are meaningful to them. The individuals
that Porras *et al.* interviewed primarily experienced their work as
meaningful because it somehow contributed to, or involved things
that they consider valuable and enjoyable. In most cases however,
these individuals also found their work meaningful because it contributed to the creation of lasting relationships with others.[38] What
this suggests is that it is an individual's investment in a system of
relations at work that ultimately makes his/her efforts seem meaningful or significant. Porras *et al.* succinctly articulate the implication
of this point with respect to the dynamics of leadership.[39] They suggest that if leaders serve a cause, the cause also serves them. If an
individual does things, and acts in ways that serve to nurture and
sustain the network of relationships within an organizational system,
then its members are more likely to recognize, value and support his/
her contributions. This also accounts for a shift in perceptions with
respect to the role of charisma that is detectible in some recent leadership literature. Whereas the possession of personal charisma used to
be considered an important prerequisite for effective leadership, the
emphasis seems now to be shifting towards causes that in and of
themselves inspire and draw people along. In other words, the goals
and priorities of an organizational system are no longer seen as
something that is defined by the passions and values of one or more of
its charismatic members, but rather as something that is continually
constituted in, and by, the relational dynamics and contextual contingencies of the system as a whole.

What this formulation of following one's passions discounts, however, is the possibility that worthy causes, or "causes with charisma"
are not necessarily the brainchild of one brilliant individual who then
disseminates the idea to others. Instead, "causes with charisma" may
emerge out of the multidirectional dynamics that exists between multiple agents within organizations.

Reconciling the pursuit of individual passions with the need to build
and sustain relationships with others is also an important theme in the

---

[38] Jerry Porras, Stewart Emery and Mark Thompson, *Success Built to Last:
Creating a Life That Matters* (Wharton School Publishing, 2006), p. 24.
[39] *Ibid.*, p. 110.

202 Business Ethics as Practice

virtue-ethics paradigm.[40] The late Robert Solomon's work, for instance, suggests that character is cultivated and maintained in the continuous interaction of individuals and groups. In and through such interactions the individual is inculcated with the virtues that are valued by the group. It is therefore hardly the case that individual passions and character traits are solipsistic idiosyncrasies that have no relationship with individuals' lives amongst others. Knights and O'Leary provide further support for this position in their critique of post-Enlightenment individualism.[41] They argue that the kind of individualism that emerged after the onset of the Enlightenment in Western society has skewed the relationship between individuals and society by placing too much emphasis on self-interest. In their view, an individual's personal interests cannot be separated from his/her membership of a particular society. "Success" is only meaningful within a community that acknowledges and rewards it in some way.[42]

Whetstone makes a similar point that in a mature organization, culture, leadership, and mission are interwoven.[43] He therefore insists that it is the internal culture of an organization that defines what is considered heroic, helpful or harmful by its members. The same is true of the dynamics of authority within an organizational system. However, describing the process by which an individual nurtures and sustains relationships with others in these terms still can't do justice to the multidirectional interactions that would allow systemic leadership to emerge. These authors' observations and proposals do not lead us to perceive leadership as a fully relational construct. If one takes seriously the contention of authors on leadership in complex adaptive systems that leaders can no longer "control" or "direct" behavior, what exactly do they do?

What would strategic leadership mean if viewed from the perspective of systemic leadership dynamics? According to Boal and Schultz there are still important things that individual leaders have to do in order to

---

[40] J. Thomas Whetstone, "A Framework for Organizational Virtue: the Interrelationship of Mission, Culture and Leadership," *Business Ethics: a European Review*, 14(4) (2005).
[41] David Knights and Majella O'Leary, "Reflecting on Corporate Scandals: the Failure of Ethical Leadership," *Business Ethics: a European Review*, 14(4) (2005).
[42] *Ibid.*, 374.
[43] Whetstone, "Framework for Organizational Virtue."

allow for the emergence of systemic leadership.[44] They argue that strategic leaders assist in providing the rationale for past actions and legitimating certain perspectives through activities such as storytelling. This in turn has an influence on patterns that emerge vicariously from within the dynamic interactions between agents. Leaders do not "control" this dynamic, but they do influence it.

Having a values-driven orientation

Many leadership authors have come to appreciate the importance of values in constituting and sustaining the relational context of leadership. However, there seem to be many different ideas as to the nature and origin of the values and priorities that circulate in, and inform, the complex system of relations within an organization. Some believe that it is a clear, well-defined *telos* that directs the complex system of relationships within an organization. Others see it as a set of principles that are rationally agreed upon and consistently enforced. There are also authors who attempt to effect some kind of reconciliation of these positions. Most leadership literature, however, draws on one of these approaches to identify values that support ethical leadership within an organization.

In their widely circulated book *Built to Last* Collins and Porras strongly emphasize the importance of a strong values-driven, or purpose-driven orientation in successful organizations.[45] Their central message is quite simple: companies that last are built on a central and enduring set of core values. In most cases, leaders were perceived as the source, or at least the role model of values that others should emulate. However, if we would view values as emergent properties within complex adaptive systems, as Chapter 4 proposes, the interaction between appointed leaders, leadership dynamics and emergent values should be reconsidered.

If the success of companies depends on their ability to balance continuity with change, the unilateral imposition of a particular set of values makes little sense. If, however, emergent values provide both continuity and direction, it becomes possible for organizations to experiment with what Collins and Porras call "big hairy audacious goals." Collins and

---

[44] Boal and Schultz, "Storytelling, Time and Evolution," 413.
[45] Jim Collins and Jerry I. Porras, *Built to Last: Successful Habits of Visionary Companies* (HarperBusiness Essentials, 2002).

Porras argue that to simultaneously preserve the basic tenets of an organization's orientation and stimulate progress constitutes a yin-yang dynamic that must always be held in creative tension. However, they do not explore how this actually occurs.

Some scholars working on leadership in complex adaptive systems offer more concrete proposals. They argue, for instance, that through "tagging," i.e. the process by which the creation of aggregates is facilitated, coordination emerges even though there is no "control" in the strict sense of the word. Tagging allows the organization to strike the ever-elusive balance between exploiting what has already been learnt and exploring new territory.

In their analysis of what it is that makes individuals, or leaders, successful Porras *et al.* draw attention to the high levels of integrity that are found among leaders who have enduring success. Porras *et al.* associate integrity with a sustained commitment on the part of individuals to both that which they consider personally meaningful and that which they believe could make a positive difference to the lives of others. Because of their apparently personal nature, one would expect such value commitments to differ significantly from one leader to the next. At first glance, therefore, this view of integrity seems to invite a very individualistic sort of value orientation, but there is an important caveat. In the course of their research, Porras *et al.* observed that most enduringly successful people believed that their service to others simultaneously served their own interest.[46] In other words, they didn't perceive it as a choice between serving *either* the one *or* the other, but rather as a case of simultaneously serving *both* the one *and* the other.

It has long been hypothesized that the impact of leaders on an organizational climate would be enhanced if leaders acted with integrity. Research studies have confirmed that there is a relationship between the effectiveness of leaders, and their perceived altruism.[47] Other findings, however, have tended to problematize the construction of a linear causal relationship between the personal value orientation of those in formal positions of authority and the value orientation of the organizational system as a whole. In one study, no direct support could

---

[46] Porras *et al.*, *Success Built to Last*, p. 99.
[47] A. S. Engelbrecht, A. S. van Aswegen and C. C. Theron, "The Effect of Ethical Values on Transformational Leadership and Ethical Climate in Organisations," *South African Journal of Business Management*, 36(2) (2005).

be found for the hypothesis that the personal integrity of transformational leaders significantly enhanced the ethical climate within the organizations that they lead. Findings such as these suggest that more complex relationships may exist between the personal value orientations of those in formal positions of authority within an organization and the value orientation of the organizational system as a whole.

In their discussion of five business ethics myths, Trevino and Brown pointed out that it is not true that ethical leadership is predominantly about leadership integrity.[48] Though individual characteristics may play their part, they do not in and of themselves translate to ethical leadership. Trevino and Brown argue that in order for ethical leadership to exist, a leader must be both a moral person and a moral manager. That is, they need not only be perceived by their colleagues and subordinates as persons of good character, but they also need to be competent and diligent in the management of the organization's ethics dimension. The personal values of an organization's formal leadership are therefore only significant inasmuch as they are drawn into the wider process of value formation in the organization and insofar as it is reflected in institutional realities. Trevino and Brown argue that supervisory leadership is as important as executive leadership in developing an organization's ethical leadership capacity.[49]

Trevino and Brown's analysis may precipitate the further question as to why all leadership studies are still exclusively directed at the role that individuals in positions of authority play. It may in fact be that the personal values of those in formal positions of authority need take no special precedence over those of other members of an organization. Values do not radiate out from the person who occupies a position of authority, but emerge spontaneously in the organizational system as the by-product of a perpetual, organization-wide process of personal adjustments, interpersonal alignments, and institutional adaptations. Leaders can contribute to the emergence of certain value orientations through what Boal and Schultz call sense-making, sense-giving and sense-taking. This informs and influences the process by which individual cognitive structures evolve and shared schemas develop. In this

---

[48] Linda Klebe Trevino and Michael E. Brown, "Managing to be Ethical: Debunking Five Business Ethics Myths," *Academy of Management Executive*, 18(2) (2004).
[49] *Ibid.*, 80.

way, strategic leaders may enhance the emergence of what they call "cognitive consensuality." This form of consensuality is replicated by what Boal and Schultz named "memes," i.e. units of cultural knowledge transmission that operate as carriers of mental representations. However, an important caveat that should be kept in mind is that the influences that strategic leaders could have in this process are never unilateral, nor are the stories they tell unequivocal accounts of reality. In fact, storytelling within organizations could go in unintended directions.

Eliciting and appreciating contention

One of the differences between traditional views of leadership and contemporary writing on the subject is the latter's disregard for the egocentric idiosyncrasies of successful charismatic individuals. The inability of many leaders of that ilk to face criticism and accommodate dissent compels contemporary observers to seek alternatives. What is more commonly celebrated in recent writing about leadership is the value of what Porras *et al.* call the "harvesting" of contention. Porras *et al.* point to the many advantages of accommodating dissent within an organization.[50] Not only does it allow ideas to be collected from the best and the brightest members of an organization, it also fosters innovation. An added benefit is the pre-emptive effect that it has with respect to the cynicism that often develops in and among employees in the absence of opportunities for open contention. In organizations where open conversations are a rare, cathartic exception, and the edifying sense of being part of a creative team is denied to employees, creative ideas become "secret assets hoarded by team members rather than a shared resource that makes the team stronger."[51] Successful organizations are spaces within which contention and challenges to the status quo are not only welcomed, but also made productive. Porras points to Commerce Bank's practice of challenging employees to regularly come up with at least one stupid rule to kill and iVillage's open strategic meetings, where the best idea prevails, as practical examples of how contention may be harnessed.[52] He also draws attention to leaders such as Paul Galvin, who founded Motorola.

---

[50] Porras *et al.*, *Success Built to Last*, p. 188.
[51] *Ibid.*, p. 189.   [52] *Ibid.*, p. 191.

Galvin's leadership was distinguished by the way in which he encouraged dissent, discussion and disagreement among his employees. According to Porras, Galvin gave individuals immense responsibility to grow and learn on their own, even if this required working through failures and mistakes.[53]

Peter Senge corroborates this view of leadership.[54] He argues that in a complex system, it is impossible for any one leader to have all the answers. Leaders therefore have to cultivate an open-minded attitude and be prepared to continually challenge their own favored views. This requires a willingness to allow dissent and a readiness to relinquish the preoccupation with consensus that was so characteristic of organizational management during the latter years of the industrial era. Strategic leaders can enhance the dialogue process in complex adaptive systems, and foster new perspectives.[55] In order to do so, dialogue cannot be aimed primarily at creating consensus.

What the studies of leadership in complex adaptive systems point out is that the way in which leaders enable emergence of certain value orientations within organizations is quite different from unilaterally "directing" the behaviors of others. Instead, "enabling" leadership entails disrupting existing patterns, encouraging novelty and then making sense of whatever unfolds.[56] Leaders in complex adaptive systems enable new perspectives on the future by utilizing conflict and embracing uncertainty. In fact, by injecting tension judiciously, spaces may open up as a result of struggles over diverse ideas. It is from within these spaces that new responses emerge. Uhl-Bien *et al.* describe the process by which leaders introduce new ideas, new people, and new resources as "dropping seeds of emergence." It is important to remember that the impact of these "seeds" will remain unpredictable.[57]

Wisdom and humility

Karl Weick defined wisdom as the balance between knowing and doubting, or behaviorally, as the balance between too much confidence

---

[53] Collins and Porras, *Built to Last*, p. 38.
[54] Peter Senge, "Systems Citizenship: the Leadership Mandate for this Millennium" in Hesselbein and Goldsmith, *The Leader of the Future*, p. 41.
[55] Boal and Shultz, "Storytelling, Time and Evolution," 415.
[56] Plowman *et al.*, "The Role of Leadership," 342.
[57] Uhl-Bien *et al.*, "Complexity Leadership Theory," 307.

and too much caution. Wisdom enables individuals simultaneously to draw on what they know and embrace that which they might not know as opportunities for creative sense-making. Successful organizational learning and knowledge creation is based on what Weick calls "heedful interrelating" and "acting thinkingly."[58] According to Weick, it is this kind of openness and readiness to exploit whatever opportunity may present itself to learn new things that facilitates the capacity for ongoing adaptations within an organization. Wise leaders are paradoxically capable of embracing both what they know and what they do not know. Such leaders seem to possess the enviable ability to deftly navigate the treacherous tightrope between too much confidence and too much caution. Wisdom comes with the realization that the process of gathering new information and gaining new perspectives is an ongoing one and that knowledge can therefore never be regarded as fixed or complete. An individual's openness to new perspectives or readiness to re-evaluate his/her own views critically need not undermine the decisiveness and confidence with which he/she acts upon his/her considered judgment. Most successful leaders have an explorer mentality, which allows them simultaneously to apply themselves in a goal-directed manner and remain open to new ideas and opportunities. According to Porras *et al.*, many of the successful people that they spoke to had come to the conclusion that "planning works, though the plan itself rarely does."[59] In other words, those who are too rigidly committed to the realization of a particular goal or outcome could easily fail to capitalize on better ideas or opportunities when they present themselves along the way.

There are many authors who recommend the example of leaders who create enabling conditions for growth in their organizations without allowing their egos to get in the way.[60] The concept of "humility" originates from the Latin word "humus," which means fertile soil. Its etymology suggests that humility has long been thought of as a source of strength in human relations. Humility should not be confused with a low self-regard. It is more properly associated with a centered, balanced, and integrated sense of self. Humility allows the individual to possess a healthy sense of his/her own strengths and weaknesses. It sustains the

---

[58] Karl Weick, "The Attitude of Wisdom" in K. Weick, *Making Sense of Organizations* (Oxford: Blackwell, 2001), p. 167.
[59] Porras *et al.*, *Success Built to Last*, p. 169.
[60] The literature on "servant leadership" is especially insightful in this regard.

balance between an individual's current abilities and his/her willingness to learn. In fact, the balance between personal humility and professional will is the distinguishing characteristic of those whom Jim Collins describes as "Level 5" leaders. According to Collins, this type of leadership is exemplified in someone like Abraham Lincoln. He describes it as a paradoxical combination of modesty and willfulness, shyness and fearlessness.

Senge and Kaufer cite an interview with Phil Caroll, the recently retired CEO of Shell Oil, to underscore the importance of humility and a leader's ability to acknowledge his/her own vulnerability: "You need a healthy dose of humility . . . The truth is everyone can see your flaws . . . if you try to hide them, they wonder what else you are hiding."[61] Individuals' ability to acknowledge their own weaknesses and to draw on other people's insights allows them to address their own "blind spots." What is more, the legion challenges of today's complex business environment make it absolutely crucial that they do so. Gaining insight into one's own weaknesses is also, as Caroll so succinctly reminds us, absolutely necessary for sustaining relationships of trust.

Fostering collaboration

There are many aphorisms in leadership literature that articulate the belief that a leader's success depends on the quality of people that he/she is able to draw on. According to Porras *et al.*, many of the successful leaders that they interviewed reiterated and confirmed the validity of truisms such as: "You're only as good as your people."[62] Since many organizations face complex challenges that require people to work collaboratively across functions, researchers at the Center for Creative Leadership (CCL) have come to view leadership as part of a process that happens throughout the organization and involves interdependent decision making. Alexander explains that the CCL's researchers define leadership as something which functions more inclusively, across functions and organizations and from the middle out.[63]

Senge and Kaufer identify three types of organizational leaders: local line leaders, executive leaders and internal networkers.[64] These

---

[61] Senge and Kaufer, "Communities of Leaders," p. 25.
[62] Porras *et al.*, *Success Built to Last*, p. 199.
[63] John Alexander, "The Challenge of Complexity," pp. 90–91.
[64] Senge and Kaufer, "Communities of Leaders," p. 23.

leaders are critically interdependent on one another. Executives may carry some responsibility for interpreting and articulating the sense of purpose and priority that exists among the members of an organizational system, but their efforts will be meaningless if this is not done in a consultative and collaborative way. They therefore have to play the multidimensional role of steward, role model and mentor. Since local line leaders are the closest to the "front lines" where organizational value is created, they are the ones who facilitate the translation of values and priorities into organizational practices. Line leaders have to believe in the importance of these values and have insight into the relationship between values and goals. Executives therefore have to work with line leaders to translate good ideas and helpful insights into day-to-day activities, governance systems and organizational structures. They have to empower line leaders to take the lead in suggesting what should be done in practical teams; in fact, to teach them the practical implications of their ideas. Their role as stewards requires that they acknowledge their own vulnerabilities and declare their willingness to follow. The third type of leader that Senge and Kaufer identify is the internal networker.[65] These leaders come from many different formal roles or functional areas. They are characterized by their mobility and ability to move freely within informal networks. As such, they are able to move across silos and to connect otherwise isolated line managers to other like-minded individuals within the organization. They play the role of "internal consultants," "thinking partners" and mentors. They also circulate emerging values through their storytelling, habits and, in some cases, humor.

As a result of what Helgesen calls "the diffusion of knowledge," a leader has to draw on specialized and embedded knowledge scattered throughout the organization. In a very real sense, the decision-making pool in the organization has expanded, and leaders have to manage by inclusion, bringing as many people to the table as is necessary to gain a proper understanding of the challenges and opportunities that present themselves in, and to, their organizations. As such, the question as to who matters strategically within an organization has to be completely rethought. Rigidly hierarchical decision-making channels and the centralization of control in formally constituted positions of power are unlikely to allow an organizational system enough

[65] *Ibid.*, p. 25.

flexibility to deal effectively with the complexity of the contemporary business environment.

O'Toole adds an Aristotelian spin to the notion of collaboration.[66] He proposes that the true task of leadership is to create an environment where each person can reach his/her full potential. From this perspective, it is the responsibility of leaders to create and sustain such opportunities for growth. O'Toole points out that leaders who are themselves passionate about what they do understand the importance of also allowing others to discover and pursue things that they care passionately about. O'Toole describes, in this regard, how employees at Google are encouraged to experiment with new ideas and are rewarded for their innovations. Google employees are paid to spend 15–20 percent of their time pursuing their "passionate distractions" through unfocused discovery. The idea is to encourage the discovery of break-through ideas during office hours, instead of forcing employees to moonlight. Employees are given the option of either spending one day a week on such activities, or accumulating days over a period of time so that they can eventually spend a few uninterrupted weeks focusing on such exploratory activities.[67] Strategies such as these not only assure employees that they are capable of making a meaningful contribution in the organizational team, but also encourage them to play a part in its success. Shared accountability is a further benefit of this collaborative approach.

Another emerging leadership strategy that involves collaboration is the notion of "virtuous teaching cycles" (VTC). VTC stands in stark contrast to traditional top-down strategies for knowledge dissemination within an organization. Tichy and De Rose argue that since some of the knowledge that is most important for the sustained success of an organization is generated at the customer interface, a top-down knowledge dissemination strategy increases the likelihood that important insights will be obliterated before their value has been harvested. VTCs create highly interactive learning opportunities, where the teacher can become the learner, and the learner the teacher. Companies like Best Buy and Intuit are reported to have had great success with this approach. They have succeeded in empowering their frontline managers to become

---

[66] James O'Toole, "The True Measure of a CEO," *The Conference Board Review* (September/October, 2005).
[67] *Ibid.*, 60.

teachers and, by implication, leaders within their organizations.[68] However, the occasional productive reversal of roles between "leaders" and "followers" can only be properly understood and appreciated within the context of the fluid relational and contextual dynamics that shape today's complex organizational environments.

From a systemic perspective, leadership emerges within an organizational system through an intuitive appreciation among all its members of their interdependency and therefore of the need to establish and sustain collaborative relationships. It is interesting to note, in this regard, that the need for each individual to courageously face up to, and acknowledge, the limitations of his/her own knowledge and insight is something that is stressed again and again by writers on leadership. Ultimately, it is this abiding sense of their own limitations that draws individuals who complement and extend one another's skill sets and competencies together within the organizational system and thus allows productive collaborative relationships to come into being.

It is helpful to draw on Uhl-Bien *et al.*'s description of various types of leadership that exist in organizations.[69] Administrative, enabling and adaptive leadership patterns co-exist in organizations and all have a role to play in the organization as complex adaptive system. Boal and Schultz support this view in arguing that cross-functional interactions create multiple constraints within complex adaptive systems through increasing interdependencies, yet manage to allow for the release of excess that can multiply the available alternatives.[70] In a collaborative organizational environment, the diverse inputs of all its participants need to contribute to the thing(s) that their working lives are directed at. These concerns need not be rooted in some final consensus on a single shared purpose. As long as there is some sense of normative congruence, it could be articulated and formulated differently by various individuals and units. As such, these ongoing deliberations cannot be contained through a unidirectional strategic process driven by a few senior executives. At the same time, it cannot be a completely random process or a process of continual, unstructured experimentation either. What some leadership literature therefore seems to hint at is a participative process in which the

---

[68] Noel M. Tichy and Chris DeRose, "Leadership Judgment at the Front Line" in Hesselbein and Goldsmith, *The Leader of the Future*, pp. 200–201.
[69] Uhl-Bien *et al.*, "Complexity Leadership Theory."
[70] Boal and Schultz, "Storytelling, Time and Evolution," 409.

members of an organization generate ideas regarding what is meaningful to the organization. When the members of an organization care about where the organization is going, they are drawn together and drawn along by a power inherent to the dynamic itself.

Charisma, rhetoric and motivation

Many people associate leadership with an individual's ability to inspire and motivate others. Personal charisma is often considered central to this ability. However, authors such as Porras *et al.* challenge us to rethink the functioning of charisma in organizations. They argue that people are more often moved and motivated by causes that have charisma, than by charismatic leaders. In other words, people are generally more likely to be moved by those causes with which they already identify and about which they have already begun to feel passionately. Because of this, those passions and goals that draw the various members and units of an organization together and give them a sense of purpose are of special importance. Due to the rich institutional, interpersonal and intraperso-nal variety that characterizes most contemporary organizations, it is not always easy to consciously articulate that which circulates among, and moves, the organizational system as a whole. Berson *et al.* point out that one of the central aspects of the way in which individual leaders influence an organization's direction is related to their ability to generate context-specific metaphors as a source of shared mental models.

They also highlight the ability of leaders to affect the intuition of followers by building the type of organizational context that encourages intuition.[71] Aristotle's analysis of the rhetorical abilities of the great orators of his day provides an interesting perspective on how a certain understanding of normative congruence may come into being. The great Greek orators had the ability to create a discursive space between them and their audience in which a sense of truth could emerge. From this Aristotelian perspective, therefore, the role of formal leadership has to do with the facilitation of interactions that allow a sense of purpose to emerge among the members of an organizational system. Open con-versations between mutually receptive colleagues in an organizational

---

[71] Yair Berson, Louise A. Nemanich, David A. Waldman, Benjamin M. Calvin and Robert T. Keller, "Leadership and Organizational Learning: Multiple Levels Perspective," *The Leadership Quarterly*, 17 (2006) 577–594.

system create an environment within which original perspectives, new energy and fresh motivation reveal themselves. In other words, what motivates people in an organization is not something that flows in one direction from the fountain of a charismatic leader's wisdom and energy to the receptive soil of his/her passively expectant followers. Motivation and inspiration is not something that the formal leaders of an organization infuse their subordinates with. Instead it is something that is continually generated in the boiler room of an organization's internal system of relations. In the open environment of contemporary organizations, everybody helps shape the goals that move the organizational system forward. As such, it is also everybody's responsibility to keep the organization's wheels turning in the right direction and at a competitive pace. That which is conventionally associated with the role and responsibilities of formal leaders therefore becomes a function of the organizational system as a whole.

Redefining authenticity and diversity

In a discussion of what Porras et al. call "The myth of authenticity," they dispute the belief that in order to be "real," leaders have to consistently reveal all that they are thinking and feeling to the world.[72] Though well intentioned, this kind of authenticity under-appreciates the value of discretion in interpersonal communication. It also underestimates the extent to which an individual's sensibilities may be informed by a variety of passions. In addition, it fails to recognize that people are often called upon to fulfill more than one role and that many people are able to do so without compromising their personal integrity. Cognitive psychologists confirm that individuals have various "selves" that may be operationalized in fulfillment of various role responsibilities. From this perspective, authenticity requires judgment as to what is appropriate within the context of a specific set of role responsibilities.

Building lasting relationships that are capable of accommodating change requires recognition of the fact that individuals do not always have to fulfill the same role. According to Porras et al., the best leaders realize that their relation to other people may change over time and that this is likely to necessitate occasional role adjustments. One day,

[72] Porras et al., Success Built to Last, pp. 167–168.

they point out, a person might work for you. The next day you might work for them. It is even conceivable that he/she might become your customer or a vendor at some future juncture. Porras *et al.* argue that, in a sense, such a person remains part of one's "virtual team" and that it is therefore important to sustain the relationship despite the role changes that may occasionally occur over time.[73]

It is also important to consider the relationship between the notion of "authenticity" and individuals' need for personal growth. The best team will only stay motivated and loyal if their work environment gives each member the opportunity to grow as a person and as a professional. The notion of authenticity should therefore not be so rigidly conceived that it excludes the possibility that team members may grow and change over time.

This may be avoided by approaching the notion of authenticity from a less individualistic and more relational perspective. Charles Taylor argues, in this regard, that an individual has a sense of self only as a result of a particular "horizon of significance." This horizon of significance is responsible for the individual's sense of value and significance within a particular context and set of relationships. From this perspective, "authenticity" or, as it is often described, "being yourself," is more properly associated with an individual's ability to gauge, and come to terms with, his/her role within a particular context and system of rela-tionships. Authenticity, thus conceived, allows for the fact that an indi-vidual's role may shift as he/she traverses the complex typography of an organization's various functional units and system of relations. Because it allows the individual to calibrate his/her role in relation to the various stakeholders with whom he/she is engaged, this view of authenticity involves a certain degree of perspectivism. However, because its per-spectivism is so thoroughly rooted in the contextual parameters of sus-tained stakeholder relationships, it avoids deteriorating into a rationale for some a-moral form of individualistic relativism.[74]

The fact that such a relational view of authenticity compels an individual to recognize all the various responsibilities that go with the different roles that he/she fulfills, both inside and outside the context

---

[73] *Ibid.*, p. 198.

[74] In this regard it is also helpful to recall Uhl-Bien's insight that many leaders have social self-concepts, i.e. a sense of self that is defined in and through their relationships to others. See Uhl-Bien, "Relational Leadership Theory."

of the organization, may actually enhance his/her ethical responsiveness. If, for instance, an individual finds him/herself in the role of having to authorize the launch of a Challenger space shuttle, this relationally conceived view of authenticity not only allows, but indeed compels him/her to be responsive to a variety of relationships. The important difference between what is suggested here and a detached form of rational self-reflexivity, is that these different perspectives only become available to the individual in and through his or her embeddedness in various relationships and tacit knowledge structures. Such an individual's decision would, for instance, be informed, not only by their sense of being responsive to management demands, but also by their sense of duty as a professional who has to be morally responsive to a broader range of stakeholders.

Since this understanding of authenticity reframes "identity" to a large extent, it also precipitates a reconsideration of what we mean by, and how we deal with, diversity. According to Thomas, the concept of "diversity" has changed significantly in recent years. He argues that it is important to distinguish between the issue of representation, which relates to the presence of a variety of races and genders in the workplace, and the issue of *diversity*, which he associated with: "the differences, similarities, and tensions that can and do exist between the elements of ... different mixtures of people."[75] In his conception, diversity management is a special kind of skill that is characterized by the ability to sense what role differences and similarities in areas such as personal style, thought processes and personality play in shaping the behavioral patterns within an organizational system. Thomas thus specifically identifies diversity management with the ability to make "quality decisions in the midst of differences, similarities and related tensions."

Differences based on race and gender are not the only factors that contribute to the complexity of an organization's internal system of relations. Mergers and acquisitions, changing customer bases, geographic relocations, product innovations and the development of new functions also have a complicating effect on the relational dynamics within an organization. Because every employee represents a singular

[75] R. Roosevelt Thomas Jnr., "Diversity Management: an Essential Craft for Future Leaders" in Hesselbein and Goldsmith, *The Leader of the Future*, pp. 47–50.

mix of traits and capacities it is important to create an environment in which various unique individual contributions are not only recognized, but drawn into the rich tapestry of organizational values and dynamics. The rich and challenging diversity of opinion within contemporary organizations should mirror the diversity of opinion in society at large. An organization that allows its priorities and activities to be shaped and informed by the full spectrum of individual human differences within its ranks is therefore much more likely to establish and sustain meaningful relationships with its various stakeholders.

Fostering trust and confidence

The internal processes that continually shape and inform the life of an organization have an important bearing on its members' capacity for trust. These processes occasionally require subtle, but significant, interpersonal adjustments and personal recalibrations on the part of employees. Since accommodations and adaptations of this nature also have a normative dimension, they often impact those things that people value and hold dear. Because of this, some people's sense of security may be undermined. This can sometimes lead to resistance. Most people experience difficulty during long periods of sustained tension and experimentation. This can lead to two common forms of avoidance, namely: the displacement of responsibility and the diversion of attention. According to Senge, scapegoating, blaming problems on authority, externalizing the enemy and shooting the messenger are all examples of how responsibility may be displaced by employees in the absence of a sense of security.[76] It is in relation to such problems that the importance of fostering trust among colleagues is often stressed in leadership literature.

Trust is often regarded as the solution to a particular type of risk. Typically, it is required in contexts where flexibility is required or when the members of an organization face many uncertainties. The renowned sociologist, Anthony Giddens points out that trust is always accompanied by an awareness of risk and incomplete information.[77] As such, trust emerges in a situation of vulnerability, where there is

---

[76] Senge, "Systems Citizenship," p. 81.
[77] Jon Aarum Andersen, "Trust in Managers: a Study of Why Swedish Subordinates Trust their Managers," *Business Ethics: a European Review*, 14(4) (2005), 392–395.

some possibility for error. The complexity of contemporary business life makes it ever more likely that agents will have to act in the absence of complete information. In these situations, individuals or groups of individuals would like to be able to expect that the word, promise, or written intentions of another individual or group can be relied upon. Trust can also be defined as the mutual confidence that no party to a relationship will exploit the vulnerability of the other.[78]

In her research, Klenke found that trust has many dimensions. She identified at least four moral values that contribute to the emergence of trust, namely: consistency, loyalty, openness and integrity.[79]

One of the more contentious issues in leadership literature relates to whether trust is exclusively a product of calculative decision making, or is based instead on emotion.[80] This debate is complicated by the fact that the employees in many organizations have little direct contact with top echelon leaders and tend therefore to rely on general perceptions circulated via the corporate grapevine. It may be that an organizational system's trust in their formal leadership is a multifaceted affair, in which informally circulated perceptions play just as important a role as direct observations of leaders' behavior. The perceptions of members of an organization with respect to their leadership may be influenced as much by what they read in the media as they are by symbolic actions like the fact that the CEO sits in an open-plan office like everyone else, or the fact that he/she communicates with his/her employees frequently or in a particular manner.[81] Within a complex adaptive system, the multidirectional interactions between agents make it impossible to tell exactly what the various influences may be.

According to social psychologists, trust is not a general attitude or disposition, but is limited instead to specific transactions and the particular people who are involved in it. Trust is what allows relationships to be sustained over time. Some authors distinguish between transactional trust and transformational trust. Transactional trust is based on

---

[78] *Ibid.*, 393.

[79] Karin Klenke, "Corporate Values as Multi-Level, Multi-Domain Antecedents of Leader Behaviors," *International Journal of Manpower*, 26(1) (2005), 50–66.

[80] Andersen, "Trust in Managers," 393.

[81] Clara Gustafsson, "Trust as an Instance of Asymmetrical Reciprocity: an Ethics Perspective on Corporate Brand Management," *Business Ethics: a European Review*, 14(4) (2005), 146.

the notion that trust is created incrementally and reciprocally – you have to give it to get it. It is based on the consistent way in which a person honors agreements and delivers on promises. It involves confidence in a person's competence to deliver what was promised or agreed upon, i.e. what is sometimes referred to as "competence trust." It also involves the belief, on the part of all those who are party to a particular transaction or agreement, that all relevant and necessary information will be disclosed in a timely and accurate manner, i.e. "communication trust."

There are, however, researchers who dispute the viability of this reciprocal and conditional understanding of trust. The notion of transactional trust requires knowledge and experience, which is not always available, or not available in sufficient measure to ensure absolute security. As such, trust requires an acceptance of what Gustafson calls "asymmetrical reciprocity." Gustafson explains that because each individual has a unique history and position in life, each person's reactions and view of the world are different. This means that you can never expect another person to respond exactly as you yourself would have done under the same circumstances. One's expectations of another can never be based on the projection of one's own values. As a result, trust is a response to relationships that can never be fully reciprocal. To trust is to rely on the goodwill of another without being able to fully approximate, fathom or predict what the implications of doing so will be. It is precisely this quality of trust that allows it to fulfill a function that contracts cannot. This important function has to do with the fact that it is impossible to fully imagine and explicitly circumscribe in contractual terms *all* that one trusts another party to do.[82] Trust, as an instance of asymmetrical reciprocity, is therefore required in all business relationships. Gustafson argues that once one accepts that there is always more to the other party than one can know, it becomes possible to respect the other person as a free moral subject.

Because one can never fully put oneself in another's shoes, two-way communication and attentive listening is very important. Many leaders are under the false impression that they know what their employees' and customers' views, wants and needs are without ever having taken the time to test their assumptions through direct engagement. The trust that customers have in a specific brand depends on the way in which each person in the organization displays a respectful interest in that

---

[82] *Ibid.*, 142–144.

which they cannot and should not assume about their customer. All the members of an organization should therefore assume an attitude of respectful, attentive listening. The trust of the organization's customers may well depend on it. It is also important to note that most employees take their cues from a trusted colleague with whom they have frequent contact, rather than from the formal directives of those who sit at the top of the organizational hierarchy. As such, the ability of colleagues to trust one another is just as important as their willingness to trust those who have been given formal authority over them.

Research by Kickul, Gundry and Posig suggests that trust emerges within the context of a two-way relationship between employees and leaders.[83] Their research also brought them to conclude that there is a meaningful correlation between the degree to which employees trust their leaders and their perceptions with respect to organizational justice. Interestingly, Kickul *et al.* also found that the more direct the contact was between leaders and their employees, the stronger those leaders' influence was likely to be.[84] Their research thus draws attention to the important role that supervisors and direct managers play in organizational leadership. In fact, it suggests that individuals who fulfill those kinds of roles may, in some respects, have more influence within the organizational system than those at the top of the managerial hierarchy. Kickul *et al.* found that of all the forms of tangible behavior that they studied, communication had the most impact on the development and perpetuation of relationships of reciprocal trust. Their findings suggest that explaining decisions fosters trust in the consistency of decision making within an organization.

The willingness to rely on another without absolute certainty as to the consequences of doing so is more easily reconciled with the notion of "transformative trust." According to Klenke, transformative trust relies on conviction, courage, compassion and community.[85] It emerges in environments where people are committed to their beliefs, and act on them with consistency. Because transformative trust involves a willingness to forego certainty, and therefore also control, it facilitates the delegation of responsibility in an organization. Compassion is required

---

[83] Jill Kickul, Lisa K. Gundry and Margaret Posig, "Does Trust Matter? The Relationship between Equity, Sensitivity and Perceived Organizational Justice," *Journal of Business Ethics*, 56 (2005), 205–218.
[84] *Ibid.*, 213.   [85] Klenke, "Corporate Values," 59.

to foster the kind of open and honest communication that allows people to contribute to the creation of meaning in an organization. Because compassion is one of the hallmarks of transformative trust, it can play an important role in drawing people in, and encouraging them to contribute to the process of meaning creation within an organization. In this way, a sense of community is created that makes people feel that they can make a difference and that they are being trusted to do so in their own terms.

Trust is built when it becomes clear that leaders are intent on creating opportunities within which other individuals and the organization as a whole can flourish. From the perspective of complex adaptive systems, it may be helpful to think of the variety of roles that various types of leaders play as "nodes" within the complex interplay of agents. Some may be enablers, who induce interactions and establish interdependencies. Others may be administrators who provide emergent patterns with structure and devise implementation plans. The important fact remains that everyone in the organization must be able to trust that others will step up to their emergent task.

Interdependence

The interdependence between an organization and the environment within which it functions is a theme that has received considerable attention in recent leadership literature. The business community's growing appreciation of the extent to which an organization's fate and fortunes are intertwined with those of its environment has underscored, for many, the importance of serving a broad stakeholder community. On various levels, business organizations are discovering that they cannot go it alone.[86] An increased awareness of the impact that an organization's business operations can have on the environmental and social systems in which it participates has precipitated a reconsideration of the nature and dynamics of stakeholder relationships. Business organizations may not necessarily be located at the pivotal central position on the stakeholder map. In other words, the relationship between a business organization and its stakeholders should not always be understood in terms of an active agent acting upon more or less passive recipients. Its position can,

---

[86] Senge, "Systems Citizenship," p. 34.

and should, change based on the complex set of interactions within which it is embedded. An organization is affected by the environment within which it functions as much as it affects its environment through its own operations, and it often finds itself acted upon by its stakeholders.

Many consumers and investors are beginning to demand that business organizations run their operations in a socially and environmentally sustainable way. The notion of sustainability goes far beyond the Corporate Social Responsibility movement's insistence on environmental and social performance. Social projects can no longer be seen merely as the way in which an organization "gives back" some of its profits to those communities who support it. Instead, the emphasis on sustainability requires a fundamental rethinking of "business as usual" and a reconsideration of the capitalist business model's preoccupation with the financial bottom-line.

The development of the notion of the "triple bottom-line" is very significant in this regard. This form of reporting has gained a lot of international support over the last few years and has succeeded in redefining the terms in which corporate success is measured. Instead of defining corporate success solely in terms of the financial bottom-line, tripe bottom-line reporting requires that organizations consider the success of their activities, not just in financial terms, but also in terms of their social and environmental impact. Economic performance also goes beyond organizations' ability to yield competitive financial returns on their stockholders' investments. It requires that organizations consider how they are impacting the broader economic system in which they participate. The taxes that organizations pay, the jobs that they create and their indirect contributions, such as the investments that they make, the innovations that they fund and the infrastructure that they build, are all significant in this regard. To gauge an organization's social performance, its relationships with all its stakeholders, including employees, customers and local communities have to be considered. In measuring an organization's social performance, the measures that it takes to create a safe, pleasant and fair working environment for its employees are just as important as its social responsibility projects within the broader community. On the environmental level, triple bottom-line reporting is pushing in the direction of full cost accounting, i.e. demanding the consideration of the environmental and social costs of an organization's operations. Ideally, all organizations should be required to work towards a zero environmental footprint, i.e. conserving, restoring and replacing the natural resources that are impacted in the course of its operations.

An awareness of the interdependency between business and the systems within which it functions requires a special kind of capacity. Senge calls this "systems intelligence," i.e. the ability to see systems and patterns of interdependency within, and surrounding, an organization.[87] There are two systems thinking skills that are particularly crucial in this regard, namely: seeing patterns of interdependency and seeing into the future. Since it is impossible to predict the future with any certainty within a complex system, the ability to work intuitively towards partnerships that could contribute valuable insights and knowledge is essential. It is therefore crucial to be able to build partnerships across boundaries. To bring parties together who have never collaborated before and who may have very different kinds of sensibilities requires time and commitment.

Boal and Schultz also argue that strategic leaders serve as "cognitive network brokers," through whom the firm interacts with a wide range of networks. However, such commitments are not only worth making, but necessary, because purely transactional business relationships are no longer adequate within the context of today's complex business environment. As such it is important for all those who contribute to the creation and maintenance of an organization's external stakeholder relationships to retain a healthy regard for the limitations of their own knowledge and perspectives.

Rethinking leadership and accountability within complex organizational systems

The emphasis that is placed on interdependence, integration and adaptation in recent leadership literature suggests that the role and responsibilities that have typically been attributed exclusively to those who were formally appointed to positions of authority within an organization should be reconceived in more systemic terms. We have seen that to this end, the dynamics of so-called "complex adaptive systems" provides an apt descriptive model. It provides, amongst other things, an account of the irregular, nonlinear patterns of stakeholder interactions within an organizational system. As such, it

[87] Senge, "Systems Citizenship," p. 39.

allows all members of the organization to assume various leadership roles, within the context of a given business episode, in response to the unpredictable iterations of an organization's complex system of relations. In some instances this may involve a pragmatic reversal of roles between those who occupy positions of authority and those who answer to them in the formal hierarchy of an organization.

Studying the dynamics of leadership within complex adaptive systems also allows one to gain insight into the ability of a complex organizational system to accommodate uncertainty and unpredictability in its internal dynamics without disintegrating as a functional unit. This is especially significant in relation to the tacit sense of normative propriety that the members of an organization develop over time as they interact with one another and observe each other's behavior. It is precisely because of the relational way in which it is continually constituted that an employee's tacit sense of propriety begins to display, over time, a certain congruence with that of his/her colleagues and superiors. From the perspective of a complex adaptive systems model, the relation between the value orientations of individual members of an organization is therefore one of *congruence*, not *consensus*.[88] It is to this relationally constituted normative congruence that a complex adaptive organizational system owes its ability to accommodate difference and dissensus, without losing its functional unity of purpose or sense of identity. What makes this normative congruence so powerful is the fact that it emerges out of ongoing experimentation and contention and therefore allows the organization to draw on the full range of talents, skills and perspectives that its diverse members have to offer.

Congruence among the different normative orientations of its individual members also facilitates a similar sort of alignment with respect to goals and priorities that move and motivate an organizational system. As such, it contributes to a tacit sense of purpose(s) and cause(s) among its members that empowers rather than compels. The congruity of value, priority and purpose that is described in the complex adaptive systems model of organizations can never be fully

---

[88] Authors such as Boal and Schultz refer to the establishment of "cognitive consensuality." I prefer not to use the term "consensus," as it has the connotation of a shared content that can be deliberately understood and described. I prefer the word congruence, as it alludes to the process of value emergence, rather than to substantive value content.

reified in a fixed constellation of deliberately articulated codes and statements. Instead, it is always understood as the emergent property of a dynamic system. This understanding of the emergence of normative congruence clearly has important implications for our understanding of the notion of accountability.

Within the context of corporate governance failures, accountability has become closely associated with the ability to name, shame and punish those individuals and organizations that are thought to be responsible. Those in positions of authority in such organizations are usually held accountable *for* what goes wrong in such situations. However, from what we have come to understand of systemic leadership, a more constructive approach would be continually to remind all those associated with an organization that they are accountable *towards* one another. To fail to act appropriately in the way that one conducts oneself in business is therefore to fail *someone*. The more positive charge of "being accountable towards" a broad group of stakeholders on an ongoing basis, would allow us to recognize corporate failures as a breakdown of stakeholder relationships.

In holding individuals and corporations accountable *for* wrongdoing, the current discourse regarding accountability relies on certain flawed assumptions. In the first place, it assumes that there is a direct cause-and-effect relationship between the decisions and actions of specific individual agents or corporate agents, and the negative outcomes or harm that resulted from it. Secondly, it assumes that agents, whether individual or corporate, make deliberate decisions based on a clear understanding of all relevant principles or behavioral guidelines. From the perspective of the complex adaptive systems model, direct cause-and-effect relationships between agents and events become much more difficult to trace. Furthermore, the view of moral agency developed in Chapter 3, and the discussion of moral epistemology in Chapter 4, suggest that a simplistic understanding of values and of the way in which moral decisions are made is inappropriate within the context of complex adaptive organizational systems.

This does not mean that it is impossible or unimportant to hold executives and their organizations accountable for wrongdoing. The law safeguards those aspects of societal life that are considered the moral minimum for interactions between agents. The legal obligations of corporations and the fiduciary duties of executives and directors remain a central part of the checks and balances on corporate abuses.

However, the legal understanding of accountability is but one piece of the puzzle. It can only guide us in those interactions where clear intentionality, negligence or recklessness can be established.[89] As a result of the multidirectional interactions within a complex network of agents and organizations, it is often difficult to do so. Thinking of accountability in purely legal terms also has the disadvantage that it focuses on the retroactive appropriation of blame, instead of pre-cipitating a critical interrogation of how past, future and present are interrelated in contingent moral responsiveness. This preoccupation with what some authors have called "blame-responsibility" thus dis-tracts people from a proper consideration of their "obligation-responsibility," i.e. the obligations that individuals and corporations have to those with whom they share a business relationship. But this may not even take us far enough.

To understand business obligations in purely legal terms represents, in a sense, a fundamental misconstrual of the very nature of respon-sibility. The notion of responsibility originates from the Latin word *respondere*, which means to answer, or to promise in return. This meaning dates back to the 1300s and denotes a more general associ-ation of the notion of responsibility with the idea of responsiveness. Unfortunately, few people still make this connection. In current lay-men's terms, responsibility currently has two meanings. Firstly, it is understood as an obligation or a duty owed by virtue of one's role identity. The connotation of responsibility with the notion of "obligation" dates from 1787 and is thus a much later development in the etymology of the concept. Secondly, responsibility is associated with a debt that results from something that one has done. Respon-sibility, understood as moral accountability for one's actions, is a hermeneutic construct that dates from 1836. What seems to get lost in some of these more contemporary interpretations of responsibility, and the accountability that is derived from them, is its original asso-ciation with the idea of "answering," or "pledging back" to those with whom one associates. In consequence, the relational dimension of accountability is often inadequately recognized and appreciated.

There are distinct advantages to adopting a more relational view of accountability. It allows an individual to establish what it means to be

---

[89] Charles E. Harris, Michael S. Prichard and Michael J. Rabins, *Engineering Ethics: Concepts and Cases*, third edition (Wadsworth, 2004).

morally responsive in more immediate and practical terms. This means that the individual members of an organization can allow their sense of responsibility to be informed by the contextual contingencies and parameters of particular stakeholder relationships and specific business episodes. It is therefore not just the formal parameters of the law that determine what is appropriate, acceptable or expected in business conduct. In the relational formation of an individual's understanding of appropriate behavior, perceptions and other intangible dynamics also play an important part. As such it is important that individual business practitioners and organizations always also consider *towards whom* they are accountable. To do so is to acknowledge that much of the value of an organization is generated in and through cooperative business relationships and that the quality of these relationships may represent an organization's most valuable assets. The emphasis in this approach to accountability is on the way in which a business organization and its employees engage with and respond to their stakeholders within an extended network of reciprocal business relationships. An understanding of the individual's own, specific moral challenges is therefore always developed *in terms of* contingent relationships. Appropriate action is adjudicated in terms of ongoing power dynamics and insights gained through experience and experimentation. The tacit sense of normative propriety that guides business conduct on both an individual and organizational level emerges in and through the continual consideration of internal and external stakeholder interactions. These tacit forms of normative orientation may resist deliberate articulation in the form of rules and procedures, but they nevertheless form the backdrop against which the actions and decisions of individuals and organizations become intelligible. As such, this relational approach to accountability acknowledges the importance of individual discretion and discernment.

It is true that, for some, such a relationally responsive and contextually contingent understanding of accountability may seem like a very insecure basis for corporate ethics. It may be argued, for instance, that such a view of individual and corporate responsibilities amounts to a form of situational ethics. It is also possible that there may be some who equate the ongoing relational recalibration of individual and organizational responsibilities with a form of moral relativism. While such fears are understandable, it has to be remembered that the normative content of moral responsibilities are not only shaped, but also limited by what is necessary to sustain relationships with various stakeholders over time. It is important to understand that a business practitioner or organization does not act in the absence of any moral expectations. Business practitioners and organizations are obliged to build relationships of trust, confidence, and respect with stakeholders. This imposes important limitations on what they can justifiably do. As a sense of moral propriety emerges in the course of specific sets of interactions, it creates strong normative expectations that guide and inform individual behavior. The kinds of moral constraints that emerge in the context of specific business relationships are often of a more demanding nature than more conventional legalistic ones. They require careful consideration and discretion in each situation. If individual employees are to build and sustain crucial relationships of trust with their organization's stakeholders, they need to participate fully in the multidirectional relational circuits within the organizational system. It is through these channels of reciprocal influence that the normative sensibilities of those who participate in the organizational system are continually shaped. An individual employee's participation in an organization's internal network of relations therefore helps to ensure that his/her moral sensibilities remain congruent with those of the organizational system.

Even though an individual employee's sense of normative propriety develops in interaction with his/her colleagues and associates at work, it is important that this does not become his/her exclusive frame of reference in matters of morality. This would amount to determinism and undermine the critical freedom that lies at the heart of moral responsiveness. Since normative expectations emerge within the context of a particular "internal" system of organizational relationships, there is always the risk that employees will become insulated against those interests that do not fall within the ambit of their own immediate concerns. The phenomenon of "groupthink" is a specific manifestation of such an insular mindset. In the process, the members of an organization run the risk of becoming inured against discourses that utilize logic contrary to their own. What safeguards the members of an organizational system against the potentially harmful effects of such insularity, is the fact that complex adaptive systems are organized as open networks of relations. As such they cannot function in isolation from one another. They are therefore unlikely to devolve into deterministic environments that undermine the possibility of dissent and criticism.

Building relationships requires a certain amount of accommodation and inclusion. Because of this, the normative orientations of organizations remain open to challenge, reform and development. However, the tacit sense of moral propriety that informs the behavior of an organization's individual employees does not develop overnight. It develops gradually over time and it is never entirely reified. As such it is always susceptible to the shaping influence of those who participate in the organizational system. An organization's agents and employees always have an opportunity to contribute to the processes of value formation that play out daily among them. While it may not be possible deliberately to impose a set of pre-formulated values on employees, the everyday decisions and actions of individuals, as well as the way in which an organization is structured can, over time, have a decisive influence on what is valued by those who participate in it.

Systemic leadership cannot flourish under just any circumstances. The organizational conditions that foster systemic leadership and a relationally responsive understanding of accountability therefore require careful consideration. It is therefore important to consider the organizational implications of this relational, responsive understanding of accountability.

As was explained above, the notion of "systemic leadership" has developed in recognition of the fact that many of the functions that were traditionally associated exclusively with formal leadership are now shared by all the members of an organizational system. Any individual who participates in the system can assume responsibility or take the lead in its various operations when, where, in the manner, and for as long as it is necessary to do so. This should, however, not be construed to mean that all the members of an organization lead at the same time, or that every decision is made collectively. Collier and Esteban point out, in this regard, that people have different capabilities, and that roles and responsibilities may occasionally be exchanged between individuals. Because of this, they conclude, the dynamics of leadership in an organization is asymmetric.[90] The co-existence of and interdependence between various forms of leadership is therefore important. The fact that adaptive leadership emerges amongst a variety of organizational members, does not render "administrative" leadership, with its more bureaucratic nature, useless or less important. All the members of an organization have to be to be empowered in a way that allows them to assume responsibility in circumstances where it is required, and draw on

[90] Collier and Esteban, "Systemic Leadership," 209.

the full array of diverse perspectives that are available in the system. A fundamental reconsideration of organizational systems, processes and procedures is required.

This has to start by recognizing the fact that the goals and priorities of complex contemporary organizations are continually shaped and informed by all who participate in them. From a systemic leadership perspective, influence is exerted in an organization's internal system of relations along shifting, multidirectional channels. This does not mean that any one of its members can entirely redefine the identity of an organization through his/her decisions, actions and attitudes. Neither does it represent an organizational dispensation where "anything goes." Instead, the actions and attitudes of individual members are taken up into, and circulated within the organizational system in a way that allows them to influence, but not determine the course of things. One might say that it is "taken together" with the actions and attitudes of others by members of an organization as they plot their daily course forward. Through their participation in an organization's internal system of relations, members' priorities and expectations are gradually shaped until a certain ineffable congruence begins to emerge among their various individual sensibilities. Though often unarticulated and inexpressible, this congruity of purpose and priority among the members of an organization has a powerful effect on their sense of common cause and normative propriety. As such, it serves as a safeguard against inappropriate behavior.

The discussion of trust earlier in this chapter drew attention to its importance in the emergence of an open organizational environment where candid but respectful communication can take place freely. If influence is to flow freely along the multidirectional channels that crisscross the system of relations within an organization, its members must feel that they are trusted and they have to believe that they can trust others with important information. Because mastery and control of all the various specialized operations of today's complex business organizations is mostly beyond the capacities of one person, it is crucial that information be shared throughout an organization. Collier and Esteban argue that sharing information generates the kind of dialogue and questioning that makes learning possible.

It is important to create open access to resources that could strengthen interdependence. Hoarding information within distinct organizational functions, often referred to as the "silo-effect," can have an extremely harmful effect on an organization's ability to remain responsive to the complex realities and unforeseeable contingencies of contemporary business environments. As a result of organizational silos, people privatize their successes, are unwilling to admit mistakes, and tend to steer clear of conversations that challenge the way they do things. This avoidance of conflict has an inhibiting effect on the multidirectional diffusion of influence within an organization's system of relations. According to Collier and Esteban, reciprocal interaction will always involve "constructive conflict." As we saw in our analysis of the leadership dynamics in successful organizations, willingness to allow all members to challenge critically and re-evaluate what is being done in and by an organization contributes to a sense of ownership. Actions, decisions, attitudes or behavior that proves somehow detrimental to the intentions of those who participate in the organizational system must be challenged and changed.

Senge argues that organizational life mirrors natural systems in its reliance on the interaction between self-reinforcing (positive) and balancing (negative) feedback.[91] Within organizations, new insights and innovations must always be balanced with a historic sense of identity and continuity. In this regard, Plowman *et al.*, as well as Boal and Schultz, point out that strategic leaders give meaning to emergent events by reframing them, interpreting them, and creating organization stories within which new dynamics make sense. To the extent that this is achieved, "creative conflict" is unlikely to drastically alter those aspects of the organizational system that are considered crucially significant by its members. It is more likely to facilitate a process of critical reconsideration in which the purposes and priorities of an organization are creatively reinterpreted in relation to new contingencies and opportunities. This process is crucial in the emergence and perpetuation of an attitude of relational responsiveness among the members of an organization.

Occasional miscalculations and misconstruals are an inevitable feature of organizational systems where responsibility is shared and discretion encouraged. That someone's powers of discretion and discernment should fail him/her during some unfortunate and unforeseeable intersection of events should be taken as a matter of course and should not dissuade an organization from empowering or trusting

---

[91] Senge and Kaufer, "Communities of Leaders," p. 26.

its people. If such incidents are aired openly in an environment of trust, they can be turned into learning and growing opportunities, not only for the individual(s) involved, but for all who participate in the organizational system. However, where there is no trusting belief in the value of open communication, this becomes impossible.

Collier and Esteban emphasize the responsibility and autonomy of every member of an organization.[92] The notion of systemic leadership does not allow the members of an organization to "pass the buck." It is always everybody's duty to take responsibility for the proper and efficient conduct of business within the organization. However, it is important to recognize that the various individual members of an organization may interpret the nature and extent of their responsibilities differently. Organizational functions like strategic planning, human resource management, supply chain management and reporting practices all pose their own special kinds of challenges to those who are charged with their execution. The way in which individual members of an organization interpret these responsibilities and exercise their discretion under various unforeseeable circumstances and in relation to all its different stakeholders ultimately determines the extent to which an organization meets its ethical obligations. In the prosecution of their various duties and responsibilities, individual corporate agents signal to those with whom they interact what can be expected, not only from them, but from all those who identify with the organization that they represent. The need to maintain trust, respect and goodwill, and to remain dedicated to the goals of a particular business association, all influence how an organization or its agents interpret the moral challenges that confront them.

The way in which an organization reports its practices is an indication of how morally responsive it is. For instance, if an organization feels compelled to remain relationally responsive to a variety of stakeholder constituencies, it is unlikely to limit the account that it gives of its activities to the accumulation of physical assets and financial gains. Corporate responsiveness requires that an organization explain how it perceives its relationships towards its stakeholders and how it intends to build and sustain these relationships. Suppliers, employees, customers, and the communities within which the organization operate all have different informational needs

[92] Collier and Esteban, "Systemic Leadership," 209.

when it comes to corporate reporting. The Global Reporting Initiative's guidelines provide an example of the various types of information that an organization may include as it gives an account of its activities.[93]

The institutionalization of a more systemic approach to leadership requires the balancing of a number of apparently contradictory imperatives within the organizational system. Collier and Esteban describe these as paradoxes that have to be accommodated within the organization. They identify at least five sets of organizational imperatives that need to be held in a kind of creative tension within the organizational system.

The paradox of *hierarchy–participation* refers to the fact that though leadership is everyone's responsibility, it is exercised by one person at a time. The fact that different people can play a leadership role does not mean that no structure is required for leadership to be exercised. Uhl-Bien *et al.*'s analysis of the co-existence of administrative, enabling and adaptive leadership roles within one organization is instructive in this regard. The bureaucratic aspects of administrative leadership and the existence of individuals that use their middle management positions have to be utilized to create the enabling conditions for the emergence of systemic leadership. To illustrate this paradox of hierarchy-participation, Collier and Esteban use the example of a jazz band, where certain unspoken conventions dictate who will be "soloing," and "comping" (supporting the lead) and how the switch between leading and supporting is initiated.

The *unity–diversity* paradox refers to the fact that though systemic leadership relies on a diversity of ideas and inputs, the need for congruence and a sense of direction remains. Conflict may exist, but in and through the process of mutual influencing, dissent and dialogue, an even stronger sense of congruence emerges.

Another paradox is that of *symmetry–mutuality*. Even though a systemic approach to leadership encourages all the members of an organization to be morally responsive, it cannot be denied that differences in capabilities, roles, responsibilities and opportunities affect the way in which this plays out in practice. These asymmetries may be temporary, but they cannot be avoided. The importance of keeping everyone engaged and committed at all times, despite shifts in roles,

---

[93] See the Global Reporting Initiative's Guidelines on www.globalreporting.org.

remains one of the central challenges of systemic leadership. Creating opportunities for everyone to share their ideas and setting up systems that can help formalize, advocate and implement these ideas play an important part in this.

In the process, however, yet another paradox is encountered: *discipline–creativity*. Not all ideas are good ones, and hence the organization must celebrate and reward creativity, but exercise discipline to select the best ideas and discard those that will not serve the organization's purposes.

When a new idea or response is identified, another paradox comes into play, namely that of *creation–destruction*. New perspectives typically challenge old ways of doing things. Organizational structures, familiar work patterns and positions of power are often dismantled. People will resist such changes since they undermine their sense of security and involve temporary discomfort. Collier and Esteban therefore emphasize the need for empathetic dialogue, open communication and the maintenance of relationships of trust.

The paradoxes are indicative of the kinds of challenges that are likely to be encountered in organizations that adopt a more systemic approach to leadership and a more relational understanding of accountability. A more systemic approach to leadership requires an understanding of systemic complexity at all levels of an organization. At every level of an organization members face different challenges. At board level, there has to be an acknowledgement of the interdependent relationships that exist between the organization and the wide network of stakeholders with whom it engages. The formal recognition of such relationships of interdependency may, in some cases, precipitate the extension of invitations for official board representation to important stakeholders. If this is not possible, interaction with external stakeholders must be proactively sought by specific board committees. Multidirectional communication is crucial if board members are to gain insight into the nature and extent of an organization's responsibilities towards its stakeholders. Board members should always remain willing to listen to the concerns of all of the organization's stakeholders.

A more systemic approach to leadership does not require that an organization's formal structures be abolished. What it means instead, is that the capacity to take responsibility when and where needed should be nurtured throughout the organizational system and among all of its members, despite, or alongside, the existence of a formal organizational hierarchy and various specialized functional units. The goal is to create organizational environments within which systemic leadership can be utilized to strengthen purposeful values-driven organizational practices. It is to this challenge that we turn in Chapter 6.

6 | *Reconsidering ethics management*

Throughout this book, questions have been raised about the way in which ethics programs are typically conceived of and implemented in organizations. It was argued that its main limitations center on the dissociation of ethics from business practice and the assumptions that underpin this dissociation. Chapter 1 drew on research that questions the effectiveness of ethics programs in terms of their motivation, formulation and integration. This analysis led to a critical re-evaluation of some of the basic assumptions that inform many ethics programs. It was suggested that if all the members of an organization are to participate meaningfully in its ethics programs, such initiatives would have to be reconceived in fundamentally different terms. This led, first of all, to a reconsideration of the nature of moral reasoning and moral agency.

Chapter 2 draws attention to the central role that deontological, utilitarian or rights-based theories continue to play in many business ethicists' understanding of ethical decision making and puts their limitations into perspective. It was argued that it is impossible to think of individuals as isolated, rational agents who are capable of objectively operationalizing these rational protocols whenever, and wherever, it is deemed necessary to arbitrate in matters of ethical significance.

In Chapter 3, an individual's sense of moral agency was described as something that is shaped and informed by tacit knowledge, an embodied sense of self, and the relationships in which he/she participates. The intimate relationship that was thus established between an individual's sense of self and his/her continuous interactions with, and observations of, others, suggested that the moral fabric of an organizational system is woven in an exceedingly intricate manner. This has significant implications, not only with respect to the question of who has the determining influence within an organization, but also for the way in which the values that inform the behavior of those who participate in the organizational system come into being. In Chapter 4,

236

it was proposed that values are emergent, embodied, metaphorical and rhetorical in nature and that the way in which normativity is treated in organizations should reflect an awareness of this.

To criticize certain theoretical approaches and the practices that they support contributes little if it is not accompanied by suggestions as to how a more viable relationship between business practice and ethics may be established. Chapter 5 explored recent leadership thinking about the way in which influence is circulated and responsibility shared throughout an organization's internal system of relations. In this last chapter, the notion of systemic leadership and relational accountability will be employed in an effort to rethink the motivation, formulation and integration of ethics programs in practical terms.

From our analysis so far, it has become clear that an organization need not necessarily function as the pivotal center point in a system of external stakeholder relations on which the fortunes of all hinge. Contemporary organizations are more likely to find themselves thoroughly entwined in a complex web of interdependent relationships with no fixed or identifiable "center." As such, they are sometimes on the receiving end of demands and problems not of their own making. However, such organizations can and should be selective in deciding with whom to enter into a relationship. Once they do decide to establish a relationship with another party, however, they have a responsibility to nurture and sustain it. Throughout, organizations should remain cognizant of the fact that their members' sense of normative propriety is continually being shaped in and by their interaction with external stakeholders.

Rethinking ethics management programs

In rethinking the motivation for ethics programs, a rationale must be found that goes beyond fear and protection against liability. This only becomes possible when corporate success is conceived of in terms much broader than financial bottom-line results. Ethics is the everyday business of business only insofar as it is part of what may broadly be thought of as the ultimate goal of all business-related activity, namely, the enhancement of life. Once we begin to think of life enhancement as the ultimate goal of business activity, a whole new perspective opens up with respect to the nature of employees' sense of normative propriety within an organization, the scope of their involvement in its formation and subtle mutations, as well as the role that an ethics program can play in all of this.

The support that ethics interventions receive within the US regulatory environment confronts us with a paradox. Organizations are encouraged to implement the basic elements of an ethics program, yet the checklist mentality that this creates often serves to undermine ethics as practice. Through my analysis, it became clear that ethics in corporate environments is not "something" that can be "managed." It is not a stagnant feature of an organizational system that can be precisely analyzed, concisely formulated, and deliberately implemented. In fact, it is reinterpreted and reiterated in all that the members of an organizational system say and do. Each and every member of an organization has to remain ethically responsive in relation to its various stakeholders. As such, ethics as practice defies "management" by means of precisely orchestrated ethics programs or interventions.

To recognize this is, in a sense, to call the whole notion of organizational ethics management into question. However, the basic elements of an ethics management program that are inscribed in the recommendations of the USFSG remain the framework within which most ethics officers must do their work. As such, it is part of the contextual and institutional contingencies that currently inform normativity in organizations. To ignore such a basic practical consideration would therefore not only be irresponsible, but would also be contrary to the approach that I have argued for thus far. The fact is that whatever approach one takes to normativity in contemporary organizations has to be responsive to existing legal and institutional parameters. Responsiveness cannot simply be equated with criticism. The only viable option, therefore, is to reinterpret the basic elements of organizational ethics programs in a way that facilitates the reconciliation of ethics and business in practice. A reinterpretation of organizational ethics programs has to start with a shift in the assumptions that typically inform their various elements. Table 6.1 represents a brief summary of what this entails.

What does this shift in assumptions mean for the way in which organizational ethics programs and initiatives are conceived? In what is to follow, a number of concrete proposals will be made on how basic elements of an ethics management process may be redesigned in accordance with this shift in assumptions. As in Chapter 1, I will focus

Table 6.1 *A shift in assumptions regarding ethics programs*

Where?	From an organization fixed as the center of a stakeholder map	To an organization as a complex adaptive system within a web of relationships
Why?	From fear of, and protection against liability	To life enhancement
	From a preoccupation with financial bottom-lines	To integrated sustainability
What?	From compliance checklists and rule-driven codes	To emergent normative congruence
Who?	From individual moral agents with clearly defined roles	To the ethical responsiveness of individual members with diverse perspectives
How?	From directive, instructional communication and training	To fostering responsiveness and discretion

on three different elements of ethics programs, i.e. how these programs are *motivated*, *formulated* and *integrated* into organizations.

Motivation

It is important to rethink fundamentally the role of ethics programs within organizations. Nietzsche once said that if people have a "why" in life, they could endure almost any "how." The answer to the "why?" question needs, however, to go beyond a financial rationale for ethics programs. What is necessary instead, is a radical reconsideration of why organizations exist and why employees work. Merely illustrating the relationship between ethics programs and financial results or highlighting reduced liability risks does not go nearly far enough in addressing this fundamental question. By representing ethics as a trade-off that constrains "business as usual," this type of rationale undermines the idea that ethics is an integral part of business practice. The way in which moral agency functions, and the relationship of values to life enhancement allow us a new understanding of the relevance of ethics programs.

The motivation for ethics programs lies in what the participants in organizational systems care about in life. It is also important to note that there is not a great deal of difference between that which motivates individuals to behave in an ethically responsive way and that which allows an organizational system to be driven by the values that emerge within it. An organization's values-proposition is ultimately its value proposition. Values emerge as people cooperate in the pursuit of what they consider important in life. The ethical question is no longer exclusively focused on what we may and may not do but rather on what makes life worthwhile for all those involved in, and with, a particular organization. In Chapter 3, the concerns of ethics initiatives were reconceived as the emergent values that inform an organizational culture. If an organization functions as an open, complex adaptive system, these emergent values are indicative of what is valued by those who participate in it, as they work to sustain its various relationships. As such, an ethics program exists in order to foster and sustain relationships with all of an organization's internal and external stakeholders. Chapter 5 drew out the implications of a more systemic view of ethical leadership. Accountability as relational responsiveness requires that each individual in each business episode ask the question: "Who am I in this situation and what is required of me in this relationship?"

An ongoing consideration of what an organization values would contribute to the emergence of a sense of normative congruence across all of its various functions. However, due to the way in which many organizations treat ethics in relation to their various functional imperatives, such an organization-wide sense of congruity is seldom allowed to emerge. Ethics programs are typically quite distinct from organizations' corporate social responsibility (CSR) projects and their environmental protection programs. It is often the case that the ethics and compliance officer of an organization, its sustainability officer, its company secretariat and its internal audit function have little or no interaction with one another. From the perspective of the organization as a complex adaptive system, these divisions have to be overcome. Internal controls, ethics initiatives and the organization's responsiveness to its social and natural environment should all reflect its commitment to life enhancement. The notion of "integrated sustainability" employed by progressive governance guidelines such as the South African King II Report reflects an awareness of the fact that an organization's long-term sustainability is linked to its ability to sustain a wide variety of stakeholder relationships through both financial and non-financial means. In terms of King II's Integrated Sustainability chapter, corporate success is redefined as the way in which an organization succeeds in terms of the "triple bottom-line," i.e. the social, environmental and economic bottom-lines. This more comprehensive assessment tool gives a better measure of an organization's willingness and ability to enhance the lives of those with whom it comes into contact.

A commitment to life enhancement requires that organizational silos be broken. If value congruence can't be established within an organization, inconsistencies and internal miscommunications soon become evident to stakeholders. Even attempts to report on "integrated sustainability" can reveal quite the opposite. Though triple bottom-line reporting has the potential to provide the public with better insight into what an organization does to sustain its various external stakeholder relationships, these reports are often put together by a public relations firm with little or no insight into the relationship between the actions of an organization and the value(s) orientation of its internal system of relations. In such reports, values-commitments often seem vague and bear little relation to the rest of their content. Triple bottom-line reports prepared by public relations companies cannot therefore meaningfully articulate that which informs the behavior of the members of an organization in all of its various functions, and which guides them in sustaining its various external relationships.

The proactive management of ethical risks is also often offered as a rationale for ethics programs. To gauge potential areas of ethical risk in an organization, its internal audit function, as well as certain compliance checks and organizational culture audits or "climate studies" are often employed. The data thus obtained is then typically used to explain to an organization's board why an ethics and compliance program is necessary. As indicated in Chapter 1, the problem with these forms of assessment is that they are based on the assumption that an organization's "culture" consists of more or less fixed, or consistent, patterns of observable behavior. As such, these forms of assessment are not able to tap into culture as an ongoing process of meaning formation within an organization. Compliance checklists and audit reports may be useful in identifying loopholes in an organization's systems and procedures, but they cannot articulate the tacit knowledge that continually informs people's behavior within those systems. Getting a sense of the values that inform behavior in an organization's internal system of relations requires a different kind of information gathering. Many surveys have attempted to combine the assessment of both formal and informal systems, but fail to provide conclusive data on how these interact in specific cases. Both in terms of form and content, these surveys cannot tap into the complex network of tacit beliefs that inform behavior within an organization.

To develop an alternative to current methods of ethical risk assessment, it is necessary to rethink both their content and their methodology. The ethical risk areas within an organization cannot be adequately appreciated without tapping into the tacit knowledge and beliefs that inform the behavior of its members. In addition, it is necessary to develop some sort of understanding of the symbolic universe within which these beliefs make sense. One has to learn how to read the repositories of tacit knowledge within an organization, such as its stories, artifacts, rituals and heroes, as well as the way in which its physical spaces are organized. According to Driskill and Brenton, an organization's "culture" is shaped by a number of elements.[1] They divide these elements into a number of categories. In their conception, values are considered a "master element," and are supported by *symbolic* elements such as symbols, stories, language and metaphors.[2] Heroes and outlaws are described as *role* elements, whereas rituals, informal rules and organizational communication style are considered *interactive* elements. Organizational history and place are considered *context* elements. Elements such as these are very hard to pinpoint through quantitative survey techniques, even when perception statements and complex factor analysis techniques are employed.

One of the strategies that has been developed to gauge the wide array of elements that continually play into the sensibilities of an organization's members is to analyze the stories that are circulated within its internal system of relations. These stories reveal the tacit knowledge with which those who participate in an organizational system inculcate one another through their continual interaction and mutual observation. Peter and Waterman's research into organizational culture has done much to draw attention to organizational

---

[1] Gerald W. Driskill and Angela Laird Brenton, *Organizational Culture in Action: a Cultural Analysis Workbook* (California: Sage, 2005), p. 42.

[2] This "master element" designation betrays the authors' foundationalist assumption that these values are stable entities that can be used to explain other phenomena. I argue for a more fluid, emergent understanding of values.

storytelling by illustrating the extraordinary powers of stories as didactic devices in the moral and practical education of managers.[3]

Gabriel argues that this preoccupation with storytelling has not always had a positive effect. It has lead, in his estimation, to an overemphasis on storytelling and a blurring of the boundaries between stories and other narratives.[4] Gabriel is more circumspect in his approach to storytelling in organizations. He suggests that organizations are by no means in the natural habitat of storytelling. Furthermore, stories always compete with other narratives. However, precisely because storytelling is a relatively special phenomenon in organizations, the stories that do exist are significant, and provide valuable clues as to the emotional and symbolic life of an organization. Stories signal what elicits strong emotions amongst organizational members and as such, they display what people care about most deeply. Stories utilize poetic tropes, such as the attribution of motive, causal connections, responsibility, blame and credit. They infuse people's experiences of the realities of organizational life with meaning instead of simply accepting or rejecting them. Stories create complex narrative structures out of simple events by interpreting the significance of particular kinds of behavior and the roles that certain individuals play, as well as the effect that these have in, and on, an organization's internal and external system of relations.[5] According to Gabriel, most stories about organizational life are negative stories, i.e. stories about suffering and misfortune. As such, they are mechanisms for psychological survival. An important characteristic of stories is the fact that they may have many different meanings, not only to different people, but to the same person. A character in a story may elicit feelings as wide ranging as fear, admiration, *and* envy. Because of this, stories offer scope for a wide range of rationalizations or even self-deceptions. It is important to pay attention to such rationalizations and self-deceptions, since they often play an important part in bringing about, or perpetuating, moral failures within an organization.

To tap into the sensibilities of an organization's internal system of relations, it may be necessary to use a more varied form of assessment, i.e. one that generates both qualitative and quantitative information.

---

[3] Yiannis Gabriel, *Storytelling in Organizations: Facts, Fictions and Fantasies* (Oxford University Press, 2000).
[4] *Ibid.*, p. 240. [5] *Ibid.*, pp. 36–41.

Driskill and Brenton suggest a number of methods for gathering cultural information, including *observation, interviews* and *surveys*, as well as *textual analysis.*[6] According to Driskill and Brenton, each of these methods taps into specific elements of an organization's cultural dynamics.

Through *observation*, those artifacts that are indicative of an organization's rules, heroes, history, values and communication style can be gauged. Such artifacts may include the way in which office spaces are arranged and the objects that are hung on the walls, as well as the style of dress that is adopted. That there are historical pictures of founders on the walls of an organization's offices, or the fact that employees are allowed to pick the artworks that surround their own workspace may, for instance, be a significant indicator of the sensibilities that prevail amongst an organization's members. The former may be indicative of a conformist sensibility among the members of an organization, whereas the latter may be a sign of a more individualistic or pluralistic orientation. Rites and rituals are also particularly rich sites for gathering data about organizational values. Latent meanings are revealed through these recurring events and the value that people attach to them. For instance, when an organization has weekly "standing space only" meetings, where people jointly come up with new ideas and challenge prevailing ones, it may be a sign that its members value open communication and dissent.

According to Driskill and Brenton, *interviews* or qualitative surveys should be employed to follow up on the things that have been observed. However, care must also be taken not to frame interview questions and survey hypotheses in a way that serves merely to confirm researchers' initial perceptions. Unfortunately, statistical surveys often contribute to the perception that an organization's culture can be reduced to a set of more or less fixed behavioral patterns, attitudes, perceptions and priorities that can be expressed in statistical terms. As such, they allow the management of an organization to believe that they can "control" their employees' behavior by "managing" culture. This reflects a fundamental misapprehension with respect to the complexity and dynamics of an organization's internal system of relations. Driskill and Brenton, however, argue that the use of multiple methods improves the validity

[6] Driskill and Brenton, *Organizational Culture in Action*, p. 65.

of the cultural interpretation and allows more credible conclusions to be drawn.

The third method for gathering cultural information that they propose, namely *textual analysis*, is very seldom employed in ethics management programs, but may be very useful. This form of analysis taps into the narrative constructions that inform both an individual's *and* an organization's sense of self.

Identifying ethical risks remains an important part of providing focus and direction to an organization's ethics program. The value of a risk analysis depends, however, on the way in which it is done. It hinges, in particular, on whether or not it allows those who employ it to tap into the tacit elements of an organization's internal life. Since there is no such thing as "an organizational culture" that can be assessed and described once and for all, it is important to tune into the tacit perceptions and expectations on which people rely for their sense of normative orientation in an organization. It is on this basis that all the various elements of ethics programs should be reconsidered.

Formulation

We turn next to a fundamental reconsideration of *how* ethics is formulated within an organization. Ethics and compliance professionals who are preoccupied with checking off all the various boxes on legal compliance and risk management checklists do little to contribute to the emergence of attitudes of relational responsiveness among the members of an organization. If an organization's values are to be associated with those tacit beliefs and unspoken rules that inform the behavior of all who belong to it, a code of ethics can't be a generic document drafted by an ethics officer or a few top managers. Nor can an organization's "core values" be identified by means of a statistical survey among its employees. Ethics and compliance officers should apply themselves instead to gaining an understanding of the tacit expectations and priorities that emerge and are circulated in an organization's internal system of relations. It is here that the key to an organizational system's normative congruence lies. If the members of an organization are obliged to act in ways that are responsive to its system of relations, then it is the duty of ethics and compliance officers to assist them in finding ways to do so. To this end, opportunities have to be created for the members of an organization to reflect on the tacit value priorities that are constantly being circulated among them in their interactions with one another.

The values that emerge within an organizational system reflect the ways in which its members seek to enhance the well-being of its shareholders, employees, suppliers, customers, host communities, and the natural environment. As such, a successful ethics program may increase shareholder value. However, it is equally important that an ethics program enhance employees' sense of purpose and meaning in their working lives, that it renders a service to an organization's customers, that it contributes to the livelihood of local communities, and that it protects and nurtures the environment. In a very real sense, those values that inform the moral sensibilities of an organization's members are as evident in its corporate social responsibility programs as they are in its internal ethics initiatives, its audit function, and its marketing campaigns. An organization's various initiatives should therefore be aligned and their success measured by the extent to which they serve its life-enhancing purposes.

Most attempts to formulate normative guidelines for an organization based on the value orientations of its members proceed from the assumption that organizational values are more or less static common points of reference. However, it has to be remembered that the values that emerge within an organization's internal system of relations reflect what its members care about and how they relate to others. Unforeseen contingencies and complications announce themselves within the life of an organization and pose new challenges. As such, any attempt to give formal expression to the values that inform life within an organization must allow for a certain degree of open-endedness. Instead of unilaterally announcing to the workforce of an organization what their values are to be, employees must be given the opportunity to give some sort of expression to the tacit perceptions and unspoken expectations that circulate among them. One way of doing this is to create opportunities for all the members of an organization to verbalize and enact what they care about in their work environment. On such occasions, people should feel free to share their experiences, feelings, and even prejudices.

One of the most effective ways of initiating these kinds of exchanges is to ask open-ended questions such as: "Tell us about your two best work-related experiences" or "What was your greatest work-related disappointment?" People are thus prompted to share what they consider the most valuable or gratifying aspects of their working lives. Indirect questions like: "What would you save from your office in case of a fire?" or "Which colleague would you miss most if he/she died, and why?" can also be very effective. Such prompts work best when they are employed within the context of a small focus group session where respondents are surrounded only by their peers. The power dynamics within the organization must be acknowledged and self-censorship due to the presence of superiors must be avoided. The accuracy of the statements that are thus elicited is less important than what they say about the things that people care about. People have to be able to talk about the things that made them happy or angry or despondent. As indicated in Chapters 3 and 4, people's emotional responses often provide important clues about their deep-seated beliefs, and such beliefs are very significant indications of an individual's values.

The formulation process also requires careful observation of the way in which the members of an organization go about their various daily activities. An organization's code of ethics or code of conduct may not be the best indicator of the values that inform its members' behavior. These values are often more accurately deduced from the way in which an organization's members conduct themselves in its everyday business operations. They are also reflected in what an organization spends its money on, how its members are rewarded and the way in which its physical and policy environments are structured. Typically, allocations within an organization's budget are very good indicators of what is valued by its members and of the care that it takes in nurturing stakeholder relationships. The question is: where is it investing its money? Is it, for instance, spent on training initiatives, new technology to drive efficiency, performance bonuses for cost-cutting, or research and development to foster innovation?

Listening to the jokes that are circulated within an organization's system of relations can also reveal much about its members' value orientations. Humor is often employed to deal with paradoxes within an organization. As such, jokes are quick to betray inconsistencies between an organization's publicly stated values and its internal realities. Humor is also a coping mechanism through which individuals and groups deal with their disappointments, fears and desires.

A thorough textual analysis of an organization's communications will often reveal whether its members' main concerns relate to stakeholder relationships. If nothing in the newsletters, memos, or strategic documents suggests that they are relationally responsive, then such an organization is not providing the space and opportunity for ethics to become part of everyday conversations and practice. According to Driskill and Brenton, there are many types of organizational texts that can fruitfully be submitted to this type of analysis, including: newsletters, annual reports, web sites, mission statements, bulletin boards, email transmissions, employee handbooks, transcripts of speeches, memos, affirmative action/diversity statements, and employee orientation materials or videos.[7] Various types of textual analysis can be employed, such as content analysis, rhetorical analysis and critical linguistic analysis.

Content analysis is clearly the easiest and most expedient way to analyze texts. It tracks the frequency with which concepts are employed in organizational communications and the level of attention that is given to particular issues. There is, according to Driskill and Brenton, software that is capable of performing a basic form of content analysis.[8] These software programs are designed to look for signs of "commonality" language and "certainty" language. The former is supposedly indicative of shared values and the latter of resoluteness, inflexibility or completeness. Researchers argue that the space that is allotted to the discussion of particular issues in an organization's texts is a good indication of what its members consider important. Information technology may also be productively employed in the analysis of whistle-blower reports. If, for instance, all the reports that come through an organization's whistle-blowing line could be captured electronically, a narrative analysis could be performed on the aggregate data. Whistle-blowers typically tell stories. They assign agency, construct cause-and-effect relationships and speak to the effect that particular actions have on an organization's internal system of relations. They often betray their feelings and verbalize their fears and disappointments. While the emotive content of such accounts may discredit them from a certain perspective, this data offers rich material for an analysis of the internal dynamics and unarticulated priorities of an organizational system. However, the danger of such an approach in its simplest form is that it could deteriorate into a form of nominalism. The emotive content of particular words, the relative importance of

---

[7] Driskill and Brenton, *Organizational Culture in Action*, p. 103.
[8] *Ibid.*, p. 107.

texts in relation to one another, and the significance of occasion and context, cannot always be adequately accounted for in content analysis. Content analyses are also incapable of gauging the significance of narrative constructions. Because of these limitations, content analyses have to be supplemented with other forms of textual analysis.

Rhetorical analysis is a technique that allows for a more in-depth investigation of those texts that have a special sort of significance within an organization, or that reflect the views of an important figure with whom many in the organization identify. For instance, the speech delivered by a CEO on arrival in an organization is significant. It indicates what he/she feels the strengths and weaknesses of the organization are, i.e. what is valuable and what is dispensable. Often, it also gives some indication of how the present is to be viewed in relation to the past. The symbols, metaphors and artifacts that are mentioned in these kinds of texts should be analyzed in order to identify the values that they reflect. Because they can account for the importance of time and place, as well as symbolic and physical contexts, rhetorical analyses are extremely valuable. The potential danger of using rhetorical analyses lies in the fact that researchers may misapprehend or underestimate the significance of different organizational texts. Our analysis of systemic leadership in Chapter 5 suggests, for instance, that a line manager's motivational talk at weekly meetings may be as significant as a CEO's speech, if not more so.

The last form of textual analysis that Driskill and Brenton recommend is critical linguistic analysis. This involves analyzing a small but culturally significant text in terms of its language and grammatical patterns to reveal its underlying preoccupations. For instance, the pronouns that are used in such texts may be significant: do leaders talk about "we" or "I"? Another potentially significant indicator is the excessive use of the word "you" under threatening circumstances. This may be a sign of finger-pointing and the abdication of responsibility. The active and passive use of language may also be telling in terms of accountability. When an agent wants to avoid direct accountability, the passive form may be employed, e.g., "The decision was made to sell a division of the company and lay off a certain percentage of staff." Verb tense could also be significant; the question here is whether the focus of communications is on the past, or whether it is more future-oriented. Certain words may also be over-used, indicating a certain orientation. The example that Driskill and

Brenton offer is the excessive use of words such as *proper, orderly* or *rational* in an embattled organization.[9]

This kind of critical linguistic analysis could clearly be valuable in gaining insight into the hidden beliefs and assumptions that are circulated among the members of an organization. It is, however, not without its problems. In some respects, it is a method reminiscent of the kind of exegesis that is more commonly applied to religious texts, and it suffers from many of the same deficiencies. Its deficiencies stem, in large part, from its implicit assumption that every text contains only one fixed meaning, which can be mined through the application of an appropriate methodology. The employment of language is, however, much more complex than that. To get a better sense of what the language of significant organizational text might reveal, the importance of the actual act of speaking must be brought into the equation, and the significance of non-textual factors, such as body language and emphasis, recognized. Critical linguistic analysis therefore requires the employment of supplementary techniques such as the observation of real events and the creation of participative, experiential exercises.

The idea that values are emergent, and not imposed properties of an organizational system, may be threatening to some because of the lack of managerial control that it implies. The question that may be raised, in this regard, relates to what is to be done when the values that emerge within an organization are considered inappropriate or misguided. For instance, what role is an ethics program to play in an organization that is focused entirely on the accumulation of profit, with little or no regard for the interests and well-being of those with whom its members engage? In contemplating questions such as these, ethics officers and managerial teams may be tempted into an even more narrowly prescriptive role for their ethics programs. However, they would do well to consider first the likely consequences of trying to impose values that the members of an organizational system do not recognize as their own. Such ethics initiatives are unlikely to elicit anything but skepticism or disdain. There is nothing so damaging as an ethics program that does not speak to the actual experiences and perceptions of those who participate in an organizational system.

---

[9] *Ibid.*, p. 108.

If change is to occur in an organization, it will be necessary first to unpack those beliefs that inform existing value priorities in its internal system of relations. It is only once this has been accomplished that such beliefs can be challenged by real actions and by exposing the members of an organization to different kinds of experiences. The impetus for organizational change could, for instance, be brought about by leaders who act differently and initiate different institutional practices.[10] One of the first things that Boeing's CEO, Jim McNerney, did after stepping in to respond to the ethical challenges that the company faced, was personally to stop using corporate jets for business trips and to rethink what was rewarded within the organization. In this case, one can describe McNerney's leadership as *enabling* the emergence of a new sense of normative orientation within the corporation.[11]

To work simultaneously with those values that are already being circulated in an organization's internal system of relations *and* facilitate the emergence of more relationally responsive moral behaviors, it is necessary to try to understand the reasons behind the importance of particular values among the members of an organization. For instance, if the imperative to pursue profit is of particular significance within an organizational system, it may be because there are many who believe that it is the only, or primary, point of entry to professional success and hierarchical progression. If beliefs of this nature are found to be detrimental to the perpetuation of relationships of trust, both within and around an organization, then a process could be initiated in which they may be reframed. In some cases, this may simply require an open discussion in which the question is posed: why do we pursue profit? In such a discussion, any number of answers may be offered. The important thing for those who are facilitating this reframing process is to continue to work with the assumptions and beliefs that are introduced by participants. If, say, a participant claims that the pursuit of profit is important because it fuels growth and creates investor confidence, further reflection could be stimulated by asking a question such as: but why do people care about this? This compels participants to examine the very basis of their personal

---

[10] As was indicated in Chapter 5, this could include both formal leaders, or individuals in positions of authority, and other leaders that come forward within the system as the opportunity arises.

[11] Ul-Bien, Marion and McKelvey, "Complexity Leadership Theory."

values in a way that they may otherwise never have had the occasion to do. It allows them to assess critically beliefs that they may simply have taken for granted. When thus prodded, a participant might, for instance, offer financial security and material comfort as a rationale for the pursuit of profit. What would be required at this point, and indeed throughout such a reframing process, is that those who take on the role of facilitators offer some kind of creative impetus that invites participants to consider what they already value from a different perspective. In this instance, it might take the form of a question like: what about quality of life and personal growth? Such a question could bring participants to consider the fact that, though their quality of life and personal growth may not be unrelated to their financial security and material wealth, they are not necessarily to be equated either.

When the members of an organization are given the opportunity to revisit the things they value and are invited to approach it from even a slightly different perspective, an opening could be created through which new frames of reference may enter the organization's system of relations. With respect to the pursuit of profit, for instance, those who have participated in such a process may begin to appreciate it within the context of their organization's long term sustainability and the general imperative to enhance the lives of all those with whom the company engages. In other words, a shift in perspective may be initiated within the organizational system, which induces its members to continue their pursuit of profit in ways that do not harm stakeholders, do not negatively impinge on their own or on their colleagues' quality of life and do not involve the exploitation of customers, communities or the environment. Instigating challenging conversations, and disrupting existing patterns of thought by eliciting tension or dissent, are important aspects of this process.[12]

When employees are given the opportunity to speak about their own experiences and beliefs, instead of trying to speak for the whole organization, it becomes easier to get a real sense of what informs their behavior. What this may reveal is that the values that are being circulated among colleagues differ somewhat from one organizational department to another. Such interdepartmental differences are not necessarily a cause for concern. In fact, they reflect the fact that employees seek a form of normative orientation that is appropriate to

[12] See Plowman *et al.*, "The Role of Leadership in Emergent Self-Organization."

their specific job-related activities. The primary concern in such instances is not whether an identical value orientation exists throughout an organization, but rather, whether a sense of normative congruence can still be detected across organizational functions. The different functional units of an organization may value different things, but they could still care about similar things. This may be thought of as a type of normative pluralism, meaning that one department's values do not have to be wrong for another's to be right. What is important, in such instances, is that the different sets of value priorities that are being circulated within the more intimate relational setting of an organization's various functional units are unpacked, so that the beliefs on which they are based may be revealed. For instance, those who work in an organization's internal audit department may value rule-abidingness, accuracy and respect. On the other hand, individuals employed in an organization's marketing department may value "out-of-the-box" thinking, creativity and dissent. Clearly, these different sets of value priorities serve the members of these units well in the performance of their respective kinds of duties. To be willing to accommodate both sets of value priorities within an organization is not to adopt a laissez-faire attitude to values or to simply accept inconsistencies within an organization's internal system of relations. Such differences can sometimes be realigned by reframing various sets of apparently inconsistent or contradictory value priorities in a way that draws out what they have in common. It is clear, for instance, that accuracy is something that makes accountants good at what they do, whereas creativity is what drives marketing ideas. When considered carefully, it is possible to discern a mediating value concept that embraces both sets of value priorities, namely: a commitment to excellence, or having a passion for what one does. The differences and tensions between people's understanding of value priorities often create the spaces from within which normative congruence emerges.[13]

It is not only the pursuit of excellence that can assume many different forms in an organization, this may be true of most of the values that shape and inform the behavior of an organization's members. If this is the case, then it would clearly be very difficult, if not impossible, for most organizations to formulate all the different values that are circulated amongst their members, in all their different iterations, in a final,

---

[13] See Boal and Schultz, "Storytelling, Time, and Evolution."

comprehensive code or policy document. However, in many, if not most, organizations a sense of normative congruence emerges amongst members in and through their ongoing interactions with one another and with others outside of their organization. In many respects, this sense of normative congruence may be more meaningful and more compelling in its influence than any formal organizational code or policy document. This is because it relies, in a sense, on a kind of relationally situated responsiveness and care. It requires members of the organization to use one another's actions and reactions, as well as the feedback of those outside stakeholders with whom they interact, as points of normative reference to ensure that their own behavior is appropriate. The sense of normative congruence that emerges among the members of an organization can therefore provide individuals with a significant form of normative orientation in their daily activities.

Recognizing the complex, relational nature of value orientation within organizations creates somewhat of a conundrum, since legislation requires that companies formally articulate their values in a code or values statement. While it may be possible to draft a code based on the normative congruence between different value orientations in an organization, such a code would require frequent reconsideration and revision. Business ethicists have long insisted that codes remain "living documents," but this is something that has seldom materialized in practice. One of the reasons for this is the cost of reprinting and redistributing codes. To the extent therefore, that this proves to be a decisive issue, organizations may have to rethink the way in which they put together and distribute such documents. After all, the necessity of printing codes in glossy brochures or permanently inscribing them on expensive plaques might justifiably be questioned. This kind of extravagant expenditure effectively impresses upon employees that the values that are described in a code or value statement are to be considered final, fixed and universally valid. It may also create the impression among the members of an organization that those in positions of authority are more concerned with public perception than the reality of organizational practice.

If values are emergent they should be articulated in a way that allows an organization's members to remain perpetually responsive to the evolving contingencies of its various relational commitments. If values are to give the members of an organization a meaningful form of behavioral orientation in the daily execution of their various responsibilities, they should be expressed with adequate specificity. If values are best expressed in the accommodating hermeneutic play of metaphors and tropes, they should not be forced into the lifeless linguistic constraints of general principles.

What all of this suggests is that organizations need an alternative to paper codes or formal declarations of principles. In contemplating such an alternative, it is important to consider the nature of its content, the manner in which it is to be disseminated and the way in which it is to be positioned. The content of such an alternative must speak to the nature of values and the way in which they actually function in organizations. It must be able to accommodate the iterability of employees' sense of normative propriety. One way of accomplishing this is to substitute definitive statements with open-ended questions. When this strategy is employed, it may no longer be appropriate to use the word "code." After all, can one really say that a set of open-ended questions is a code? Johnson & Johnson's Credo has long been considered one of the most successful expressions of an organization's values. It is interesting to note that Johnson & Johnson does not refer to its credo as a "code"; they insist that what they have is a "credo," i.e. a creed that reflects the beliefs and commitments of their organization's members.[14] The Johnson & Johnson Credo is instructive with respect to the kind of relational responsiveness that is envisaged in this approach. It speaks directly to its specific business purpose, namely supplying high quality products to doctors, nurses, patients, mothers and fathers. It does not address customers in general terms, but identifies them in terms of their specific role responsibilities. Such a code enables employees to think about moral responsiveness in specific terms. The Johnson & Johnson Credo is also unique in that it puts customers first, and shareholders last, thereby reflecting the value priorities of the organization.

The so-called "mirror test" remains one of the most effective tools in ethics management programs. It gives individuals a few basic questions to ask themselves when they are trying to determine the ethical propriety of a particular course of action.[15] What is proposed here

---

[14] See the complete Johnson & Johnson Credo at www.jnj.com/our_company/our_credo/.
[15] The mirror test is a communication and training tool employed by many ethics officers to stimulate ethical decision making. It includes five questions: 1) Is it legal? 2) Does it comply with the company's code? 3) How would this look in

in terms of mechanisms that could supplement, perhaps even replace codes, is a twist on the mirror test. Instead of circulating a code document, one could, for instance, confront employees with certain open-ended questions, such as "Who am I in this situation, and how do I take care of this stakeholder?" on an ongoing basis. An initiative that challenges the members of an organization with open-ended questions is not focused on the application of general principles to specific situations. It does not ask of employees to consider, first and foremost, whether something is legal or not. Its purpose, instead, is to encourage individuals to remain continually attuned and responsive to the various relationally defined parameters and expectations that their involvement with others, both inside and outside of an organization, imposes on their behavior. It also challenges the members of an organization to find ways to secure and contribute to those things that draw them together in common cause.

In order to reflect the trope-like character of values, the members of an organization could consider the use of metaphors, pictures, or even music in the articulation of what they care about. Care should be taken to create a rhetorical space that is accommodating of the complex relational processes through which values continually emerge within an organizational system. The articulation of an organization's values should be such that it challenges its members to view their own responsibilities from a relational perspective. Because these relationally defined responsibilities are always tied to the singular contingencies of a particular context, the different functional units or departments within an organization should be free to choose their own priorities. The members of such teams do, however, need to be challenged to consider how their specific priorities relate to the concerns of the organization as a whole.

An organization's articulation of its members' value orientations must stimulate further reflection and encourage discretion. It should attempt to give expression to whatever sense of normative congruence has emerged among the members of an organization, but should encourage, at the same time, criticism and dissent. The question that it should confront the members of an organization with is this: how does what you do serve to enhance the lives of all those with whom the

---

the newspaper? 4) Does it comply with the golden rule, "Do unto others what you want them to do to you"? and 5) How does this make me feel?

organization comes into contact? It must, in a sense, tell the story of what an organization's members care about and explain how each part and member of the organization has a role in caring for and nurturing that which draws them together. This story has many intricately connecting plotlines, and the characters within it are often paradoxical figures who play more than one role, but throughout its many complications, a certain inexpressible logic announces itself that somehow puts the paradoxes and particulars in perspective and makes sense of it all. It is against the backdrop of this perpetually unfolding story that the members of an organization are always acting and responding.

In terms of code dissemination, organizations should reconsider the common practice of sending each of its employees a glossy printed document for safekeeping and future reference. Instead, they could intermittently send all the members of an organization a "fill in the blanks" chart, which allows everyone to contribute in a continuous process of reinterpretation and rearticulation. It may also be a good idea to give the various functional units or departments within an organization the opportunity to fill in the blanks together, to write their own stories and to choose their own metaphors. An organization should display the various inputs that are thus collected with pride, as they are an indication of its members' ongoing commitment to those things that draw them together.

Table 6.2 contains a summary of the shifts that need to occur in the way in which organizational values are conventionally conceived. It explains why codes cannot be formulated and implemented in the way in which organizations have traditionally gone about it.

Integration

We turn next to a fundamental reconsideration of *how* ethics is integrated into organizational practice. What our analysis so far suggests is that nothing less than a total paradigm shift is required in the way in which this aspect of organizational ethics is conventionally understood. The management of an organization can no longer satisfy themselves that they have integrated ethics into their organization's practices once they have transferred all the relevant and necessary information to their employees about their company's rules and policies. The implementation of top-down leadership directives will

Table 6.2 *Redefining values*

Values as codified principles	Values within ethics as practice
Values are epistemic principles that distinguish right from wrong	Values represent what we care about and who we are
Values are universal and permanent	Values are emergent
Theoretical values guide business practice	Moral values and business values are not different in kind
Values are expressed in codes	Values are reflected in budgets, strategy documents, stories, and jokes
Values are directive, behavioral guidelines	Values are relational and responsive
Values are truth statements	Values are tropes

not suffice in establishing relational accountability. One-directional, directive communication clearly cannot inspire thoughtful responsiveness amongst the members of an organization. It is only through this kind of responsiveness that it becomes possible to integrate ethics and practice in a meaningful manner. Every member of an organization must seek to take care of the internal and external relationships to which the company owes its existence and well-being. Communication and training therefore have to be fundamentally rethought. In addition, the organization's policies and system of rewards and punishments must be reconsidered from the perspective of shared accountability and systemic leadership. Last but not least, care should be taken to ensure that a concern for moral responsiveness is reflected in the way that the organization reports on its various activities.

Institutionalizing systemic leadership

If ethical leadership is a capacity of the organizational system as a whole and if accountability is to be defined in relational terms, then organizational ethics, compliance, governance and CSR functions have to be reconceived in different terms. It was argued earlier in this chapter that these functions all derive their justification from the values that an organization is committed to. If this is the case, then they should not exist in isolation of one another. It is, however, unrealistic to think that departmental boundaries, role responsibilities and distinct job descriptions can, or should, be dismantled in order to make shared responsibility for organizational values possible. Research into leadership in complex adaptive systems has indicated that the emergent congruence of organizational concerns is perfectly reconcilable with diversity in roles and relational responses. However, more frequent interactions are required between these functions to ensure that their various specific goals and priorities remain sufficiently congruent.

The cross-functional task team

One way of ensuring that regular and meaningful interaction takes place between the ethics, compliance, governance and CSR functions of an organization is to create a cross-functional task team. Such a team could be called the "Ethics Task Team" or "Sustainability Task Team," or even something like "Relationship Custodians." Each of these names has distinct advantages and disadvantages. "Ethics," especially in the US context, has the unfortunate connotation of organizational policing against moral failures. "Sustainability" is currently exclusively associated with CSR, and people might find it difficult to see the link with governance and ethics. A more general name, less tainted by existing connotations, may therefore be preferable. An organization could even consider tying the name of such a task team more directly to its specific reason for existence or its brand. A telecommunications provider could, for instance, call its cross-functional task team the "Connectors." The idea is to link this group of people directly to what an organization cares about and pursues in its everyday operations.

The members of such a cross-functional task team would be in a better position to tap into an organization's various relational circuits than a single ethics officer. One may even describe them as an embodiment of the *enabling* kind of leadership that Uhl-Bien *et al.* referred to. By virtue of their position and assigned authority, they may have distinct functions from which they can contribute to the emergence of broader systemic dynamics.[16] They may not be hierarchically superior, but their unique expertise, access to resources and frequent interactions with a variety of stakeholders put them in a

---

[16] Uhl-Bien *et al.*, "Complexity Leadership Theory."

position to enable the emergence of normative congruence within the broader system.

Such a team would have two basic functions. The first is to detect emergent value priorities as they begin to announce themselves in the relational dynamics of an organizational system. The second is to tell organizational stories that allow those who hear or read them to get a sense of the congruence of value and purpose that guide and orientate all who participate in the organizational system.

To carry out the first of these mandates, team members would have to pool their collective observations and experiences in order to develop insight into how values manifest on various levels and in different units within an organization. Their task would also require them to consider together how these values attain and sustain their power of influence. The idea is to tap into the tacit knowledge that exists within the various functions represented on the team in order to interpret the way in which values emerge out of everyday behaviors and interactions in the organization.

The cross-functional task team's second mandate requires that they unravel the relationships between agents, emotions and beliefs that inform the normative congruence within the organization. It should also provide the opportunity for people in the various functions to learn from each other and to be made aware of how certain organizational practices and systems contribute to the emergence of values. The idea is not to seek consensus or uniformity, but to create awareness of how the organization's values manifest in its various iterations. The cross-functional task team enhances collaboration across organizational silos, and as such, allows tensions, disagreements and different perspectives to surface.

When such a cross-functional group exists, it can continually provide board members with "snapshots" of the organizational culture in its different manifestations. Using these snapshots, the board has to gauge the degree of congruence in values and purpose that exists among the various individuals and units within the organization. They must also be able to present critical perspectives that precipitate an ongoing concern for moral responsiveness at all levels of the organization. The cross-functional task team should inform the board of emergent patterns within the organization's various functions, and help the board to interpret the underlying beliefs, symbols, artifacts and heroic acts that may serve to sustain specific values. As such, they play the role of storytellers. According to Boal and Schultz, organizational storytellers create temporal coherence by grouping events together and suggesting certain plots.[17] They devise an organizational biography of sorts, point out recurring themes, and attempt to make sense of seemingly random events by constructing certain paths from the past, into the present, towards the future. In my mind, it is important to emphasize the fact that these forms of coherence are constructed, and that they do not represent "facts" found.

The fact that enabling leadership functions exist cross-functionally does not undermine the need for and legitimacy of more administrative leadership functions of a bureaucratic and hierarchical nature. An organization's board of directors, company secretariat and board committees are good examples in this regard. However, from the perspective of furthering the emergence of value congruence throughout the system, the nature of a board's corporate governance duties also needs to be reinterpreted. This is because accountability is no longer to be understood only in terms of legal accountability for corporate failures, but rather in terms of the need to sustain relationships of trust and cooperation. The board must therefore position itself to become an important custodian of all of the organization's relationships. It is the board's duty to ensure that all of the organization's relationships are sustained by directing members' attention to those structures, practices or beliefs that may prove detrimental to it.

Integrated sustainability

If integrated sustainability is to be the measure of an organization's success, a stakeholder perspective is crucial. A more realistic approach to the role that an organization plays in stakeholder relationships should therefore be adopted. This involves a greater appreciation for the fact that when an organization and its stakeholders commit to long term relationships with each other, all are likely to be affected, no matter how the balance of power may shift between them. The perpetuation of stakeholder relationships often requires that parties make compromises on a structural, procedural, contractual and financial level, but it also involves many small, less obvious interpersonal accommodations and personal adjustments. Organizations therefore

---

[17] Boal and Schultz, "Storytelling, Time, and Evolution," 411–428.

inevitably become part of complex webs of multidirectional influences by virtue of the relationships that they sustain with various external stakeholders. They rely on multidirectional communication processes to gather relevant information and to read and sustain the dynamics of their various stakeholder relationships.

From a systemic leadership perspective, it is no longer possible to exclusively hold an organization's board or executives responsible for the perpetuation of such relationships. Each individual member must understand his/her role in the organization's relational system. This means that workplace democracy, supply chain relationships and stakeholder engagement models have to be reconsidered.

"Democracy," in an organizational context, has unfortunately lost much of the positive connotations of freedom, rights and justice that its evocation in the political arena elicits. Trade union activity and arbitration processes are typically seen as a way to maintain the balance of power between the workers and management of an organization. It is often an adversarial relationship in which each party has to make trade-offs in the process of protecting its interests. Workplace democracy should not be burdened with this association by being made synonymous with trade union activity or dispute resolution. In its broadest terms, workplace democracy means that the rights, benefits and duties of belonging to a community are applied to the organizational context. The members of an organization should trust one another to do whatever is necessary and appropriate to sustain the relationships on which their organization relies. Each employee in a complex organizational environment contains a unique repository of knowledge, skills and practices that makes this possible. Not to give every individual the opportunity to contribute what he/she alone has to offer is therefore to weaken the relational fabric that secures an organization's fortunes.

Traditionally, willingness and ability to take the initiative and assume responsibility has been associated with the notion of "leadership." However, in a complex organizational environment, this is something that everyone is expected to do. As such, "leadership" may be thought of as an emergent capacity of an organization's entire internal system of relations. However, it is also something that requires constant encouragement. One way of doing so is to honor individuals on all levels of an organization's hierarchy for the initiative and discretion that they have shown in sustaining relationships of trust and cooperation, both inside and outside the organization. For instance, a small prize, like an afternoon off, for the "leadership act of the month" can be awarded to a deserving employee in the lower echelons of the organization. This sends the message that "leadership" is expected, and rewarded, amongst all employees.

Newsletters can be used as open forums where people can discuss and contest organizational practices and decisions. It should be clear to everybody that leadership is not something that only those who have risen to positions of authority within an organization are capable of. Instead, it is something that is manifested every time a member of the organization is morally responsive and takes care of the internal and external relationships on which the organization relies.

Supply chain relationships are an important part of an organization's complex system of relations. These are often thought of as part of an organization's "external" relationships. However, it is hard to sustain strict distinctions between "internal" and "external" relationships, since the boundaries between "inside" and "outside" often become blurred in a complex system of relations. For example, the fact that many organizations outsource the manufacturing of their products makes them no less responsible for these products, or the harmful effects that may result from their production. Apart from such considerations, however, procurement is typically one of the areas of organizational life that is fraught with a whole range of ethical risks. Because of this, it is very important for an organization to consider carefully with whom it enters into a supplier relationship. Some ethics programs have included measures aimed at ensuring that an organization's suppliers conform to its own ethical priorities and imperatives. Typically, contracts are made contingent to suppliers' willingness to formally commit themselves to an organization's "Supplier Code of Conduct." The formal signing of such codes can, however, easily amount to lip-service. It is better for an organization to think of, and treat, its suppliers as an integral part of its system of relationships. Suppliers form part of its capacity to respond to all of its various relationships. In a very real sense, suppliers are the hands and legs of the organizational body, and should not be treated as add-ons that have short-term, instrumental purposes only. If, therefore, an organization is careless in choosing its suppliers and is inadequately attuned to the values that emerge in supplier relationships and within supplier organizations, it will risk poisoning its own organizational environment. In view of such considerations, it may even make sense to include representatives from supplier organizations in some meetings of the cross-functional task team. In supplier relationships, it is important that organizations understand one another's value priorities and expectations and find ways to facilitate some sort of normative congruence between their respective practices. With some suppliers, it may not be possible to find an easy alignment of practices. If this is the case, the ethical risks of this non-alignment must be monitored on a continual basis.

Other stakeholders, like customers, local communities, environmentalists or lobbyists, are often viewed as external parties who merely have to be informed of organizational decisions and surveyed to establish their perceptions of the organization. The problem here is that external stakeholders are often viewed as adversaries that the organization must report to, or explain itself to. The organization feels compelled to account *for* its actions and their consequences. This puts the organization in a defensive mode, which is not conducive to building and sustaining relationships of trust and mutual respect. Stakeholders should be viewed, instead, as important allies. As advocates, supporters, and the critical conscience of the organization, they could count among its most precious assets. This is only possible if there is a relationship of trust between an organization and its stakeholders. If the stakeholder dynamic is shaped and informed by little more than sporadic exchanges of an instrumental nature, it becomes very difficult to create or sustain a sense of real relational commitment. Relationships of trust and loyalty evolve in the course of regular interactions, where issues that are significant to those involved are discussed in an open and honest way. If the opportunity for such interactions arises only rarely, they are unlikely to be of a particularly meaningful kind. An effort must therefore be made to create more frequent opportunities for interaction. Such meetings should not always be dominated by some urgent instrumental purpose or crisis of conflict. The intensity, tone, and subject matter of these exchanges must be adapted to suit the timing, context and purpose of the interaction. Some interactions may be more social, some more informational. On other occasions, the organization may invite criticism or dissent. All of these form part of a healthy relationship.

Ethics and compliance offices or functions within organizations

The way in which the "ethics function" within organizations operates will also have to be reconsidered from a systemic leadership perspective. The question that needs to be addressed is how one should describe the ethics and compliance officer from a systemic leadership perspective. Do we want to maintain a strict *administrative* or bureaucratic leadership role for ethics and compliance officers, or would a cross-functional task team who act as *enabling* leaders across the various functional units provide enough administrative support? The even more radical question has to be raised. If we are hoping for emergent, adaptive ethical leadership throughout the organization, should we be doing away with ethics and compliance functions altogether? In a sense, from the *adaptive* leadership perspective, every member of an organization actively contributes to its "ethics function" when he/she conducts him/herself in a relationally responsive way in the organizational system. As such, the ethics function is a function of the entire organizational system. Every one of its members manifests and influences an organizational system's emergent value orientations in the way in which he/she relates and responds to others. However, this may not mean that there is no room for ethics officers, or a dedicated ethics function/office within an organization. In fact, it would not be wise to suggest a "one-size-fits-all" approach to all organizations' ethics and compliance functions. In each organization, the balance has to be found between bureaucratic structures, enabling distributed leadership roles, and the adaptive leadership that emerges amongst all organizational members. Organizational size, age, industry and a variety of other factors will all play a role in determining this balance.

What seems inevitable is that in each and every organization, the role and function of the ethics and compliance officer may have to be carefully reconsidered. An organization's ethics officer may have to become less of the sole agent in charge of "rolling-out" its ethics program, and more of an initiator, instigator, and facilitator of conversations that allow members of the organization to develop a sense of what moral responsiveness in various situations could entail. Opportunities must be created for the sharing of specific anecdotes or stories of hopes, fears, successes and failures. The more concrete and particular these interactions are, the more they will allow members of the organization to become attuned to the tacit sense of normative congruence that emerges amongst them on an ongoing basis. These incidents or experiences must not be treated as precedents, or as exemplars of moral behavior that have to be copied. Instead, the variety of stories that are shared should always invite different stories to be told. It is the cumulative effect of different expressions of what members of the organization care about that allows a sense of normative congruence to emerge.

Ethics officers may, in addition, have to become interpreters of the ways in which an organizational system's value priorities become manifested in everyday corporate life. In the first place, the normative imperatives and priorities that emerge within an organization have to be read in all of their specific iterations. As interpreters, ethics officers require hermeneutic skills. They have to be able to read an organizational system's relational dynamics, in both its positive and less fortunate iterations, and interpret the specific actions and decisions of those who participate in it. The goal of this interpretative process is not to formulate certain "conclusions" regarding the organization's tacit sense of normative congruence in general terms. It is rather to allow the contextual specificity of decisions and actions to elicit an ongoing process of questioning what the organization cares about in its everyday activities.

To keep abreast of developments and incidents within their organizations, ethics officers will require the help and support of a cross-functional task team. As discussed earlier, this task team can bring information and insights to the table that are impossible for one individual to gather. In this regard the ethics function of an organization has to draw in a more decentralized team of interdisciplinary and cross-functional experts and the balance between the enabling role of the ethics officer and that of other leaders must be found.

There remains much to commend in having a central "location" that has specific responsibility for enabling, articulating and assessing the emergent value congruence within the organization. Though impossible to direct in any linear way, or "control" in the strict sense of the word, there is room for a function whose primary role relates to ethics. If this responsibility is completely diffused, it is easy to see this priority dissipate under the pressures of everyday organizational life. The organization's willingness to allocate resources to such a function is in itself a tacit message of the importance it places on having a strong values orientation. Furthermore, an ethics officer is the one individual who has access to the many different iterations of an organization's normative concerns. Because of the variety of perspectives that an ethics officer is exposed to, he/she can develop a sense of how values emerge, lose their significance and re-emerge across organizational functions. By circulating these stories (with all identifying particulars removed) in audiences that would otherwise not have access to them, ethics officers can allow others in the organization to become more attuned to the dynamics of various forms of normative orientation. It is therefore important that specific anecdotes, stories and experiences are shared with a cross-functional task team in order to stimulate discussion and reconsideration of values throughout the organizational system. As such, the ethics office creates a space within which it becomes possible for all the members of an organization to collaborate in the protection of that which they consider valuable.

Another ongoing task of an ethics and compliance function is to play a role in enabling the relational responsiveness that sustains normative congruence within an organization. As the initiator, instigator and facilitator of conversations regarding what moral responsiveness would entail within various organizational functions, the ethics officer may be required to speak many different organizational "languages." As translator an ethics officer must not only understand how values become manifested in the various parts of an organizational system, but must also be capable of formulating their interpretative observations in an idiom that is familiar and accessible to its different specialized audiences. Those who work in an organization's information technology department may, for instance, express themselves differently about values than those who work in research and development. This means that an ethics officer must know a fair amount about what different people in their organization do, and how it all fits together functionally. Visiting the various locations in which an organization's members work, attending meetings within its various departments, and striking up informal canteen conversations are just some of the ways in which an ethics officer might attempt to familiarize him/herself with the various idioms in which an organizational system might express its priorities and expectations.

An ethics officer should attempt, where possible, to assist the members of an organization in becoming more attuned to the tacit knowledge that informs their behavior. One of the ways of doing so is to utilize instances within which the normative congruence between members of the organization seems to have broken down. It is typically in the breakdown of relationships that tacit expectations register themselves most clearly. For instance, the ethics officer can help an individual consider why his/her behavior was deemed inappropriate by others in the organization. This would entail engaging in open-ended conversations about what informed his/her understanding of a specific situation, and speculating on how others might perceive such behavior and what their expectation might be in specific contexts. As such, the ethics officer becomes the mediator that can assist in fostering an environment where people are attuned to the various relational dynamics that inform an organization's sense of normative congruence.

As a close-reader of organizational texts, he or she should be skilled in interpreting specific statements, actions and decisions within the context of the emergent values of the organizational system.

An ethics officer should pay close attention to all organizational communication, budget decisions and strategic developments and raise questions regarding the organizational system's ability to allow moral responsiveness amongst all its members. To raise awareness of the implications that business decisions have in terms of the organization's tacit sense of normative propriety, ethics officers must request a seat at the table of as many decision-making forums as possible. It is crucial, for instance, to share stories and anecdotes that will allow board members a glimpse of the various iterations of the organization's emerging sense of normative congruence. The circulation of stories should, however, not stop at the boardroom. For this kind of communication to be successful, an ethics officer needs to build and sustain good relationships with various decision makers in an organization. The importance of establishing a direct reporting relationship between the ethics officer and the CEO or Chairman of the Board, has been stressed by many ethics management consultants. However, this is by no means the only important relationship that an ethics officer must sustain. Nurturing trusting relationships with other senior executives, as well as middle managers, will allow ethics officers the opportunity to talk about values to the people who witness their various manifestations at the coalface. Oftentimes, ethics officers can have a much more meaningful impact by building and sustaining such informal networks.

It is crucial to identify as many individuals as possible who are willing to contribute to the ongoing consideration of the organization's emergent sense of normative congruence and to instigate such conversations in various forums. Instead of formally appointing certain individuals as "ethics champions," all employees should be given the opportunity to champion the cause on a daily basis, and should be reminded of that role. The question that remains is whether reminding members of the organization of this role would lend enough impetus for them to take up this responsibility. As such, it may be necessary for the ethics officer to recognize individuals who did succeed in taking up the challenge in some way. This could be done informally, or by means of feedback into the organization's performance management system.

Ethics and compliance officers are often seen as "police officers." This is unfortunate, because ethics officers should act as supporters of the relationships that sustain organizational life. If this is a persistent belief within a specific organization, it may even make sense to split the roles of ethics custodian and compliance officer. Depending on the nature of the organization and its industry, compliance may require a very strict bureaucratic, hierarchical approach. By default, the person responsible for the compliance function in such an organization will need to be an "administrative" leader. Administrative leadership could, however, be supplemented by enabling leaders in various organizational functions, and could even assist in assigning and managing the resources that makes enabling leadership within the organization as a whole possible. It cannot be denied that an organization's compliance officer is appointed in a position of authority. This role is unfortunately just one of the cards that is dealt to these officers within the compliance environment, especially within the US. One therefore has to recognize the fact that a compliance officer does have a role to play in ensuring that members of the organization have access to various forms of normative orientation that can assist them in the use of their discretion. As has been suggested in this chapter, this can take place through formal and informal processes. Establishing and maintaining systems of discipline and reward is part of this.

An ethics officer, on the other hand, has to be able to go beyond administrative functions in fulfilling his/her task. His/her "authority" should therefore be understood in slightly different terms. The core function of an ethics officer is not so much to "enforce the rules," but rather to confront members of the organization with the relational implications of everyday business decisions. An ethics officer's authority and influence only has value insofar as it is perceived as something which serves the ongoing consideration of whether the organization is being morally responsive in all its operations. In order to contribute to the relational responsiveness across organizational functions, the ethics officer must play many roles. Theirs is a paradoxical charge that requires unique capacities. The care that they take in evaluating everyday behavior in terms of its moral responsiveness can be both nurturing and challenging. It is nurturing in that it creates a space within which a consideration can be given to how everyday business interactions affect the normative congruence that emerges in the organization. Yet, since such discussions are not always welcome, the ethics officer must be the one to instigate, mediate and facilitate difficult conversations regarding issues that would otherwise not be raised.

The ethics officer's role is to facilitate relationally responsive behavior among the members of an organizational system by personally acting with an appropriate sort of discretion in their dealings with others. If, therefore, these officers are to act as "role models" to their colleagues in an organization, it is most definitely not as the living emblem of some immutable moral ideal. An ethics officer should display the capacity for ongoing questioning and thoughtful deliberation, instead of being the one with "all the right answers." The focus is always on practical discretion. It is also important that an ethics officer remains humble and accessible by admitting mistakes and retaining a healthy sense of humor.

Training and communication

Ethics training in organizations

The Federal Sentencing Guidelines' training and communication requirements pose additional challenges to the implementation of some of the ideas that have been developed in this book. This is especially true with respect to the idea of moral agency and the way in which values emerge in complex adaptive organizational systems. If they are to be meaningfully employed, training programs have to somehow accommodate the fact that agency and values are embodied, relational and contextual.

In his research on workplace dynamics in developed economies, McKinsey found that complex interactions, in which people are required to deal with ambiguity and draw on their tacit knowledge and experience to solve problems, are valued more than routinized, transactional interactions.[18] This he ascribes to the fact that goals are shifting, that the stakes in business decisions are often high, that information is frequently ambiguous or incomplete, that decisions are commonly circulated through multiple feedback loops, and that many participants contribute to decisions under severe time constraints.

The content of training programs must speak to these realities and engage individuals on multiple levels. The idea that training consists of a deliberate "transfer" of formalized knowledge has to be reconsidered. Eraut makes a number of interesting observations in this regard. He distinguishes between codified knowledge, cultural knowledge and personal knowledge.[19] Codified knowledge refers to textual material containing organization-specific information, such as manuals, records, plans, policies and correspondence. This is by no means the most important form of knowledge when it comes to organizational values. Social activities and work experience create cultural knowledge that is typically not codified and is learnt through participation. The knowledge that individuals carry with them and which informs the way in which they think, interact and perform in various situations, can be described as personal knowledge. Eraut argues that tacit knowledge and skills are based on cultural and personal knowledge, rather than codified knowledge. This kind of knowledge is acquired informally through participation in group activities, by collaborating with colleagues, by working with clients and by tackling challenging tasks on the job. "Training" people by informing them about the content of an organization's code of ethics and other relevant policy documents does little to introduce them to the subtle and complex web of tacit beliefs that orientate participants in an organization's system of relations. Those who join an organization must, instead, become attuned to its particular relational dynamics and unspoken expectations. This allows them to acquire, over time, a sense of normative propriety that is congruent with the values that emerge and are circulated throughout the organizational system.

---

[18] Eric Sauve, "Informal Knowledge Transfer," *T+D* (March, 2007).
[19] Michael Eraut, "Informal Learning in the Workplace," *Studies in Continuing Education*, 26(2) (2004), 247–273.

Informal learning that taps into personal and cultural knowledge is essential in sustaining a sense of normative congruity among the members of an organizational system. This kind of learning can be described as implicit, i.e. it occurs independently of conscious attempts to learn and without explicit knowledge of what was learnt.

Another form of learning is reactive learning. Though intentional and more explicit, this form of learning takes place in the midst of action, with little time for consideration. Most ethics training programs make the mistake of focusing exclusively on deliberative learning based on a conscious, goal-oriented form of knowledge transference and focused activities such as problem solving. However, in practice, decisions are often made instantaneously, as a kind of a reflex reaction, or intuitively. Though conclusions drawn on the basis of deliberative or analytic decision making may play a role in informing individuals' behavior, they are by no means the only or even decisive factors that play into people's perceptions and actions.[20]

The possibility of problem solving as such must be viewed from a different perspective. Eraut found that reasoning in the workplace is typically schema-driven, rather than algorithmic. People have certain images of appropriate or inappropriate action and are more likely to match a situation with what they already know and believe than to employ a formal paradigm to "rationally" conceive a completely novel or unprecedented course of action. In situations where decisions are made instantaneously, without conscious deliberation, people are therefore more likely to base their actions on their tacit understanding of existing patterns of behavior. When acting and reacting intuitively, therefore, most people tend to act in a fairly routinized manner. Eraut's observations provide insight into how the tacit sense of normative propriety shapes and informs the day-to-day behavior of individuals. It also explains how the normative congruity between individual perceptions, actions and decisions is sustained in an organizational system.

The question is how implicit and reactive learning strategies can be integrated within ethics programs. To address these aspects of learning, ethics programs must focus on helping individuals understand why they intuitively react to situations in the way that they do. Individuals should also be encouraged to consider why others in the

[20] *Ibid.*, 250.

Table 6.3 *Ethics training from two perspectives*

Ethics training	Typical ethics training programs	The practice of "training"
What?	Focus on "downloading content"	Story-telling, jokes, activities that involve people's bodies, emotions, loyalties
How?	Seldom pay attention to the tacit knowledge that inform people's behavior	Explore rich metaphoric language
Who?	Use hired trainers	Tap into existing communities of practice
Goal	Apply "theory" to "practice" through the use of case studies	Foster moral responsiveness through experiential exercises

organization experience their decisions and actions in a certain way. The goal of an ethics program therefore shifts from formal instruction in a pre-established ethics curriculum, to an exploration of the tacit frames of reference that inform behavior. Table 6.3 illustrates the way in which the target audience, goal, content, and format of ethics training change when it is aimed at addressing, exploring and harnessing tacit knowledge within an organization.

Since an individual possesses tacit knowledge without being aware of it, it is extremely difficult, if not impossible, to articulate it deliberately. It is therefore unlikely to be very useful to simply ask people to explain a decision that they had made instantly and intuitively. This only compels people to concoct some sort of acceptable rationalization. Instead, one would want to encourage members of the organization to provide each other with feedback on how particular decisions and actions are perceived and how they affect relationships.

Training material will also have to draw on symbols, artifacts, stories and metaphors to help participants explore the complex fabric of their tacit moral knowledge in an indirect way. For instance, asking participants to find a picture that best describes an organization or its management will allow them to explore references within their symbolic universe. Such pictures may provide a useful form of articulation for unexpressed beliefs about an organization or its management. A wall-collage of all the pictures that the members of an organization choose to represent their perceptions about an organization could be constructed to identify overlaps, discontinuities and areas of uncertainty. Another way to develop a sense of people's tacit beliefs is to ask individuals to create a symbol or metaphor by completing a statement such as: "management is like ... "

Storytelling may also be a helpful strategy. Callahan makes a distinction between storytelling and narrative that is potentially significant in the use of this strategy in ethics training.[21] A narrative is more open-ended than a story. Callahan argues that storytelling is usually employed to give in an explanation and justification of events in order to persuade an audience. Narrative, on the other hand, can, and should, be able to accommodate anecdotes the significance of which is not immediately clear. This would, of course, include anecdotes of people's lives at work: how they do things and who they work with, as well as what they love and hate. The length of an anecdote is not important. Surprising insights can unexpectedly rise to the surface in the course of a narration.

Callahan suggests that "anecdote circles" be used to facilitate narration among colleagues. An anecdote circle basically comprises a gathering of employees who share anecdotes with each other. The goal of an anecdote circle is not to interview people, or to ask for people's judgments and opinions. Instead, the idea is to generate more anecdotes. This is done by asking participants for examples of particular types of experiences instead of requesting an explanation or justification of their actions or decisions. Anecdotes reveal values and themes that are operative within an organizational system. The way to get an anecdote circle going, according to Callahan, is to draw a time-line and ask participants to populate it with significant events, such as the things that they enjoyed, or dreaded. Another strategy is "ditting," i.e. encouraging participants to try and trump each other's stories with even better ones. A good question to ask to get "ditting" going is: can anyone do better than that?

[21] Shawn Callahan, "How to Use Stories to Size up a Situation," *Anecdote White Paper*, Number 1 (September, 2004).

Jokes and humor contain anecdotes that provide insight into the tacit knowledge that exists in an organizational system. Humor elicits emotional and visceral responses and taps into repositories of common beliefs within an organizational system. In a study of the use of humor in business ethics programs, Lyttle found that the use of self-effacing humor is important in establishing the trust that allows persuasion to take place.[22] The research focused on the use of cartoons and mini-cases as part of the Lockheed Martin "Ethics Challenge" board game, which is used annually in their ethics training program. It is not the use of cartoons that makes this type of training effective, but rather its employment of humor. The research found that the persuasive effect is stronger when ironic humor is used. In order to understand irony, there has to be an understanding of both the surface meaning and the ironic meaning. Irony reflects an awareness that all is not what it seems at face value, and hence is helpful in getting a sense of what people tacitly believe. Gabriel points out that organizational jokes can have both subversive effects and in other cases reinforce and sustain organizational controls.[23] Joking allows criticism to be voiced in a light-hearted manner and taboo subjects to be addressed. It can also undermine the sanctity and legitimacy of authority. At the same time, however, it can diffuse tense situations, build collective solidarity and legitimize power disparities. Gabriel points out that compliance and resistance are not mutually exclusive. Through humor, criticism can be accommodated and a space for dissent can be created without a complete and sudden overhaul of organizational systems. Jokes will, however, always signal which values may be under threat or suspicion within the organization's tacit knowledge structures.

Gabriel puts his finger on one of the most important aspects of storytelling: "Stories continually test and redraw the boundaries between the managed and the unmanaged."[24] It allows people to write and rewrite their identities and renegotiate the things that an organization cares about. Identities are fragmented, tentative and experimental and training must provide participants with the opportunity to revisit both their own sense of self and the way in which they

---

[22] Jim Lyttle, "The Effectiveness of Humor in Persuasion: the Case of Business Ethics Training," *The Journal of General Psychology*, 128(2) (2001), 206–216.
[23] Gabriel, *Storytelling in Organizations*, pp. 121–123.   [24] *Ibid.*, p. 128.

see the organizational system in which they participate. In many cases, traumatic events precipitate this kind of reconsideration. Nostalgia, suffering and insults are therefore useful and important triggers for organizational storytelling. The emotional content of stories narrated as a result of some form of loss provides important perspectives on what people care about most within an organization. Stories of suffering precipitate a consideration of what causes pain and anguish, and hence, what is valued in the organization. Insults signal what people see as essential to their identities and what they are proud or ashamed of. It is the link between suffering, insults and nostalgia and individuals' and organizations' sense of self that makes storytelling so valuable in gauging the values that inform the relational dynamics within an organizational system.

Nostalgia is reflection on an organizational system's current state as much as it is reminiscence about its past. It allows identities to be reconsidered and, in some cases, reveals those things that may in the past have allowed individuals or an organization a sense of self-worth. Gabriel argues that nostalgia can offer some consolation for the injury that the impersonal life of organizations can inflict on an individual's narcissism.[25] It reassures people that their lives had been significant, meaningful, or pleasurable. Nostalgia is not an unequivocally constructive or destructive form of organizational storytelling, as it can have both positive and negative effects. As a window onto the complex dynamics within an organization's system of relations, it is valuable. Changes in the physical environment in which people work and the loss of valued colleagues or leaders can all contribute to nostalgic stories. One way to initiate a process of nostalgic recollection among colleagues is to ask them to choose a metaphor from a list that best describes their organization. The list that is presented to participants could include metaphors like that of a family, which has been found to be central to nostalgic feelings. One can also precipitate nostalgic recollection by asking participants to write the obituary of a valued colleague or leader as part of the training exercise. These imaginary obituaries are bound to contain many clues as to what is valued among colleagues in an organizational system.

These are all strategies that may be employed in formal training programs to elicit and expose people to the tacit perceptions and

---

[25] *Ibid.*, p. 186.

expectations that inform the relational dynamics within an organizational system. It is also important, however, to capitalize on the informal learning that is continually taking place within an organization. Ethics training does not end with the few formally arranged occasions where deliberate efforts are made to sensitize people to the tacit perceptions and unarticulated expectations of their colleagues. The most important forms of learning within an organizational system are informal, implicit and ongoing. It is crucial therefore to identify and participate in the day-to-day practices in and through which informal learning takes place in an organizational system.

The members of an organization often learn informally through their participation in so-called "communities of practice." Communities of practice refer to a form of social learning that occurs when groups of people share information and collaborate in the development of new perspectives, solutions or innovations. The information that is shared in communities of practice is aimed at orientating participants in the conventions, expectations and dynamics of a particular organizational context. It is not necessarily advice aimed at solving specific problems. It usually takes the form of peer-to-peer interactions, which creates a safe environment for emotional and instructional support. The value of communities of practice lies in their ability to allow relevant knowledge to be made available spontaneously and on an ongoing basis. It changes the one-directional, top-down flow of information in an organization by allowing employees to participate in many multi-pronged, fluid conversations.[26]

Trust is an essential prerequisite for knowledge sharing in organizations. As Callahan explains, sharing knowledge is a natural human phenomenon, and it is unfortunate that organizations so often create barriers that make this impossible. Callahan suggests that when they are allowed to flourish, communities of practice facilitate information sharing, which reinforces an organizational system's tacit knowledge.[27] They enrich that part of an organizational environment that relates to its participants' area of interest, by adding additional layers of meaning to existing artifacts and by creating new ones. In the sustained communication within such communities, new questions are

---

[26] Sauve, "Informal Knowledge Transfer," 23.
[27] Shawn Callahan, "Want to Manage Tacit Knowledge? Communities of Practice Offer a Versatile Solution," *Anecdote White Paper* (2007).

continually raised, which allows an organizational system to respond to new or unprecedented challenges. Knowledge is not locked up within particular individuals. Through storytelling, questioning, and experimenting with new tasks, the capacity of the entire group to respond intuitively to challenges is enhanced. Communities of practice also function as initiation rites through which new members are made part of the inner circle of organizational life. Within such a context, mentoring becomes a spontaneous process of sharing, rather than a top-down instructional and directional interaction between superiors and subordinates.

Communities of practice do not have to be created. They emerge spontaneously within organizations. These communities can be identified by asking the members of an organization some open-ended questions. One can enquire whom employees refer to when they are in need of information or orientation, or whether they are aware of groups of people who draw together in times of crisis. Asking an organization's systems administrator about the existence of online or email groups within the organization may also help to identify such communities. If there is an online system for booking meeting rooms in an organization, its records may reveal patterns of regular meetings amongst certain individuals, which may be indicative of a community of practice. Though such groups cannot be engineered, it is possible to create an environment within an organization that welcomes and supports communities of practice.

There are various forms of information technology that can help to support and sustain communities of practice.[28] An organization could, for instance, create an online "space" for its employees that allows them to interact with one another in such communities of practice. Such spaces should be capable of facilitating document dissemination, the sharing of professional expertise, storytelling, creative thinking, and the sharing of personal experiences and perspectives. To this end email list-serves, asynchronous tutorial software (like Blackboard or WebCT), synchronous online interactions (e.g., HorizonWimba or Centra), webcasts, online group meeting-spaces or online conference calling (e.g., Skype) may be employed.

---

[28] Lex Chalmers and Paul Keown, "Communities of Practice and Life-Long Education," *International Journal of Life-long Education*, 25(2) (March–April, 2006), 139–156.

Through communities of practice, personal, cultural and codified knowledge components are all brought into play. Within the context of ethics training, such communities can play an important role in ensuring that individuals remain responsive to the specific ethical demands which they face within an organizational system. Instead of scheduling separate ethics training sessions, organizations could identify existing communities of practice and challenge them with a moral dilemma related to their immediate area of interest or expertise. What I have in mind here is not some general case study that is circulated for discussion. Instead, a moral dilemma that forms part of the everyday activities of the group must be identified. An employee's participation in such a collegial engagement could be viewed as the fulfillment of their annual ethics training requirement. Not only are participants likely to gain much more from such an opportunity for reflection and interaction, it could also make a valuable contribution to the tacit knowledge that is circulated within an organization's system of relations. With the permission of participants, the stories, experiences, jokes and perspectives that are offered in such engagements could be shared with the rest of an organization through newsletters or websites.

One of the basic problems with many ethics training programs is that their content is structured on the basis of a strict theory vs. practice distinction. Typically, ethics programs include some information and, in some cases, conversations regarding an organization's values, after which decision-making skills are taught. These guidelines and skills are then "applied" or "tested" in case study discussions. My analysis suggests that the deliberate application of formal normative imperatives to practical problems does not play a significant role in shaping people's everyday conduct at work. Explicit deliberation on the implications of values in practice does not succeed in tapping into the personal and cultural knowledge that inform people's everyday decision making. It is much more useful to challenge people with experiences that draw on what they already know, or to confront them with tricky situations that tap into their intuitive responses. In an organization's ethics training, people's visceral responses to everyday experiences should therefore be identified so that they may be used as learning opportunities. For example, a significant experience such as moving to a new building could be unpacked to create the opportunity for storytelling, nostalgia or even expressions of repressed anger and frustration. New opportunities for such experiences can also be created. Dancing, singing, gardening and exercising are all activities that people enjoy after hours, but which they rarely have the opportunity to indulge in with colleagues at work. Activities such as these involve bodily interaction and as such, tap into tacit repositories of meaning and significance. In South Africa, for example, gumboot-dancing is used to great effect in teambuilding within mining communities. A dance can deal with hierarchies, cooperation, and honor in ways that defy rational articulation or formulation. Every organizational system is likely to present its own unique opportunities for such forms of collegial engagement and they should be creatively employed in ethics programs.

Communication

The communication of ethical values is perhaps the aspect of ethics programs that ethics officers spend the most time and money on. Poster campaigns, newsletters, games and marketing materials such as clothing, stationery, etc. have all been used to raise people's awareness of ethics programs. Communication strategies of this kind are also used to market whistle-blowing lines and encourage people to report misconduct. However, the question is whether these initiatives really tap into the tacit knowledge that inform people's understanding of values and shape their behavior. Communications that require people to read, or actively deliberate, are likely to have a fairly limited effect on the web of perceptions, beliefs and knowledge that informs every individual's moral sensibilities.

More informal forms of communication on ethics-related topics are more likely to be effective. It seems paradoxical, however, to try to "design" or "engineer" more spontaneous forms of communication. It is clearly impossible to plan and execute a communication strategy aimed at informal communication. However, it may be possible to create opportunities and spaces in which such forms of communication can emerge. One way of doing so, for example, is to create virtual conversation spaces, by either utilizing existing communities of practice, or by creating new list-serves. Other spaces, such as "Speaker's Corners" or "Graffiti Walls" could also be created to stimulate organizational storytelling or to facilitate constructive expressions of dissent. In some organizational systems it may also be possible to circulate ethics-related jokes or arrange a monthly "Comedy Hour" to get people talking and thinking about the way that things are done in their collegial circle.

In some cases, it may be helpful to stimulate conversations about topics that are of particular concern at certain times of the year. Addressing issues at the precise time when they are of the greatest interest and concern to the members of an organization is important, because, as research has shown, people tend to draw on tacit knowledge and develop new insights only when they really need to. For instance, the practice of gift-giving presents many employees with dilemmas around the holidays each year. One way to get an organization talking about what constitutes an appropriate gift is to tap into water-cooler conversations about it. The anecdotes that people offer informally about particularly nice gifts that they have received, could, for instance, elicit vigorous discussion on this topic. This is especially true in cases where the gift that was accepted is deemed inappropriate by certain members of the organization, since it reveals differences in the tacit expectations that exist within the organization. The key is an awareness of the issue and a willingness to utilize everyday conversations as opportunities for reflection.

Another idea is to stimulate organizational storytelling around certain themes. The first few introductory paragraphs of a story depicting a real situation where an employee is confronted with a conflict of interest could be composed and individuals or departments within the organization could be asked to complete it. Comparing the different endings that are thus proposed, and seeing how they relate to the real-life ending, could initiate interesting and meaningful conversations among colleagues and between different departments. The challenge is to get busy employees to participate in such initiatives. It may therefore be helpful to offer a small reward, like an afternoon off, for the department or individual who comes up with the most interesting ending to such a story.

Because every organization also participates in a wider network of relationships, such conversations cannot be limited to internal communication. This wider relational system somehow has to be drawn into the conversation so that the congruency of values to which such interactions contribute might extend beyond an organization's boundaries. Relationships are sustained through frequent, multidirectional communication. Spaces and opportunities must be created for other stakeholders, like suppliers, contractors, customers, investors, and community members to become part of an organization's story-telling practices. When the members of an organization are exposed to multiple different narratives, their tacit understanding of the values that inform the relational dynamics of the organizational system is enhanced. This is one of the great benefits of creating multi-discursive communicative spaces in an organizational system. Strategies similar to those proposed above can be employed to create spaces within which this kind of multidirectional communication can take place. Exposing the members of an organization to the stories that their suppliers and customers tell gives them the opportunity to compare what they believe about themselves with the perceptions of others.

The use of ethics help-lines and hotlines is an important part of dealing with ethical failures in organizations. The success of an ethics help-line is often dependent on the approachability of the ethics officer and his/her team. An open-door policy is extremely important, as are informal interactions between the ethics officer and employees over lunch-hours, after meetings, and at social events. Trust and a comfortable rapport are gradually built up over time and in the course of multiple interactions.

Many organizations find it difficult to make their ethics hotlines or whistle-blowing lines work. Although these kinds of confidential reporting systems are often made available at great cost, many companies find that their employees do not to use them. The willingness of employees to report misconduct through an organization's whistle-blowing line depends on many factors, like the way in which reporting is portrayed within an organizational system, confidence in the way the line functions and people's actual experiences when they call such lines. In some ethnic cultures, industries or organizational systems there may already be strong beliefs about whistle-blowing that influence people's perception of such reporting systems. It is important to gain insight into these systemic variables before a hotline is established. For instance, if a hotline system is being implemented in a country where people associate whistle-blowing with the way in which some of their fellow citizens informed on others during wartime and thus betrayed their own people, such an approach may have to be reconsidered.

People are more likely to become involved when they witness misconduct if they feel some form of responsibility towards those who stand to be affected. It is therefore helpful to make each and every individual aware of their role as custodian of an organization's relationships. If each individual feels responsible for protecting the organizational system in which he/she participates, communicating ethical concerns simply becomes a part of the relational dynamic. When this happens, whistle-blowing may no longer be necessary, since it would become possible to raise concerns and express dissent within an organization's system of relations. As such, ongoing communication may provide the key to an environment within which whistle-blowing is appropriate only in exceptional cases.

Policies, discipline and reward

Policies

The fact that the most important information regarding an organization's value system is shared in an informal, implicit and tacit manner does not mean that no explicit reinforcement of these values is necessary. Policies create clear parameters and make it easier to manage the contingencies of everyday business life. However, it is too often the case that policy environments do not reflect organizational values and in fact send mixed messages regarding what the organization actually cares about. A disparity between an organization's tacit knowledge and its structural realities can create confusion or cynicism. It is very important that the entire policy environment be reviewed in order to ensure that it reinforces the organization's values. This requires hermeneutic skills, patience and a willingness to interrogate the most intricate parts of an organization's formal policy environment. A cross-functional task team can be very helpful in gathering and analyzing all the different organizational functions' or units' policies.

The policies of an organization must be assessed in terms of their content, form and function. In terms of policy content, it is important to distinguish between explicit content and implicit content. One should "read between the lines" to get a sense of what exactly a policy is communicating to employees. Simple documents like a dress code policy or a diversity policy can communicate implicit meanings that may undermine organizational values. While respect for all and diversity of opinion may be an important part of an organization's values, its dress code may focus predominantly on women's attire, communicating subtle sexist biases. An organization's diversity policy could be so focused on meeting race and gender quotas that it fails to encourage diversity of thought and opinion. In other organizations creative thinking and the willingness to challenge the status quo may be valued, but strict hierarchical decision making may nevertheless be enforced through policies. Policies should be just another iteration of what an organization cares about. They should not contradict or betray these concerns by placing other priorities on the table. What should be sought is normative congruence. Policies should not contradict one another or communicate a disparate set of values.

Policies must be enforced consistently. There can be no normative congruence within an organizational system if policies are applied inconsistently, especially if the perception exists that policies are only developed with lower level staff members in mind, and do not apply to managers and senior executives. It is important to ensure that policies set parameters that are realistic and that all levels of staff and all the various functional units within an organization feel comfortable with. Note, however, that the consistent application of an organization's policies should not amount to a simplistic "one-size-fits-all" approach. The various departments and units within an organization have unique tasks and ways of doing things, and the application of policies must be responsive to these contextual dynamics. A balance must be sought between allowing some room for different departments to develop their own job-specific ways of doing things, and setting clear parameters that may not be violated under any circumstances. Policies must therefore be general enough to allow for a degree of contextualization, without being so vague that they become meaningless. Striking such a balance requires insight into how the various departments within an organization function. A cross-functional task team could provide valuable insights in this regard; the insider knowledge that they could provide should inform policy development and revision.

Policies must be revisited to ensure that they keep up with the emergent values that sustain organizational relationships. In some cases, it may be necessary to get rid of policies that create unnecessary red-tape or unduly limit people's discretionary powers. Policies should not act as disincentives for the use of discretion. If an organization's policies force its members into a regime of mindless compliance, it effectively excludes those relational and contextual considerations that are crucial to appropriate behavior. An organization's policy environment must be tailored to its purpose and its level of development. It may be that some organizations in certain industries prefer a more rule-driven environment. Other organizations may have such a strong sense of value congruence among their members that detailed policies seem superfluous. Under such circumstances, people may experience the imposition of an excessively circumscribed policy environment as an affront to their intelligence and an encumbrance to their powers of discretion.

Policy environments can have a detrimental effect on people's willingness to exercise their discretion, as well as on their personal commitment to what the policies are aimed at securing in the first place. It is important to draw out the relationships between the policies and values of an organization so that it is clear to all that the organization's policies exist to protect what they care about. The members of an organization must have insight into the values that lend policies their right to exist. This insight allows them to use their discretion in making decisions. It is also important, in this regard, to challenge the members of an organization to think beyond their own narrowly circumscribed role-responsibilities and consider the wider implications of their actions. People should be ready to assume responsibility for a situation or problem even when there are others whose job description may be more directly related to the issue at hand. Discretion involves the willingness and ability to be responsive, no matter what is required to accomplish the task at hand.

It is always possible, of course, that someone might use their discretion and make a decision that, in retrospect, proves to have been inappropriate. As is the case with all experiential learning, mistakes must be treated as opportunities to gain new perspective. Such learning experiences could be made productive by inserting them into an organization's internal discourses. A story could, for instance, be constructed, in which the personal and specific details of the actual case are omitted, but which nevertheless gives an account of the kinds of contingencies and considerations that informed the protagonists' actions and decisions. Circulating such as story could do much to ensure that a congruency of values and norms is sustained among the members of an organizational system.

Performance management

An organization's performance management system has a profound effect on its ethics program. People get a sense of what is valued within an organizational system by looking at what is rewarded and punished. Rewards and punishments also play a significant part in the power dynamics within an organization. Individuals' sense of self is produced as they attempt to come to terms with the power dynamics, subtle expectations and unarticulated beliefs that exist within every organizational system. Employees might become sensitized to the congruence of values within an organizational system, but it is the way in which these values are reflected in the performance management system and disciplinary processes that influences the power dynamics within such a system. It is important to ensure that an organization's performance management system is congruent with the emergent values and priorities that are circulated among its members. People should be rewarded for acting as custodians of that which an organization's members value. If the distinction between external and internal goods is abandoned (as I have suggested in Chapter 4), meeting profit targets and sustaining business relationships can, and should, be part of the same values orientation. Good business and ethical considerations need not be seen as trade-offs, but rather as two ways of attending to the same priority.

It is also important to allow the members of an organization to give input on its performance management system. In most organizations, individuals get the opportunity to discuss performance expectations with their direct superior during annual performance appraisals. However, the single conversation that employees have with their direct superiors under the pressurized circumstances of an annual performance review does not give them a fair or adequate opportunity to express their views about an organization's performance management system.

Performance management takes place in both formal and informal ways and it is the latter that are rarely adequately recognized or addressed. Day-to-day expressions of appreciation or concern are just as important as formal recognition, possibly even more so. The members of an organization must be able to ask for feedback when they are in need of it and must feel free to question their colleagues' responses to, and appraisals of, their efforts. Informal rewards, like a compliment, or an expression of gratitude, go a long way in encouraging appropriate, relationally responsive behavior. This is a central part of supervisors' and managers' performance management responsibilities. Sometimes honor is more important than money because it enhances an individual's sense of self and raises him/her in the esteem of his/her colleagues in the organizational system. An individual's rise within an organizational system can often be attributed to frequent rewards of this nature. Rituals or artifacts that have symbolic meaning can also reward individuals in a significant way. For example, an organization could instigate a ritual in which employees who have served their customers well have their morning coffee served to them by their manager. Though financial rewards and promotions will always remain important in rewarding employees for their efforts, these other, more informal and less tangible forms of recognition can provide more regular forms of interpersonal feedback.

Disciplinary processes are an unfortunate, but necessary, part of organizational life. Their role is to help reinforce normative parameters within an organizational system. However, as a number of philosophers have pointed out, discipline also influences people's sense of identity and agency. It can initiate a state of social control in which individuals begin to police themselves. This self-policing can become so powerfully compelling that creative forms of discretion become impossible. In rule-driven, predictable organizational environments that function as closed systems, such a form of social control may be seen as an efficient management strategy. However, in complex organizational systems and business environments, where individuals are continually confronted with novel and unforeseen problems, discretion is crucial. Individuals must be able to respond creatively to whatever situation presents itself. It is important, therefore, not to discipline individuals in a way that labels them as criminals, misfits or failures. It is better to focus on the way in which individuals had misread, or misinterpreted their responsibilities within the context of a specific set of relational dynamics. An offender is therefore not a criminal, but someone who failed to act as custodian of that which his/her co-participants in an organization system care about.

This does not mean that offenders should simply be excused, or that no punishment should be meted out. If someone rides roughshod over the values of his/her colleagues, or damages the relationships on which they all rely for their livelihood, he/she should be held to proper account. Disciplinary cases should, however, always precipitate a reconsideration of how it was possible for an individual to misread or remain unaffected by the normative beliefs and expectations that are continually circulated among colleagues in an organization's system of relations. What were the power relationships and structural constraints that allowed the individual to believe that a particular action or decision was appropriate, when it was not? Finding out "who did it?" should never be the main concern in a disciplinary process. Rather, the question should be: "how did this happen and how could it have been avoided?" Disciplinary processes should be seen as a way of tapping into the tacit messages that are circulated among individuals within an organization and an opportunity to reflect on previously undetected ethical risk areas. Indiscretions should be used as learning experiences on all levels of an organization. They give participants in an organizational system the opportunity to see how structures and policies, as well as formal and informal communication, inform people's perceptions, beliefs and behavior.

Ongoing assessments and reporting

Most organizational ethics programs start and end with an assessment of the organization's ethical risks, the success of its ethics programs and the sustainability of all of its operations. This is clearly a more complicated process than providing a set of statistics that describe the status quo, and addressing problematic areas with a list of compliance measures. Trends that had emerged in audits and assessments, disciplinary cases and whistle-blowing reports have to be analyzed and interpreted on an ongoing basis. It involves tapping into the sense of normative congruence that is emerging in and through everyday business behavior. This changes our perspective on what a "report" or "an audit" really is. It is at best a snapshot that must constantly be challenged, reframed, and inserted into the broader perspective of organizational histories. The kind of qualitative assessment, such as textual analysis, that has been proposed as part of all the other aspects of an ethics program, applies to the gathering of data in the reporting phase too.

The ethics office is responsible for facilitating the gathering of information across organizational functions and for integrating it to provide a perspective on emergent patterns within the organizational system. The importance of sharing this information with the board and disseminating it to various line managers across organizational functions cannot be overemphasized. People become most frustrated if they participate in an information-gathering exercise but never receive feedback on the findings. Information on both the explicit and implicit elements of an organizational system's relational dynamics should be shared through formal and informal channels. It is, however, important that these findings should not be presented as fixed characteristics of the organization, nor should they resort to over-generalizations. Sharing stories and cases of real incidents may be more helpful in getting a sense of the organization's tacit normative congruence.

The fact that contemporary organizations are all part of complex webs of relationships means that information dissemination cannot stop at internal assessments and reports. An organization's members must make its various partners and stakeholders aware of what is valued within its system of relations. Triple bottom-line reporting can play an important part in this. A triple bottom-line report attempts to articulate the ethical commitments of all of the various functions of an organization. As such, it provides a sense of how the values that are circulated within an organization's system of relations inform all of its operations and functions.

A triple bottom-line report cannot be randomly pieced together from the disparate bits of information that have been gathered from various departments in an organization. It should instead be the product of the collaborative efforts of a cross-functional team of insiders, who have a sense of the value commitments of those who participate in the organization. Such a report's introduction should speak of what is valued within an organizational system within specific business episodes, and explain how it is tied in with the organization's business purposes. Its description of an organization's governance processes and the way in which its board functions should display a commitment to accountability as relational responsiveness. When reporting on an organization's policy environment, a triple bottom-line report should contain more than the usual "check-the-box" enumeration of standard policy documents. Policies must be linked to the specific values that they seek to secure. In all areas of performance, whether economic, social or environmental, the values that inform the actions and decisions of an organization's members should be made clear. Triple bottom-line reports are no more than window-dressing exercises if they fail to show how people work together to sustain relationships across organizational functions.

The communication between an organization's ethics office, its corporate social responsibility division, its environmentalists, and those who work in its internal audit function must serve to inspire collaboration within the rest of the organization. It should demonstrate that it is possible for everyone to consider their impact on normative congruence within the organization, despite differences in their immediate concerns and specific responsibilities. This open communicative style and orientation should characterize interaction throughout the organizational system. The human resources function of an organization must, for instance, understand how it is related to the information technology and marketing functions. If such an understanding does exist, it makes the process of gathering information and formulating reports easier and more meaningful. It also allows stakeholders to get a sense of what those who participate in the organizational system strive for in all of the organization's business operations.

Reports are formal, explicit forms of communication. However, they also communicate in implicit ways. The structure, layout, pictures and style of communication say a lot about what is valued in an organization. Shrewd readers will find as much in what an organization excludes from its report as they do in what it does include. Stakeholders can play an important role in reflecting on the implicit messages that a report conveys. It is important to remember that stakeholders are part of an organization's network and are capable of interpreting and contributing to the tacit knowledge that is circulated among its members. In the final analysis it is important to accept the fact that all reporting is an exercise in sense-making, executed from a very specific point of view. It is not the only way to read the organization's dynamics. As such, tapping into different stakeholder perceptions remains an important check on simplistic depictions of organizational realities.

The way forward

The main argument of this book has been that ethics should be part of everyday business practice and not mere compliance with legislation and regulations. If ethics is something that has to be attended to only because legislation or regulation calls for it, it is positioned as a trade-off, as something that has to be done in order to be allowed to get on with business-as-usual. When this is the case, organizations simply ask themselves: what do we have to put in place to comply? Consequently, they spend as little time, money and effort on their ethics programs as they think they can get away with. If ethics programs are designed and implemented with this kind of mindset, they are likely to suffer from a number of serious defects. In the first place, they will lack legitimacy. Those to whom they are supposedly addressed will soon recognize them for what they are: mere window-dressing exercises. Such ethics programs are also unlikely to influence people's sense of normative orientation or affect the way in which they understand and exercise their moral agency. Finally, there is little chance that ethics programs of this nature could effect an integration of ethics into people's everyday working lives. Institutionalizing codes, policies and various kinds of checks-and-balances may seem reassuring from a compliance perspective, but it is unlikely to have any meaningful effect on the moral responsiveness of those who participate in organizational systems.

To break out of this compliance mindset, it is necessary to consider again why business organizations exist in the first place. To many this will seem self-evident: business exists to make profit. This book does not dispute this. What it does dispute though, is that profit is an end in itself. People care about profit, salaries, bonuses, and company cars because they want to live a certain kind of life. In most cases, they want this kind of life because they believe that it makes them "somebody." Money, and the things that it can buy, give people a sense of identity and make them feel valued and respected. The irony is that many people lose themselves, destroy their relationships, and harm their communities in the single-minded pursuit of money. We therefore need to rethink the relationships between people's sense of themselves, their sense of agency, and the things that they value in life. It is in, and through, the interactions between our sense of self, the power relationships in which we function, and the truths that we tacitly possess, that the fabric of morality is woven. The first part of this book represents an attempt to unravel these intricate relationships and to provide a new framework for understanding moral reasoning, moral agency and moral epistemology. The last two chapters try to show how insight into this intricate moral fabric changes how people practice ethics and how we conceive of ethics programs in organizations. Many more chapters will be needed to draw out all the implications of treating ethics as part of the everyday business of business. There was only space in this book to consider the implications of this approach for ethics professionals, whether academics, practitioners, or both. It remains for people in the various professions, and across different industries, to unpack the specific practical implications of this approach in their own working lives and organizations. This book therefore ends in an opening.

Index